£10.50

OXFORD STUDENT TEXTS

Series Editor: Steven Croft

John Ford

'Tis Pity She's a Whore

Edited by Richard Gill

Oxford University Press

OXFORD

UNIVERSITY PRESS

Great Clarendon Street, Oxford OX2 6DP

Oxford University Press is a department of the University of Oxford.
It furthers the University's objective of excellence in research, scholarship,
and education by publishing worldwide in

Oxford New York

Auckland Cape Town Dar es Salaam Hong Kong Karachi
Kuala Lumpur Madrid Melbourne Mexico City Nairobi
New Delhi Shanghai Taipei Toronto

With offices in

Argentina Austria Brazil Chile Czech Republic France Greece
Guatemala Hungary Italy Japan South Korea Poland Portugal
Singapore Switzerland Thailand Turkey Ukraine Vietnam

Oxford is a registered trade mark of Oxford University Press
in the UK and in certain other countries

© Richard Gill 2012

The moral rights of the author have been asserted

Database right Oxford University Press (maker)

First published 2012

British Library Cataloguing in Publication Data

Data available

ISBN: 978-0-19-912955-3

1 3 5 7 9 10 8 6 4 2

Typeset in India by TNQ Books and Journals Pvt. Ltd.

Printed in China by Printplus

Paper used in the production of this book is a natural, recyclable product made from
wood grown in sustainable forests. The manufacturing process conforms to the
environmental regulations of the country of origin.

The publishers would like to thank the following for permission to reproduce
photographs:

Page 4: Masters of the Bench of the Honourable Society of the Middle Temple; page 10:
The Bridgeman Art Library; page 11: Nico Tondini/ Robert Harding World Imagery/
Corbis; page 14: Provost and Fellows of Worcester College, Oxford; page 17: Fulcanelli/
Shutterstock; page 20: Cameraphoto Arte Venezia/ The Bridgeman Art Library; page 200:
Stephanie Maze/ Corbis; page 207: The National Gallery, London; page 216: The Yorck
Project: 10.000 Meisterwerke der Malerei/ DIRECTMEDIA/ GmbH.; page 237: Photo
Scala, Florence, courtesy of Ministero Beni e Att. Culturali

Contents

Acknowledgements

The text of the play is taken from John Ford:*'Tis Pity She's a Whore and Other Plays*, edited by Marion Lomax (Oxford World's Classics, 1995).

Extracts from the *Authorized Version of the Bible* (*The King James Bible*), the rights in which are vested in the Crown, are reproduced by permission of the Crown's Patentee, Cambridge University Press.

Acknowledgements from Richard Gill

I would like to thank Jan Doorly, John Florance, Tony Moore, Hannah Parsons and Miriam Stevenson for the help they have given me.

For Joan Ward

Editors

Steven Croft, the series editor, holds degrees from Leeds and Sheffield universities. He has taught at secondary and tertiary level and headed the Department of English and Humanities in a tertiary college. He has 25 years' examining experience at A level and is currently a Principal Examiner for English. He has written several books on teaching English at A level, and his publications for Oxford University Press include *Exploring Literature*, *Success in AQA Language and Literature* and *Exploring Language and Literature*.

Richard Gill, who was Head of English at Wyggeston and Queen Elizabeth I College, Leicester, now works part-time at the Richard Attenborough Centre, Leicester University. He has published books on Jane Austen, Shakespeare, and Tennyson, as well as a book on the study of English Literature. In this series, he has edited *John Donne: Selected Poems*, Christopher Marlowe's *Dr Faustus* and *W.B. Yeats: Selected Poems*.

Foreword

Oxford Student Texts, under the founding editorship of Victor Lee, have established a reputation for presenting literary texts to students in both a scholarly and an accessible way. The new editions aim to build on this successful approach. They have been written to help students, particularly those studying English literature for AS or A level, to develop an increased understanding of their texts. Each volume in the series, which covers a selection of key poetry and drama texts, consists of four main sections which link together to provide an integrated approach to the study of the text.

The first part provides important background information about the writer, his or her times and the factors that played an important part in shaping the work. This discussion sets the work in context and explores some key contextual factors.

This section is followed by the poetry or play itself. The text is presented without accompanying notes so that students can engage with it on their own terms without the influence of secondary ideas. To encourage this approach, the Notes are placed in the third section, immediately following the text. The Notes provide explanations of particular words, phrases, images, allusions and so forth, to help students gain a full understanding of the text. They also raise questions or highlight particular issues or ideas which are important to consider when arriving at interpretations.

The fourth section, Interpretations, goes on to discuss a range of issues in more detail. This involves an examination of the influence of contextual factors as well as looking at such aspects as language and style, and various critical views or interpretations. A range of activities for students to carry out, together with discussions as to how these might be approached, are integrated into this section.

At the end of each volume there is a selection of Essay Questions, a Chronology, and a Further Reading list.

We hope you enjoy reading this text and working with these supporting materials, and wish you every success in your studies.

Steven Croft   *Series Editor*

John Ford in Context

The lives of the English playwrights

William Shakespeare is exceptional and an exception. Exceptional because of the range of his material, the dramatic and poetic force of his language and his creation of rich and distinctive characters, and an exception because, as a playwright celebrated for about 400 years, scholars have thoroughly researched his life and times. Shakespeare is named in well over 200 documents (many of them legal), and in addition there are stories, many from his years in Stratford, that may contain elements of truth.

For a man born in the sixteenth century who was not a noble, a great deal is known about Shakespeare. Just how much becomes clear when comparisons are made with the lives of those playwrights born shortly before or just after him. For instance, there is a record of Shakespeare's baptism on 26 April 1564 and some, though not compelling, evidence that he was born three days earlier. But very little is known of the life of John Webster (author of *The Duchess of Malfi*) before he was admitted to the Middle Temple (see page 2) in 1598, and the early life of William Rowley (author of the sub-plot in Thomas Middleton's *The Changeling*) is a blank. And had they been famous for 400 years, research might have unearthed more material about Cyril Tourneur (author of *The Atheist's Tragedy*) and Thomas Dekker (author of *The Shoemaker's Holiday*). The fact is that most of Shakespeare's contemporaries, with the exceptions of Christopher Marlowe and Ben Jonson, excited almost no scholarly interest until the first decades of the twentieth century.

Ford's early life

In the case of John Ford, editions of his plays were published in the early nineteenth century, and critical comments were made by Charles Lamb (1808) and William Hazlitt (1820), but it was in the twentieth century that he began to be regarded as an important playwright. Biographical interest has followed, but the results of research are still patchy. It is known that he was the second son of a country gentleman from Devon and that he was baptized on 12 April 1586 in St Michael's, Ilsington, a small settlement in south Devon on the edge of Dartmoor, roughly half-way between Ashburton and Bovey Tracey.

The Fords were a well-established land-owning family with powerful connections. Elizabeth Ford, his mother, was the niece of John Popham, who was to become the Lord Chief Justice. The social setting of *'Tis Pity She's a Whore* might be described as middle class. There are no kings. Soranzo is described as a Spanish nobleman, and the Cardinal says that Grimaldi is *nobly born;/ Of princes' blood* (III.ix.57–58), but the chief business of the plot concerns the family of Florio, a successful and possibly only recently established merchant of Parma. Many of the scenes are set in or near his house.

The next known event in the life of John Ford is 26 March 1601, when he matriculated (was recognized as a member) at Exeter College, Oxford. At 15 he was not unusually young; when John Donne matriculated at Hart Hall, Oxford in 1584, he was recorded as being 11 years old. What may be deduced from John Ford's matriculation is that he had either attended a grammar school (a school that taught Latin grammar) or been educated at home by a private tutor. It is worth pointing out that in the play, Florio's son Giovanni has been educated at university and his developing views, sharply rebutted by his sometime teacher the Friar, form the play's chief intellectual thread.

The Middle Temple

Ford did not stay at Oxford long; on 16 November 1602 he entered the Middle Temple in London. This was a self-governing body that specialized in legal training. As there was no limit to the period of study, young men who were rich enough to pay could stay in residence as long as they liked. Ford was suspended in 1605 for failing to pay for his food and drink, but reinstated in 1608. He may have been in trouble with the Middle Temple authorities in 1617 because of his participation in a protest against the wearing of lawyer's caps in the dining hall. However, as there was another John Ford in residence, it is not certain whether it was the playwright who was censured. There is no record of what else he did there, and no record of his completing his legal training.

The London Inns of Court, which included the Middle Temple, are important in the history of English Renaissance drama. Several of the early seventeenth-century playwrights were associated with these institutions for talented, ambitious young men. Francis Beaumont (author with John Fletcher of *The Maid's Tragedy*) was a member of the Inner Temple; John Marston (author *The Malcontent*) had gone to Middle Temple about a decade before Ford, and Thomas Middleton (author of *The Revenger's Tragedy, Women Beware Women* and *The Changeling*) was a member of Gray's Inn. Drama was fashionable and had about it an attractively dangerous air of adventure; the playwrights of the Inns of Court tackled murder, madness and incest. Furthermore, the dining halls of the Inns of Court were easily adapted for the performance of plays (see the illustration overleaf).

Plays, poetry and prose

Ford was typical of his times in that he was a poet and writer of prose as well as a playwright. His poetry is early: *Fame's Memorial* and *Funeral Tears*, which are elegies on the death of Charles Blount, Earl of Devonshire (1606), and *Christ's Bloody Sweat* (1613). His prose works were *Honour Triumphant* (1606), *The Golden Mean* (1613) and *A Line of Life* (1620). The latter two works advocate a stoical patience in the face of troubles.

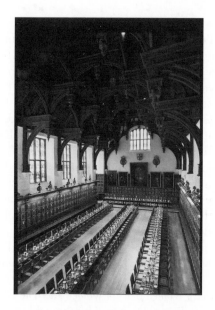

Middle Temple Hall was built between 1562 and 1573, and remains
virtually unchanged

His first play, *An Ill Beginning Has a Good End*, dates from
1613, and *The Witch of Edmonton*, a collaboration with Dekker
and Rowley, from 1621. There were further collaborations: *The
Spanish Gypsy* in 1623 with Rowley and Middleton, and with
Dekker, *The Bristol Merchant* and *The Fairy Knight*, both first
performed in 1624 and now lost.

It was common practice to collaborate on plays. When there
was more than one playwright attached to a company of actors, it
was a convenient way of producing plays quickly. New work was
in constant demand, and most plays were only performed a few
times. Collaboration also provided an opportunity for new
playwrights to learn their craft. The plot was probably devised by
one playwright, and his collaborators worked on individual
sections such as sub-plots, comic elements, prologues and
epilogues. Shakespeare collaborated with John Fletcher in writing

The Two Noble Kinsmen (1613), the main plot being Shakespeare's and the sub-plot Fletcher's.

The first play of which Ford was the sole author was probably *The Lover's Melancholy*, first performed in 1628 and published the following year. It is not known when most of Ford's plays were written. It is often supposed that *'Tis Pity She's a Whore* was written in 1631, but all that is known definitely is that it was published in 1633. That year also saw the publication of *The Broken Heart* and *Love's Sacrifice*. *Perkin Warbeck* was published in 1634 and *The Fancies Chaste and Noble* in 1638. *The Lady's Trial* was first acted in 1638 and published in 1639.

Nothing is known about Ford after 1639. It is assumed that he left the Middle Temple and returned to Devon. No date for his death has been found.

Italy

Many plays of the English Renaissance are set in Italy. Shakespeare's *The Merchant of Venice* and *The Two Gentleman of Verona* include their settings in their titles. Altogether, 11 of Shakespeare's plays are set in Italy, and that figure excludes the Roman plays. Although Shakespeare's geography is not always reliable, he certainly understood how some Italian cities worked. He knew, for instance, that because Venice consisted of about 200 tiny, built-up islands, all its daily needs – including food – had to be supplied by merchants. He also knew that Venice, in order to protect its republican status, allowed only foreigners to command its forces. Othello is able to command there because he is a foreigner.

Shakespeare was not the only playwright to locate plays in Venice; Jonson set *Volpone* there. Venice is the most popular Italian setting, but Shakespeare set *Romeo and Juliet* in Verona and Mantua, Marston's *The Malcontent* is set in Genoa, and the title of Webster's *The Duchess of Malfi* indicates its Amalfi location.

'Tis Pity She's a Whore is set in Parma. Is this significant? It could just be a matter of Italians being thought of as passionate (even lustful) and unscrupulous. Playwrights assumed that audiences knew that the political philosopher Niccolò Machiavelli (1469–1527), who frankly acknowledged the moral vacuum of Italian statecraft, was Italian. Sometimes, therefore, there is nothing specific about the Italy of the English stage. The setting of *The Revenger's Tragedy* is simply Italy. Nothing more is needed to account for its atmosphere of corruption.

John Ford certainly does more than simply indicate a setting for his play. He makes a number of references to Italian cities: Giovanni has been to university in Bologna (I.i.49), Philotis is urged to go to a convent in Cremona (IV.ii.25), Richardetto pretends to be a doctor from Padua (II.i.55) after he is reported to have died on the way to Leghorn (II.ii.76), and the Banditti come from the *mountains of Liguria* (V.iv.5). Local colouring is also present in references to Duke Monferrato, wars against Milan, the love poet Sannazaro, Rome, the presence of the Friar and the Cardinal, and the snatches of Italian conversations and songs with which Annabella taunts Soranzo (for instance, IV.iii.59).

But what is to be made of this local colouring? Is there anything like a consistent sense that this is an Italian play? The question raises one of the most interesting problems of English Renaissance drama: do playwrights strive to create a world other than the one they and their audiences know, or are the characters and their various social situations essentially English and, more particularly, from London? The critic A.D. Nuttall argued that Shakespeare presented other societies as distinct from his own (*A New Mimesis*, Methuen, 1983), while G.K. Hunter claimed that Shakespeare regarded human nature as unchanging from place to place (*Dramatic Identities and Cultural Tradition*, Barnes & Noble, 1978). In the wake of Hunter's work, *'Tis Pity She's a Whore* has been described as a 'city tragedy' (Verna Foster, in *John Ford: Critical Re-Visions*, edited by Michael Neill, Cambridge University Press, 1988) and a play whose life seeks to come to terms with contemporary London (Leah Marcus, *Puzzling*

Shakespeare: Local Reading and its Discontents, University of California Press, 1988).

Two points, one particular and one general, must be conceded to the view that Italy in any detailed sense is of little importance as the setting of the play.

- Some passages sound English. Bergetto's talk about the horse with its tail where its head ought to be (I.iii.38–41) recalls the kind of trick associated with London fairs. Also, his account of being roughed up in the street (II.vi.73–80) fits English urban thoroughfares, in which overhanging house frontages provided shelter and the centre of the street was a channel to carry away muck and rainwater. However, this arrangement was not confined to England.

- The general point is that one of the chief features of the Renaissance stage was its flexibility. The open acting space, be it large as in the outdoor playhouses or smaller as in the indoor hall playhouses (see page 12) could represent interiors, exteriors, the court, the countryside, foreign lands and, when required, very specific locations. The effect of this may well have been to create a specifically theatrical world rather than a world that represented a particular place.

The case that, at least for some of the scenes, an audience should think of *'Tis Pity She's a Whore* as a play with an Italian setting rests on the recognition that certain important features make good sense if viewed in that context.

- Ford presents his characters as having a sense, though perhaps a crudely popular one, of national identities. There would be no point presenting Soranzo and Vasques as Spaniards in a foreign land if that land – Italy – did not have an identity making it a different place from Spain.

- The English believed that Italians were keen on duelling. This was not a matter of prejudice. Italian 'professours' of fencing established themselves in London, and one of them, Vincentio Saviola, wrote a fencing manual, published in 1595. Shakespeare probably used Saviola's manual in *Romeo and Juliet* (first printed in 1597), a play that contains several duels.

7

Ford's duel in I.ii follows Shakespeare in that it arises from a long-standing antagonism, though unlike Shakespeare the dispute is a matter of personal rivalry rather than the mutual animosities of two families (see Interpretations page 219).

- Ford has a feel for the political arrangements in Parma. The city had come under the control of the Pope in 1531. In 1545 it was presented to the Farnese family, relatives of the Pope. This might go some way towards explaining why the chief civil authority in the play is the Cardinal. There are no dukes, counts or kings. The Cardinal is something of a despot. When he refuses to hand Grimaldi over, the cry is *Dwells Justice here?* (III.ix.63), but no one questions that he has the authority to act.

- In relation to the presentation of papal power, it is worth following up an observation by Martin Wiggins (in his New Mermaids edition of the play, see Further Reading page 257) that the play might have been intended to be 'a period piece set in the recent past'. Grimaldi is said to have fought in the wars between the Papal States and Milan (I.ii.82–83), which happened from 1547, and the poet Sannazaro died in 1530 (II.ii.5). Furthermore, the codpiece (III.i.14) was no longer worn in the 1630s and, unlike in other plays, there are no references to guns. Perhaps Ford is deliberately imagining a mid-sixteenth century date as well as an Italian setting.

- The economics of the play are also right. Hippolita (sneeringly?) calls Annabella *Your goodly Madam Merchant* (II.ii.49). Annabella is wealthy because her father is a merchant who, as he says of himself, is *blessed with enough* (I.iii.9). Parma thrived on trade, and merchants built themselves grand houses. Parma was known for its cheese, and although Martin Wiggins thinks the reference may well be to a drink, Poggio's remark about Bergetto saying he *loved parmesan* (I.iii.61) is right both as a celebrated local product and as a comically inept piece of wooing. The word *Parmesan* entered the English language in 1556. (Supporters of the England/London focus of Renaissance drama will point out that merchant activity is central to many contemporary plays, in particular those of Ben Jonson.)

- Perhaps the most interesting of the play's 'Italian' features is its sense of public spaces. *'Tis Pity She's a Whore* certainly requires scenes in which the sense of a private space is vital (see Interpretations page 198), yet many of its scenes are clearly set in the streets and open spaces of Parma. Ford presents the spectacle of Italian life, its sense of parade and display. The note is struck by Putana when, elevated on the balcony, she says to Annabella: *Observe* (I.ii.109). Putana's remark is prompted by the entrance of Bergetto and Poggio, but it sums up a world in which characters are both observers and observed. Bergetto is such a figure. He asks Poggio to *Mark my pace* (I.ii.123) and, significantly, with the exception of II.vi, all his scenes are public, including his death scene (III.vii) and the appeal to the Cardinal (III.ix).

- Some critics have called the manner of the play 'baroque'. The word has a number of meanings, but in both literature and the visual arts it might be said to indicate a liking for expansive gestures and rich emotional colouring. Although the design of baroque art (particularly its architecture) was classical, the intention was to arouse strong emotions in the viewers. Italy, including Parma, was the home of such art, particularly in church building and religious painting. In England the word is often applied to the elaborate and inventive language of the devotional poet Richard Crashaw (1613–1649). When used of *'Tis Pity She's a Whore* it makes sense of staging and gesture. Giovanni addresses the dead Annabella, decked out in her blood-soaked wedding dress, in expansive language: *How over-glorious art thou in thy wounds* (V.v.103). *Over-glorious* means superlatively lovely. Such high claims are distinctly baroque, as is also Giovanni's entrance in the last scene with Annabella's heart on his dagger (see Interpretations page 243).

- Did Ford know that Parma is an appropriate setting for the public aspects of the play? It has (and had in the seventeenth century) splendid public areas. For instance, west and east of the cathedral there are magnificent piazzas (see the illustration overleaf).

9

The public square in front of the cathedral, bell tower and baptistery
in Parma

In keeping with its public character, certain characters
consciously conduct themselves in a theatrical way. Bergetto
practices his affected walk (I.ii.123), and Richardetto describes
himself as *a looker-on,/ Whiles others act my shame* (II.iii.3–4).
Hippolita gains access to Soranzo's wedding banquet by
disguising herself as one of the players in a masque (IV.i.35). In
IV.iii Vasques uses theatrical language to describe his own
actions: he is an actor who gives his *cue with cunning* (267). In the
final crisis of his life, Giovanni presents himself in theatrical
terms. At the conclusion of the scene in which he kills
Annabella, he encourages himself to *boldly act my last and greater
part* (V.v.106). Characters who consciously speak of actions in
theatrical terms are features of Renaissance plays, the most
important being Hamlet. In the case of Ford, it can be taken as
an aspect of the public nature of Italian city life. And there is a
further factor. Did Ford know that in the Farnese Palace in the

centre of Parma there was the enormous Teatro Farnese, built in 1617–1618 and capable of seating 3000 spectators? It was used, though only rarely, for spectacular productions. (See Interpretations page 199.)

Ford's theatre

Hall playhouses

Ford was a Caroline playwright; that is to say, the plays of which he was the sole author were all written under Charles I, who reigned from 1625–1649. Moreover, Ford wrote for the hall playhouse.

The Teatro Farnese at the Farnese Palace in Parma

Hall playhouses differed from amphitheatres such as the Globe because they were indoors. The first of these was the Blackfriars, which was probably on the upper floor of what had been a monastic building. First used in 1576, it closed in 1584, and then from 1596 (when it was bought by Richard Burbage) Shakespeare's late plays – *The Winter's Tale, The Tempest, The Two Noble Kinsmen* – were performed there. Its stage was smaller and narrower than the open-air theatres, the width being about 7–8 metres, compared with 13–14 at the Globe. Importantly, the fixtures of the stage were probably very similar to the amphitheatres. At the back of the stage there was a tiring house with three entrances, the central one of which worked as an inner stage or discovery space. There was almost certainly a balcony above the central entrance. In the auditorium, there was probably a three-sided gallery, so people sitting on the two sides would be above the players on the stage.

Several factors combined to make hall theatres distinctive.

- Because they were smaller and enclosed there was, potentially, greater intimacy between players and audiences. Soliloquies might seem more private and more inwardly anguished, and perhaps sympathy for the plight of the characters was sharper.

- This in turn meant that certain scenes were difficult to manage. On the vast stage of the Globe, Shakespeare could invite his audiences to imagine battles, but skirmishing in the hall theatres would be in danger of looking ridiculous (see Interpretations page 219). Spectacles, however, could be staged. Some of the actions must have owed much to the court traditions of masques – elaborate entertainments using song, dance, music and poetry, performed by players in richly decorated costumes.

- Plays performed in hall playhouses were often literally quieter. Musicians played hautboys (woodwind instruments) instead of the much louder cornets. There was probably little use of drums.

- The hall playhouses were increasingly associated with court circles; the audiences included the fashionable and elegant.

This was, in part, a function of geography: the halls were north of the river in areas where the affluent lived. Theatre-going was part of the social round, a chance to show oneself finely clothed in a public place. The theatre historian Andrew Gurr writes: 'it became acceptable for fashionable ladies to occupy the boxes alongside the stage, the social advantage of parading oneself at the Blackfriars or the Cockpit came second only to an appearance at the Court itself' (*The Shakespearean Stage, 1574–1642*, see Further Reading).

- An aspect of this public display was sitting on the stage itself. For 2 shillings, gentlemen could sit on a bench placed on the stage. Perhaps their presence drew attention to the theatricality of Caroline life. And did playwrights think that this was in keeping with the Italy they were presenting – cities where rich young men swaggered to impress ladies and intimidate rivals?

- The hall playhouses were more expensive than the open-air theatres. Admission to the Globe or the Fortune ranged from a single penny to sixpence, whereas entrance to the hall started at sixpence and went up to 2 shillings and sixpence. Again, Gurr sums up the situation: the lowest fee at the Blackfriars 'would buy you the luxury of a Lord's room at the Globe'.

The Cockpit

Potentially, a great deal is known about the hall theatre for which Ford wrote his plays – the Cockpit in Drury Lane. This relies on two assumptions made when attempting a historical reconstruction.

The Cockpit Theatre was built in 1616 for the theatrical manager Christopher Beeston on the site of a cockpit, which was built about 1609. Cockpits were usually circular or many sided, so the gamblers could be near the fighting birds. (One survival is The Fighting Cocks Inn, an octagonal wooden structure, in St Albans.)

At this point the first assumption must be made: that a detailed design for a theatre by Inigo Jones, made in 1616 (see the

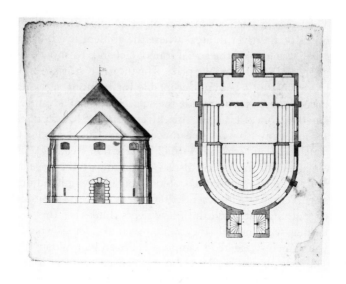

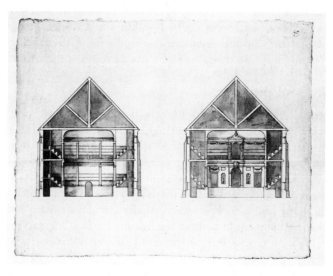

Plans for a theatre by Inigo Jones, believed to be for the Cockpit in
Drury Lane

illustration opposite), is of the Drury Lane Cockpit. The date is right and the shape – a semi-circular auditorium – is consistent with the design of cockpits. Furthermore, Jones was the architect to the king, and a later work of his – the Cockpit-in-Court, built as a royal theatre in Whitehall, 1629–1630 – shows a number of similarities with the Drury Lane design.

The second assumption is that the theatre Ford wrote for is basically the Cockpit as drawn by Jones, in spite of the fire of 1617. This was caused by a riot of London apprentices. This assumption can be made with some confidence. Damage to the Cockpit was caused chiefly to books and costumes; the only structural damage was the loss of some tiles. We may assume, then, that Jones's drawing is pretty much the Cockpit (or the Phoenix, as it was sometimes called after the fire).

The shape of the Cockpit may owe something to the original building, as it is semi-circular at the auditorium end. Perhaps this rested on the original foundations. The end behind the stage is square, and may well have been an addition to the 1609 cockpit. The building was smaller than Blackfriars, though the actual performing area was, at 7.2 x 4.6 metres, probably about the same size as Blackfriars. Because Jones's drawing is so precise, several features and their dimensions are evident. At the auditorium end there was an entrance lobby, which had two staircases. These gave access to the galleries. At the other end, behind the stage, there were two further staircases, which served seating behind the stage and the upper stage.

The stage itself was 1.2 metres high and the area behind the tiring house facade was 3 metres in depth. There were two galleries, each with four steps of benches. The upper gallery was 5.4 metres above the stage. To those peering over the front, the drop might have induced giddiness or even fear. Also, the fact that there was seating alongside the stage meant that spectators would have been able to see into the discovery space.

From a theatrical point of view, the exciting aspect of Jones's design is that it shows us what the tiring house facade looked like. Apart from the sketchy drawing of a performance at the Swan, probably in 1596, by Johannes de Witt, it is not known what a tiring house looked like. Careful study of stage directions has led to agreements on entrances, discovery space and balcony. But nothing is known about style or decoration. The Jones drawing is therefore invaluable. However, although it tells us what Ford's audiences saw behind and above his players, it probably tells us nothing about the Globe. This is because Inigo Jones had come under the influence of Italian architecture. His design for the Cockpit was almost certainly not in the style that would have been found in the Globe or the Swan.

Jones's contacts with Italy are relevant to the Cockpit design. He went to Italy soon after his father's death in 1597, staying for up to six years. He almost certainly visited Venice, where he would see the works of Andrea Palladio, the most accomplished and imaginative classicist of his (or any) day. Jones matters in the history of English architecture, because he brought Palladian classicism to England. The other influence that Jones probably absorbed was from Florence, where Bernardo Buontalenti designed both the scenery and the costumes for the masques staged in the Medici court. Later in his career, Jones was also a designer of masques, the first of which, with a text by Ben Jonson, was performed on Twelfth Night 1605.

Jones went to Italy again in 1613–1614. The details of his journey have survived. He went to Milan, Venice, Padua, Bologna, Florence, Rome, Naples and Turin. One of the most important of his visits was to Vicenza. Here he would have seen several Palladian palaces and the huge Teatro Olimpico, which opened in 1585. This has a sumptuous tiring house like the front of a palace – two storeys of classical openings enriched by statues. On the flanks there are entrances, and niches filled with more statues. Palladio died before the theatre was finished, so the work passed to Vincenzo Scamozzi, who added an artful perspective of a grand Renaissance street seen through the great central arch. (The Teatro Olimpico was the inspiration for the Teatro Farnese in Parma, see page 11.) Did Jones learn from this that a tiring house should be in the Palladian manner? Though

The stage of the Teatro Olimpico at Vicenza has a sumptuous tiring
house and a perspective of a Renaissance street

little can be deduced from it concerning Ford's play except that
the city was one that the English thought was worth visiting,
Jones also went to Parma.

Although on a much smaller scale than the Vicenza theatre,
the tiring house at the Cockpit looks like the frontage of an
Italian palace. The left and right entrances (1.8 x 1.2 metres) are
surmounted by swags (mouldings representing material knotted
in two places to form a big curve and two short vertical drops).
Between the doors and the big central doorway, there are niches
with statues like the ones in the flanks of the Teatro Olimpico.
The central doorway is large (2.4 x 1.2 metres) and is surmounted
by a cartouche (an elaborate shield), which connects it to a first
floor opening (the balcony). This is of the same size and
proportions as the central doorway but looks larger because it is

more elaborate. It is flanked by columns with statues, upon whose heads rest urns. The top of the opening is a broken pediment – a triangular moulding with a gap between the two upper elements. An urn is placed in the gap. This opening functioned as the upper stage. To either side of the upper opening there are three rows of seats. The Cockpit, therefore – to adapt the language of the twentieth-century theatre – was 'in the round'.

Jones's drawing shows that there was no trapdoor in the stage. This might suggest that plays that required spirits or devils to rise onto the stage were no longer performed. Certainly the religious element in *'Tis Pity She's a Whore* requires no external 'divine' interventions. Religion is a matter of moral behaviour regulated by the conscience.

The tiring house, and probably parts of the galleries, would be painted, and prominent features such as the statues would be gilded. The appearance would be in keeping with the expensive character of the theatre.

The play in the theatre

Given that one of the features of the seventeenth-century stage was its versatility (see page 7), it is very difficult to be certain that the physical features of a theatre would oblige playwrights to create particular kinds of stage action. Nor is it possible to be certain exactly what kinds of dramatic effects the design of a theatre would make possible. Yet if Jones's drawing represents the Cockpit, speculation as to how *'Tis Pity She's a Whore* was staged is something it is difficult to resist. What then can be said about the play and the playhouse?

- As noted above, the front of the tiring house would have looked like a large house in a street of an Italian city. In certain scenes, it would take no imaginative effort for an audience to regard it as the front of Florio's house. This is true of the second and third scenes. The fact that Grimaldi and Vasques fight outside Florio's house might indicate the wealth of the girl the suitors are pursuing, and that wealth is further evident when Annabella and Putana enjoy a parade of the suitors from their balcony.

• There is a moment in the second scene when the action begins to be very intimate. When Giovanni says *Here's none but you and I* (184), the audience must assume that Annabella and Giovanni are no longer in the street. Perhaps the tiring house facade would have been imagined as a courtyard or garden in Florio's house. That transition (were there specific actions to indicate a change of location?) underlines what has been said about the character of the play (see page 9). The dramatic life of *'Tis Pity She's a Whore* consists of a sharp contrast between the public and the private. The street scenes are obviously public, as are also the two banqueting scenes – the wedding feast (IV.i) and the birthday celebration (V.iv). In a theatre where wealthy people were, so to speak, on public display, the strutting and posing – indeed, the play acting – of the characters on stage would be convincingly in tune with the theatre in which their actions were being presented. But what then of the intimate scenes, the post-consummation scene of the young lovers (II.i) and the anguish of Soranzo in his study (II.ii)? These must have been enacted in the discovery space, and perhaps props – a bed, a desk – helped to define the space as private.

• It is not easy to assess just what the experience of an audience watching from the upper gallery would have been. In a small space, the upper gallery would have seemed to most people dizzyingly high. Perhaps the banqueting scenes were choreographed so that movements and grouping brought out the ritualized aspects of public feasting. As for the intimate scenes, perhaps the considerable height had another effect. Being so high up, did the audience feel like divine spectators responding with a blend of pity and horror to the workings of human passion? The upper tiers of theatres were not called 'the gods' until 1752, but audiences might have at least looked down at the terrible doings of Annabella and Giovanni like aghast guardian angels, pitying their antics. And that might have induced a fearful terror as to where this would lead.

- Mention has already been made of the 'quieter' aspects of plays in hall playhouses. In spite of its obvious debt to *Romeo and Juliet* (see Interpretations page 211), Ford's play does not begin with a street brawl. Instead there is a dispute, and in the second scene a duel between two old soldiers. The fight between Bergetto and *a swaggering fellow* (II.vi.74) takes place offstage. Nevertheless, there remains the matter of how the Banditti were presented. How many would be needed, and what kind of actions would they perform? If they acted with calculated menace, there would not need to be many, and their sudden entrances might have been sufficient to create the sense of violence. They could quickly overwhelm Putana, and in the case of Giovanni's death in the final scene, the stage direction indicates how the fight was staged: *They surround and*

The auditorium of the Teatro Olimpico, Vicenza

wound him (V.vi.83). Giovanni is quickly wounded – *He falls* (85) – and the Banditti exit four lines later.

• There is one further fight: the murder of Bergetto (III.vii). This occurs in a scene that must have been particularly interesting when performed in the enclosed space of the Cockpit. The Cockpit had high windows giving the gallery some light, but the strong likelihood is that the stage was also lit with candles. The number of candles could, of course, be reduced to indicate a night scene. The aim of those presenting the play must have been to give the impression of a darkness in which the wrong person can be attacked, while at the same time allowing the audience to see the credible confusion of the characters. In the banquet scenes the candles would become part of the festive atmosphere.

It is worth asking whether the subject of incest became the theme of a play because the audience was wealthier and (perhaps) more sophisticated than in the amphitheatres. In the open air there could be bloody revenge as in *Hamlet*, but a matter as delicate as incest might have suited people who, because of their social status, had the feeling of being part of a privileged audience. Was there even daring in going to see *'Tis Pity She's a Whore?*

All theatre blends the public and the intimate. In a play set in the theatrical public spaces of an Italian city state, Ford finds an interesting and appropriate way of bringing together the private and the public. The soliloquy is always intimate, even when the character addresses the audience. Working with this understanding, Ford makes much of the overheard soliloquy. Annabella's eloquent soliloquy of female abandonment (V.i) is overheard by the Friar. He does not make of it what we might. And perhaps that is the point; the Friar overhears as do the audience. Both have to make up their minds as to what is significant in the action of the play.

'Tis Pity She's a Whore

The Scene

Parma

The Persons of the Play

Florio, *a citizen of Parma*
Giovanni, *son of Florio*
Annabella, *daughter of Florio*
Bonaventura, *a friar, tutor to Giovanni*
Putana, *tutoress to Annabella*

Soranzo, *a nobleman*
Vasques, *servant to Soranzo*
Richardetto, *a supposed physician*
Hippolita, *wife of Richardetto*
Philotis, *niece of Richardetto*
Donado, *a citizen of Parma*
Bergetto, *nephew of Donado*
Poggio, *servant to Bergetto*

A Cardinal, *nuncio of the Pope*
Grimaldi, *a Roman gentleman*
Banditti
Officers
Attendants

Act I Scene I

Enter Friar and Giovanni

FRIAR   Dispute no more in this, for know, young man,
These are no school-points; nice philosophy
May tolerate unlikely arguments,
But Heaven admits no jest; wits that presumed
On wit too much, by striving how to prove   5
There was no God, with foolish grounds of art,
Discovered first the nearest way to Hell;
And filled the world with devilish atheism.
Such questions, youth, are fond; for better 'tis,
To bless the sun, than reason why it shines;   10
Yet he thou talk'st of is above the sun –
No more! I may not hear it.

GIOVANNI   Gentle Father,
To you I have unclasped my burdened soul,
Emptied the storehouse of my thoughts and heart,
Made myself poor of secrets; have not left   15
Another word untold, which hath not spoke
All what I ever durst, or think, or know;
And yet is here the comfort I shall have?
Must I not do what all men else may – love?

FRIAR   Yes, you may love, fair son.

GIOVANNI   Must I not praise   20
That beauty, which if framed anew, the gods
Would make a god of, if they had it there,
And kneel to it, as I do kneel to them?

FRIAR   Why, foolish madman!

GIOVANNI   Shall a peevish sound,
A customary form, from man to man,   25
Of brother and of sister, be a bar
'Twixt my perpetual happiness and me?

Say that we had one father, say one womb
(Curse to my joys) gave both us life and birth;
Are we not therefore each to other bound   30
So much the more by nature; by the links
Of blood, of reason? nay, if you will have't,
Even of religion, to be ever one:
One soul, one flesh, one love, one heart, one all?
FRIAR   Have done, unhappy youth, for thou art lost.   35
GIOVANNI Shall then, for that I am her brother born,
My joys be ever banished from her bed?
No, Father; in your eyes I see the change
Of pity and compassion: from your age,
As from a sacred oracle, distils   40
The life of counsel. Tell me, holy man,
What cure shall give me ease in these extremes?
FRIAR   Repentance, son, and sorrow for this sin
   – For thou hast moved a Majesty above
With thy unrangèd almost blasphemy.   45
GIOVANNI   O do not speak of that, dear confessor.
FRIAR   Art thou, my son, that miracle of wit
Who once, within these three months, wert esteemed
A wonder of thine age, throughout Bologna?
How did the university applaud   50
Thy government, behaviour, learning, speech,
Sweetness, and all that could make up a man!
I was proud of my tutelage, and chose
Rather to leave my books than part with thee.
I did so: but the fruits of all my hopes   55
Are lost in thee, as thou art in thyself.
O Giovanni! Hast thou left the schools
Of knowledge, to converse with lust and death?
For death waits on thy lust. Look through the world,
And thou shalt see a thousand faces shine   60
More glorious than this idol thou ador'st:

Leave her, and take thy choice; 'tis much less sin,
Though in such games as those, they lose that win.
GIOVANNI It were more ease to stop the ocean
  From floats and ebbs, than to dissuade my vows.   65
FRIAR Then I have done, and in thy wilful flames
  Already see thy ruin; Heaven is just,
  Yet hear my counsel.
GIOVANNI   As a voice of life.
FRIAR Hie to thy father's house, there lock thee fast
  Alone within thy chamber, then fall down   70
  On both thy knees, and grovel on the ground.
  Cry to thy heart, wash every word thou utter'st
  In tears (and if't be possible) of blood:
  Beg Heaven to cleanse the leprosy of lust
  That rots thy soul. Acknowledge what thou art,   75
  A wretch, a worm, a nothing: weep, sigh, pray
  Three times a day, and three times every night.
  For seven days' space do this, then if thou find'st
  No change in thy desires, return to me:
  I'll think on remedy. Pray for thyself   80
  At home, whilst I pray for thee here – away,
  My blessing with thee; we have need to pray.
GIOVANNI All this I'll do, to free me from the rod
  Of vengeance; else I'll swear, my fate's my god.
       Exeunt

Act I Scene II

  Enter Grimaldi and Vasques ready to fight
VASQUES Come sir, stand to your tackling; if you prove
  craven, I'll make you run quickly.
GRIMALDI Thou art no equal match for me.

VASQUES   Indeed I never went to the wars to bring
   home news, nor cannot play the mountebank for a   5
   meal's meat, and swear I got my wounds in the field.
   See you these grey hairs? They'll not flinch for a
   bloody nose. Wilt thou to this gear?
GRIMALDI   Why slave, think'st thou I'll balance my
   reputation with a cast-suit? Call thy master, he shall   10
   know that I dare –
VASQUES   Scold like a cot-quean – that's your
   profession. Thou poor shadow of a soldier, I will
   make thee know my master keeps servants, thy betters
   in quality and performance. Com'st thou to fight or   15
   prate?
GRIMALDI   Neither with thee. I am a Roman and a
   gentleman; one that have got mine honour with
   expense of blood.
VASQUES   You are a lying coward, and a fool. Fight, or   20
   by these hilts I'll kill thee – brave my lord! – You'll
   fight.
GRIMALDI   Provoke me not, for if thou dost –
VASQUES   Have at you! (*They fight, Grimaldi hath the worst*)
      Enter Florio, Donado, [and] Soranzo
FLORIO   What mean these sudden broils so near my
   doors?   25
   Have you not other places but my house
   To vent the spleen of your disordered bloods?
   Must I be haunted still with such unrest
   As not to eat, or sleep in peace at home?
   Is this your love, Grimaldi? Fie, 'tis naught.   30
DONADO   And Vasques, I may tell thee, 'tis not well
   To broach these quarrels; you are ever forward
   In seconding contentions.
      Enter above Annabella and Putana
FLORIO   What's the ground?

SORANZO   That, with your patience, Signiors, I'll
    resolve:
    This gentleman, whom fame reports a soldier,   35
    (For else I know not) rivals me in love
    To Signior Florio's daughter, to whose ears
    He still prefers his suit, to my disgrace –
    Thinking the way to recommend himself
    Is to disparage me in his report.   40
    But know Grimaldi, though, may be, thou art
    My equal in thy blood, yet this bewrays
    A lowness in thy mind; which wert thou noble
    Thou wouldst as much disdain, as I do thee
    For this unworthiness; [*to Donado and Florio*] and on
        this ground   45
    I willed my servant to correct this tongue,
    Holding a man so base no match for me.
VASQUES   And had not your sudden coming prevented
    us, I had let my gentleman blood under the gills; [*to
    Grimaldi*] I should have wormed you, sir, for running   50
    mad.
GRIMALDI   I'll be revenged Soranzo.
VASQUES   On a dish of warm broth to stay your
    stomach – do, honest innocence, do; spoon-meat is a
    wholesomer diet than a Spanish blade.   55
GRIMALDI   Remember this.
SORANZO   I fear thee not, Grimaldi.
        Exit Grimaldi
FLORIO   My Lord Soranzo, this is strange to me,
    Why you should storm, having my word engaged:
    Owing her heart, what need you doubt her ear?
    Losers may talk by law of any game.   60
VASQUES   Yet the villainy of words, Signior Florio, may
    be such as would make any unspleened dove choleric.
    Blame not my lord in this.

FLORIO   Be you more silent.
  I would not for my wealth my daughter's love   65
  Should cause the spilling of one drop of blood.
  Vasques, put up, let's end this fray in wine.
    Exeunt [Florio, Donado, Soranzo, and Vasques]

PUTANA   How like you this, child? Here's threatening,
challenging, quarrelling, and fighting, on every side,
and all is for your sake; you had need look to yourself,   70
charge, you'll be stol'n away sleeping else shortly.

ANNABELLA   But, tutoress, such a life gives no content
  To me, my thoughts are fixed on other ends;
  Would you would leave me.

PUTANA   Leave you? No marvel else; leave me no   75
leaving, charge; this is love outright. Indeed I blame
you not; you have choice fit for the best lady in Italy.

ANNABELLA   Pray do not talk so much.

PUTANA   Take the worst with the best – there's
Grimaldi the soldier, a very well-timbered fellow: they   80
say he is a Roman, nephew to the Duke Monferrato;
they say he did good service in the wars against the
Milanese, but faith, charge, I do not like him, an't be
for nothing but for being a soldier; not one amongst
twenty of your skirmishing captains but have some   85
privy maim or other, that mars their standing upright.
I like him the worse, he crinkles so much in the hams;
though he might serve if there were no more men, yet
he's not the man I would choose.

ANNABELLA   Fie, how thou prate'st.   90

PUTANA   As I am a very woman, I like Signior Soranzo
well; he is wise, and what is more, rich; and what is
more than that, kind; and what is more than all this, a
nobleman; such a one, were I the fair Annabella myself,
I would wish and pray for. Then he is bountiful;   95
besides he is handsome, and, by my troth, I think

wholesome (and that's news in a gallant of three-and-twenty); liberal, that I know; loving, that you know; and a man sure, else he could never ha' purchased such a good name with Hippolita, the lusty widow, in her 100 husband's lifetime: and 'twere but for that report, sweetheart, would 'a were thine. Commend a man for his qualities, but take a husband as he is a plain-sufficient, naked man: such a one is for your bed, and such a one is Signior Soranzo, my life for't. 105

ANNABELLA   Sure the woman took her morning's draught too soon.

Enter Bergetto and Poggio

PUTANA   But look, sweetheart, look what thing comes now: here's another of your ciphers to fill up the number. O, brave old ape in a silken coat! Observe.

BERGETTO   Didst thou think, Poggio, that I would spoil 110 my new clothes, and leave my dinner, to fight?

POGGIO   No sir, I did not take you for so arrant a baby.

BERGETTO   I am wiser than so: for I hope, Poggio, thou never heard'st of an elder brother that was a coxcomb, didst, Poggio? 115

POGGIO   Never indeed sir, as long as they had either land or money left them to inherit.

BERGETTO   Is it possible, Poggio? O monstrous! Why, I'll undertake, with a handful of silver, to buy a headful of wit at any time; but sirrah, I have another 120 purchase in hand, I shall have the wench, mine uncle says. I will but wash my face, and shift socks, and then have at her i'faith! – Mark my pace, Poggio.

[Walks affectedly]

POGGIO   Sir, I have seen an ass and a mule trot the Spanish pavan with a better grace, I know not how 125 often.

Exeunt [Bergetto and Poggio]

31

ANNABELLA   This idiot haunts me too.

PUTANA   Ay, ay, he needs no description. The rich
magnifico that is below with your father, charge,
Signior Donado his uncle – for that he means to make   130
this, his cousin, a golden calf – thinks that you will be
a right Israelite, and fall down to him presently: but I
hope I have tutored you better. They say a fool's
bauble is a lady's playfellow: yet you having wealth
enough, you need not cast upon the dearth of flesh at   135
any rate. Hang him, innocent!

    Enter Giovanni [below]

ANNABELLA   But see, Putana, see: what blessèd shape
    Of some celestial creature now appears?
    What man is he, that with such sad aspect
    Walks careless of himself?

PUTANA   Where?

ANNABELLA   Look below.   140

PUTANA   O, 'tis your brother, sweet –

ANNABELLA   Ha!

PUTANA   'Tis your brother.

ANNABELLA   Sure 'tis not he; this is some woeful thing
    Wrapped up in grief, some shadow of a man.
    Alas, he beats his breast, and wipes his eyes
    Drowned all in tears: methinks I hear him sigh.   145
    Let's down, Putana, and partake the cause;
    I know my brother, in the love he bears me,
    Will not deny me partage in his sadness.
    My soul is full of heaviness and fear.

    Exeunt [Annabella and Putana]

GIOVANNI   Lost, I am lost: my fates have doomed my
    death.   150
    The more I strive, I love; the more I love,
    The less I hope: I see my ruin, certain.
    What judgement or endeavours could apply

To my incurable and restless wounds
I throughly have examined, but in vain.   155
O that it were not in religion sin
To make our love a god, and worship it.
I have even wearied Heaven with prayers, dried up
The spring of my continual tears, even starved
My veins with daily fasts. What wit or art   160
Could counsel, I have practised; but alas
I find all these but dreams, and old men's tales
To fright unsteady youth; I'm still the same.
Or I must speak, or burst; 'tis not I know,
My lust, but 'tis my fate that leads me on.   165
Keep fear and low faint-hearted shame with slaves!
I'll tell her that I love her, though my heart
Were rated at the price of that attempt.
Oh me! She comes.
        Enter Annabella and Putana
ANNABELLA   Brother.
GIOVANNI [*aside*]   If such a thing
As courage dwell in men, ye heavenly powers,   170
Now double all that virtue in my tongue.
ANNABELLA   Why brother, will you not speak to me?
GIOVANNI   Yes; how d'ee sister?
ANNABELLA   Howsoever I am, methinks you are not well.
PUTANA   Bless us, why are you so sad, sir?   175
GIOVANNI   Let me entreat you leave us awhile, Putana.
    Sister, I would be private with you.
ANNABELLA   Withdraw Putana.
PUTANA   I will. [*Aside*] If this were any other company
    for her, I should think my absence an office of some   180
    credit; but I will leave them together.
        Exit Putana
GIOVANNI   Come sister, lend your hand, let's walk
    together.

    I hope you need not blush to walk with me;
    Here's none but you and I.
ANNABELLA   How's this?   185
GIOVANNI   Faith, I mean no harm.
ANNABELLA   Harm?
GIOVANNI   No good faith; how is't with 'ee?
ANNABELLA [*aside*]   I trust he be not frantic – [*to him*] I
    am very well, brother.
GIOVANNI   Trust me but I am sick; I fear so sick,   190
    'Twill cost my life.
ANNABELLA   Mercy forbid it! 'Tis not so, I hope.
GIOVANNI   I think you love me, sister.
ANNABELLA   Yes, you know I do.
GIOVANNI   I know't indeed – y'are very fair.   195
ANNABELLA   Nay, then I see you have a merry sickness.
GIOVANNI   That's as it proves. The poets feign, I read,
    That Juno for her forehead did exceed
    All other goddesses: but I durst swear
    Your forehead exceeds hers, as hers did theirs.   200
ANNABELLA   Troth, this is pretty.
GIOVANNI   Such a pair of stars
    As are thine eyes, would (like Promethean fire,
    If gently glanced) give life to senseless stones.
ANNABELLA   Fie upon 'ee!
GIOVANNI   The lily and the rose, most sweetly strange,   205
    Upon your dimpled cheeks do strive for change.
    Such lips would tempt a saint; such hands as those
    Would make an anchorite lascivious.
ANNABELLA   D'ee mock me, or flatter me?
GIOVANNI   If you would see a beauty more exact   210
    Than art can counterfeit, or nature frame,
    Look in your glass, and there behold your own.
ANNABELLA   O you are a trim youth.
GIOVANNI   Here.

Offers his dagger to her

ANNABELLA   What to do?

GIOVANNI   And here's my breast, strike home.
Rip up my bosom; there thou shalt behold   215
A heart, in which is writ the truth I speak.
Why stand 'ee?

ANNABELLA   Are you earnest?

GIOVANNI   Yes, most earnest.
You cannot love?

ANNABELLA   Whom?

GIOVANNI   Me. My tortured soul
Hath felt affliction in the heat of death.
O Annabella, I am quite undone.   220
The love of thee, my sister, and the view
Of thy immortal beauty hath untuned
All harmony both of my rest and life.
Why d'ee not strike?

ANNABELLA   Forbid it my just fears;
If this be true, 'twere fitter I were dead.   225

GIOVANNI   True, Annabella; 'tis no time to jest.
I have too long suppressed the hidden flames
That almost have consumed me; I have spent
Many a silent night in sighs and groans,
Ran over all my thoughts, despised my fate,   230
Reasoned against the reasons of my love,
Done all that smoothed-cheek Virtue could advise,
But found all bootless; 'tis my destiny
That you must either love, or I must die.

ANNABELLA   Comes this in sadness from you?

GIOVANNI   Let some mischief   235
Befall me soon, if I dissemble aught.

ANNABELLA   You are my brother Giovanni.

GIOVANNI   You,
My sister Annabella; I know this:

And could afford you instance why to love
So much the more for this; to which intent 240
Wise Nature first in your creation meant
To make you mine: else't had been sin and foul
To share one beauty to a double soul.
Nearness in birth or blood doth but persuade
A nearer nearness in affection. 245
I have asked counsel of the holy Church,
Who tells me I may love you, and 'tis just
That since I may, I should; and will, yes will:
Must I now live, or die?

ANNABELLA   Live; thou hast won
The field, and never fought; what thou hast urged, 250
My captive heart had long ago resolved.
I blush to tell thee – but I'll tell thee now –
For every sigh that thou hast spent for me,
I have sighed ten; for every tear, shed twenty:
And not so much for that I loved, as that 255
I durst not say I loved; nor scarcely think it.

GIOVANNI   Let not this music be a dream, ye gods,
For pity's sake I beg 'ee.

ANNABELLA   On my knees, (*she kneels*)
Brother, even by our mother's dust, I charge you,
Do not betray me to your mirth or hate; 260
Love me, or kill me, brother.

GIOVANNI   On my knees, (*he kneels*)
Sister, even by my mother's dust I charge you,
Do not betray me to your mirth or hate;
Love me, or kill me, sister.

ANNABELLA   You mean good sooth then?

GIOVANNI   In good troth I do, 265
And so do you I hope: say, I'm in earnest.

ANNABELLA   I'll swear't; and I.

GIOVANNI   And I, and by this kiss –

(*Kisses her*)
Once more, yet once more; now let's rise, by this,
I would not change this minute for Elysium.
What must we now do?
ANNABELLA   What you will.
GIOVANNI   Come then,   270
After so many tears as we have wept,
Let's learn to court in smiles, to kiss and sleep.
      Exeunt

Act I Scene III

Enter Florio and Donado
FLORIO   Signior Donado, you have said enough;
I understand you, but would have you know
I will not force my daughter 'gainst her will.
You see I have but two, a son and her;
And he is so devoted to his book,   5
As I must tell you true, I doubt his health:
Should he miscarry, all my hopes rely
Upon my girl. As for worldly fortune,
I am, I thank my stars, blessed with enough.
My care is how to match her to her liking;   10
I would not have her marry wealth, but love,
And if she like your nephew, let him have her.
Here's all that I can say.
DONADO   Sir, you say well,
Like a true father, and for my part, I,
If the young folks can like ('twixt you and me),   15
Will promise to assure my nephew presently,
Three thousand florins yearly during life,
And after I am dead, my whole estate.

FLORIO 'Tis a fair proffer, sir; meantime your nephew
    Shall have free passage to commence his suit: 20
    If he can thrive, he shall have my consent.
    So for this time I'll leave you, signior.
      Exit
DONADO   Well,
    Here's hope yet, if my nephew would have wit;
    But he is such another dunce, I fear
    He'll never win the wench. When I was young   25
    I could have done't i'faith, and so shall he
    If he will learn of me;
      Enter Bergetto and Poggio
                        and in good time
    He comes himself.
    How now Bergetto, whither away so fast?
BERGETTO   Oh uncle, I have heard the strangest news   30
    that ever came out of the mint, have I not, Poggio?
POGGIO   Yes indeed, sir.
DONADO   What news, Bergetto?
BERGETTO   Why look ye uncle? My barber told me just
    now that there is a fellow come to town, who   35
    undertakes to make a mill go without the mortal help
    of any water or wind, only with sandbags: and this
    fellow hath a strange horse, a most excellent beast, I'll
    assure you uncle, (my barber says), whose head, to the
    wonder of all Christian people, stands just behind   40
    where his tail is; is't not true, Poggio?
POGGIO   So the barber swore forsooth.
DONADO   And you are running thither?
BERGETTO   Ay forsooth uncle.
DONADO   Wilt thou be a fool still? Come, sir, you shall   45
    not go; you have more mind of a puppet-play, than on
    the business I told ye. Why, thou great baby, wilt never
    have wit; wilt make thyself a May-game to all the world?

POGGIO   Answer for yourself, master.

BERGETTO   Why uncle, should I sit at home still, and   50
not go abroad to see fashions like other gallants?

DONADO   To see hobby-horses! What wise talk, I pray,
had you with Annabella, when you were at Signior
Florio's house?

BERGETTO   Oh, the wench! Uds sa' me, uncle, I tickled   55
her with a rare speech, that I made her almost burst
her belly with laughing.

DONADO   Nay I think so, and what speech was't?

BERGETTO   What did I say, Poggio?

POGGIO   Forsooth, my master said that he loved her   60
almost as well as he loved parmesan, and swore (I'll be
sworn for him) that she wanted but such a nose as his
was, to be as pretty a young woman as any was in Parma.

DONADO   Oh gross!

BERGETTO   Nay uncle, then she asked me whether my   65
father had any more children than myself: and I said,
'No, 'twere better he should have had his brains
knocked out first.'

DONADO   This is intolerable.

BERGETTO   Then said she, 'Will Signior Donado, your   70
uncle, leave you all his wealth?'

DONADO   Ha! that was good, did she harp upon that
string?

BERGETTO   Did she harp upon that string? Ay that she
did. I answered, 'Leave me all his wealth? Why, woman,   75
he hath no other wit; if he had he should hear on't to his
everlasting glory and confusion: I know', quoth I, 'I am
his white boy, and will not be gulled'; and with that she
fell into a great smile, and went away. Nay, I did fit her.

DONADO   Ah sirrah, then I see there is no changing of   80
nature. Well, Bergetto, I fear thou wilt be a very ass
still.

BERGETTO   I should be sorry for that, uncle.

DONADO   Come, come you home with me; since you are no better a speaker, I'll have you write to her after   85 some courtly manner, and enclose some rich jewel in the letter.

BERGETTO   Ay, marry, that will be excellent.

DONADO   Peace, innocent.

Once in my time I'll set my wits to school;   90
If all fail, 'tis but the fortune of a fool.

BERGETTO   Poggio, 'twill do, Poggio!

Exeunt

Act II Scene I

Enter Giovanni and Annabella, as from their chamber

GIOVANNI   Come Annabella, no more sister now,
But love, a name more gracious; do not blush,
Beauty's sweet wonder, but be proud to know
That yielding thou hast conquered, and inflamed
A heart whose tribute is thy brother's life.   5

ANNABELLA   And mine is his. O, how these stol'n
    contents
Would print a modest crimson on my cheeks,
Had any but my heart's delight prevailed.

GIOVANNI   I marvel why the chaster of your sex
Should think this pretty toy called maidenhead   10
So strange a loss, when being lost, 'tis nothing,
And you are still the same.

ANNABELLA   'Tis well for you;
Now you can talk.

GIOVANNI   Music as well consists
In th'ear, as in the playing.

ANNABELLA   O, y'are wanton!
Tell on't, y'are best, do.

GIOVANNI   Thou wilt chide me then.   15
Kiss me, so: thus hung Jove on Leda's neck,
And sucked divine ambrosia from her lips.
I envy not the mightiest man alive,
But hold myself in being king of thee,
More great, than were I king of all the world: 20
But I shall lose you, sweetheart.

ANNABELLA   But you shall not.

GIOVANNI   You must be married, mistress.

ANNABELLA   Yes, to whom?

GIOVANNI   Someone must have you.

ANNABELLA   You must.
GIOVANNI   Nay, some other.
ANNABELLA   Now prithee do not speak so without jesting;
   You'll make me weep in earnest.
GIOVANNI   What, you will not!   25
   But tell me sweet, canst thou be dared to swear
   That thou wilt live to me, and to no other?
ANNABELLA   By both our loves I dare, for didst thou
    know
   My Giovanni, how all suitors seem
   To my eyes hateful, thou wouldst trust me then.   30
GIOVANNI   Enough, I take thy word. Sweet, we must part:
   Remember what thou vow'st; keep well my heart.
ANNABELLA   Will you begone?
GIOVANNI   I must.
ANNABELLA   When to return?
GIOVANNI   Soon.
ANNABELLA   Look you do.
GIOVANNI   Farewell.
    Exit [*Giovanni*]
ANNABELLA   Go where thou wilt, in mind I'll keep thee
    here,   35
   And where thou art, I know I shall be there.
   Guardian!
    Enter Putana
PUTANA   Child, how is't child? Well, thank Heaven, ha?
ANNABELLA   O Guardian, what a paradise of joy
   Have I passed over!   40
PUTANA   Nay, what a paradise of joy have you passed
   under! Why, now I commend thee, charge; fear
   nothing, sweetheart. What though he be your
   brother? Your brother's a man I hope, and I say still,
   if a young wench feel the fit upon her, let her take   45
   anybody, father or brother, all is one.

ANNABELLA   I would not have it known for all the
     world.
PUTANA   Nor I indeed, for the speech of the people;
     else 'twere nothing.
FLORIO (*within*)   Daughter Annabella!   50
ANNABELLA   O me, my father! – Here, sir! [*To Putana*] –
     Reach my work.
FLORIO (*within*)   What are you doing?
ANNABELLA   So, let him come now.
     Enter Florio, Richardetto like a Doctor of Physic, and
     Philotis with a lute in her hand
FLORIO   So hard at work, that's well; you lose no time.
     Look, I have brought you company: here's one,
     A learnèd doctor, lately come from Padua,   55
     Much skilled in physic; and for that I see
     You have of late been sickly, I entreated
     This reverend man to visit you some time.
ANNABELLA   Y'are very welcome, sir.
RICHARDETTO   I thank you mistress.
     Loud fame in large report hath spoke your praise,   60
     As well for virtue as perfection:
     For which I have been bold to bring with me
     A kinswoman of mine, a maid, for song
     And music, one perhaps will give content.
     Please you to know her.
ANNABELLA   They are parts I love,   65
     And she for them most welcome.
PHILOTIS   Thank you, lady.
FLORIO   Sir, now you know my house, pray make not
     strange,
     And if you find my daughter need your art,
     I'll be your paymaster.
RICHARDETTO   Sir, what I am
     She shall command.

FLORIO   You shall bind me to you.   70
  Daughter, I must have conference with you
  About some matters that concerns us both.
  Good master doctor, please you but walk in,
  We'll crave a little of your cousin's cunning:
  I think my girl hath not quite forgot   75
  To touch an instrument; she could have done't –
  We'll hear them both.
RICHARDETTO   I'll wait upon you, sir.
    Exeunt

Act II Scene II

Enter Soranzo in his study, reading a book
SORANZO   'Love's measure is extreme, the comfort,
    pain,
  The life unrest, and the reward disdain.'
  What's here? Look't o'er again: 'tis so, so writes
  This smooth licentious poet in his rhymes.
  But Sannazar thou liest, for had thy bosom   5
  Felt such oppression as is laid on mine,
  Thou wouldst have kissed the rod that made the smart.
  To work then, happy Muse, and contradict
  What Sannazar hath in his envy writ.
  'Love's measure is the mean, sweet his annoys,   10
  His pleasure's life, and his reward all joys.'
  Had Annabella lived when Sannazar
  Did in his brief encomium celebrate
  Venice, that queen of cities, he had left
  That verse which gained him such a sum of gold,   15
  And for one only look from Annabell
  Had writ of her, and her diviner cheeks.

O how my thoughts are —
VASQUES (*within*)   Pray forbear; in rules of civility, let
  me give notice on't: I shall be taxed of my neglect of   20
  duty and service.
SORANZO   What rude intrusion interrupts my peace?
  Can I be nowhere private?
VASQUES (*within*)   Troth you wrong your modesty.
SORANZO   What's the matter Vasques, who is't?   25
    Enter Hippolita [in mourning clothes] and Vasques
HIPPOLITA   'Tis I:
  Do you know me now? Look, perjured man, on her
  Whom thou and thy distracted lust have wronged.
  Thy sensual rage of blood hath made my youth
  A scorn to men and angels, and shall I   30
  Be now a foil to thy unsated change?
  Thou know'st, false wanton, when my modest fame
  Stood free from stain or scandal, all the charms
  Of Hell or sorcery could not prevail
  Against the honour of my chaster bosom.   35
  Thine eyes did plead in tears, thy tongue in oaths
  Such and so many, that a heart of steel
  Would have been wrought to pity, as was mine:
  And shall the conquest of my lawful bed,
  My husband's death urged on by his disgrace,   40
  My loss of womanhood, be ill rewarded
  With hatred and contempt? No, know Soranzo,
  I have a spirit doth as much distaste
  The slavery of fearing thee, as thou
  Dost loathe the memory of what hath passed.   45
SORANZO   Nay, dear Hippolita —
HIPPOLITA   Call me not dear,
  Nor think with supple words to smooth the grossness
  Of my abuses; 'tis not your new mistress,
  Your goodly Madam Merchant, shall triumph

On my dejection; tell her thus from me,   50
My birth was nobler, and by much, more free.
SORANZO   You are too violent.
HIPPOLITA   You are too double
In your dissimulation. Seest thou this,
This habit, these black mourning weeds of care?
'Tis thou art cause of this, and hast divorced   55
My husband from his life and me from him,
And made me widow in my widowhood.
SORANZO   Will you yet hear?
HIPPOLITA   More of thy perjuries?
Thy soul is drowned too deeply in those sins;
Thou need'st not add to th'number.
SORANZO   Then I'll leave you;   60
You are past all rules of sense.
HIPPOLITA   And thou of grace.
VASQUES   Fie, mistress, you are not near the limits of
reason: if my lord had a resolution as noble as virtue
itself, you take the course to unedge it all. Sir, I
beseech you do not perplex her; griefs, alas, will have   65
a vent. I dare undertake Madam Hippolita will now
freely hear you.
SORANZO   Talk to a woman frantic! Are these the fruits
of your love?
HIPPOLITA   They are the fruits of thy untruth, false man.
Didst thou not swear, whilst yet my husband lived,   70
That thou wouldst wish no happiness on earth
More than to call me wife? Didst thou not vow
When he should die to marry me? For which
The devil in my blood, and thy protests,
Caused me to counsel him to undertake   75
A voyage to Leghorn, for that we heard
His brother there was dead, and left a daughter
Young and unfriended, who with much ado

I wished him to bring hither: he did so,
And went; and as thou know'st, died on the way.   80
Unhappy man, to buy his death so dear
With my advice! Yet thou for whom I did it
Forget'st thy vows, and leav'st me to my shame.
SORANZO   Who could help this?
HIPPOLITA   Who? Perjured man, thou couldst,
If thou hadst faith or love.
SORANZO   You are deceived.   85
The vows I made, if you remember well,
Were wicked and unlawful; 'twere more sin
To keep them than to break them. As for me,
I cannot mask my penitence. Think thou
How much thou hast digressed from honest shame   90
In bringing of a gentleman to death
Who was thy husband; such a one as he,
So noble in his quality, condition,
Learning, behaviour, entertainment, love,
As Parma could not show a braver man.   95
VASQUES   You do not well; this was not your promise.
SORANZO   I care not; let her know her monstrous
      life.
Ere I'll be servile to so black a sin,
I'll be a corse. – Woman, come here no more,
Learn to repent and die; for by my honour   100
I hate thee and thy lust; you have been too foul.
      [*Exit Soranzo*]
VASQUES   This part has been scurvily played.
HIPPOLITA   How foolishly this beast contemns his
      fate,
And shuns the use of that which I more scorn
Than I once loved, his love. But let him go;   105
My vengeance shall give comfort to his woe.
      She offers to go away

VASQUES   Mistress, mistress, Madam Hippolita, pray, a
    word or two.

HIPPOLITA   With me, sir?

VASQUES   With you, if you please.   110

HIPPOLITA   What is't?

VASQUES   I know you are infinitely moved now, and you
    think you have cause: some I confess you have, but
    sure not so much as you imagine.

HIPPOLITA   Indeed.   115

VASQUES   O, you were miserably bitter, which you
    followed even to the last syllable. Faith, you were
    somewhat too shrewd. By my life, you could not have
    took my lord in a worse time since I first knew him:
    tomorrow you shall find him a new man.   120

HIPPOLITA   Well, I shall wait his leisure.

VASQUES   Fie, this is not a hearty patience, it comes
    sourly from you; troth, let me persuade you for
    once.

HIPPOLITA [aside]   I have it, and it shall be so; thanks,   125
    opportunity! [To him] Persuade me to what?

VASQUES   Visit him in some milder temper. O, if you
    could but master a little your female spleen, how
    might you win him!

HIPPOLITA   He will never love me. Vasques, thou hast   130
    been a too trusty servant to such a master, and I believe
    thy reward in the end will fall out like mine.

VASQUES   So, perhaps too.

HIPPOLITA   Resolve thyself it will. Had I one so true, so
    truly honest, so secret to my counsels, as thou hast   135
    been to him and his, I should think it a slight
    acquittance, not only to make him master of all I
    have, but even of myself.

VASQUES   O, you are a noble gentlewoman!

HIPPOLITA   Wilt thou feed always upon hopes? Well, I   140
    know thou art wise, and seest the reward of an old
    servant daily what it is.
VASQUES   Beggary and neglect.
HIPPOLITA   True; but Vasques, wert thou mine, and
    wouldst be private to me and my designs, I here   145
    protest, myself and all what I can else call mine,
    should be at thy dispose.
VASQUES [*aside*]   Work you that way, old mole? Then I
    have the wind of you. [*To her*] I were not worthy of it
    by any desert that could lie within my compass; if I   150
    could –
HIPPOLITA   What then?
VASQUES   I should then hope to live in these my old
    years with rest and security.
HIPPOLITA   Give me thy hand: now promise but thy
        silence,   155
    And help to bring to pass a plot I have,
    And here in sight of Heaven, that being done,
    I make thee lord of me and mine estate.
VASQUES   Come, you are merry; this is such a happiness
    that I can neither think or believe.   160
HIPPOLITA   Promise thy secrecy, and 'tis confirmed.
VASQUES   Then here I call our good genii for witnesses,
    whatsoever your designs are, or against whomsoever, I
    will not only be a special actor therein, but never
    disclose it till it be effected.   165
HIPPOLITA   I take thy word, and with that, thee for
        mine.
    Come then, let's more confer of this anon.
    On this delicious bane my thoughts shall banquet:
    Revenge shall sweeten what my griefs have tasted.
        Exeunt

Act II Scene III

Enter Richardetto and Philotis

RICHARDETTO   Thou seest, my lovely niece, these strange mishaps,
How all my fortunes turn to my disgrace,
Wherein I am but as a looker-on,
Whiles others act my shame and I am silent.

PHILOTIS   But uncle, wherein can this borrowed shape   5
Give you content?

RICHARDETTO   I'll tell thee, gentle niece.
Thy wanton aunt in her lascivious riots
Lives now secure, thinks I am surely dead
In my late journey to Leghorn for you
(As I have caused it to be rumoured out).   10
Now would I see with what an impudence
She gives scope to her loose adultery,
And how the common voice allows hereof;
Thus far I have prevailed.

PHILOTIS   Alas, I fear
You mean some strange revenge.

RICHARDETTO   O, be not troubled;   15
Your ignorance shall plead for you in all.
But to our business: what, you learnt for certain
How Signior Florio means to give his daughter
In marriage to Soranzo?

PHILOTIS   Yes, for certain.

RICHARDETTO   But how find you young Annabella's love   20
Inclined to him?

PHILOTIS   For aught I could perceive,
She neither fancies him or any else.

RICHARDETTO   There's mystery in that which time must show.
She used you kindly?

PHILOTIS Yes.

RICHARDETTO And craved your company?

PHILOTIS Often.

RICHARDETTO 'Tis well; it goes as I could wish.   25
I am the doctor now, and as for you,
None knows you; if all fail not, we shall thrive.
    Enter Grimaldi
But who comes here? I know him: 'tis Grimaldi,
A Roman and a soldier, near allied
Unto the Duke of Monferrato, one   30
Attending on the nuncio of the Pope
That now resides in Parma, by which means
He hopes to get the love of Annabella.

GRIMALDI Save you, sir.

RICHARDETTO And you, sir.

GRIMALDI I have heard
Of your approved skill, which through the city   35
Is freely talked of, and would crave your aid.

RICHARDETTO For what, sir?

GRIMALDI Marry, sir, for this –
But I would speak in private.

RICHARDETTO Leave us, cousin.
    [*Exit Philotis*]

GRIMALDI I love fair Annabella, and would know
Whether in arts there may not be receipts   40
To move affection.

RICHARDETTO Sir, perhaps there may,
But these will nothing profit you.

GRIMALDI Not me?

RICHARDETTO Unless I be mistook, you are a man
Greatly in favour with the Cardinal.

GRIMALDI What of that?

RICHARDETTO In duty to his grace,   45
I will be bold to tell you, if you seek

To marry Florio's daughter, you must first
Remove a bar 'twixt you and her.
GRIMALDI   Who's that?
RICHARDETTO   Soranzo is the man that hath her heart,
And while he lives, be sure you cannot speed.   50
GRIMALDI   Soranzo! What, mine enemy! Is't he?
RICHARDETTO   Is he your enemy?
GRIMALDI   The man I hate
Worse than confusion –
I'll kill him straight.
RICHARDETTO   Nay, then take mine advice,
Even for his grace's sake, the Cardinal.   55
I'll find a time when he and she do meet,
Of which I'll give you notice, and to be sure
He shall not 'scape you, I'll provide a poison
To dip your rapier's point in; if he had
As many heads as Hydra had, he dies.   60
GRIMALDI   But shall I trust thee, doctor?
RICHARDETTO   As yourself;
Doubt not in aught. [*Aside*] Thus shall the fates
    decree:
By me Soranzo falls, that ruined me.
    Exeunt

Act II Scene IV

Enter Donado, Bergetto, and Poggio
DONADO   Well, sir, I must be content to be both your
secretary and your messenger myself. I cannot tell
what this letter may work, but as sure as I am alive, if
thou come once to talk with her, I fear thou wilt mar
whatsoever I make.   5

BERGETTO   You make, uncle? Why, am not I big enough
to carry mine own letter, I pray?

DONADO   Ay, ay, carry a fool's head o' thy own. Why,
thou dunce, wouldst thou write a letter and carry it
thyself?   10

BERGETTO   Yes, that I would, and read it to her with my
own mouth; for you must think, if she will not believe
me myself when she hears me speak, she will not
believe another's handwriting. O, you think I am a
blockhead, uncle. No, sir; Poggio knows I have indited   15
a letter myself, so I have.

POGGIO   Yes truly, sir, I have it in my pocket.

DONADO   A sweet one no doubt, pray let's see't.

BERGETTO   I cannot read my own hand very well,
Poggio; read it, Poggio.   20

DONADO   Begin.

POGGIO (*reads*)   'Most dainty and honey-sweet mistress, I
could call you fair, and lie as fast as any that loves you,
but my uncle being the elder man, I leave it to him as
more fit for his age and the colour of his beard. I am   25
wise enough to tell you I can board where I see
occasion, or if you like my uncle's wit better than mine,
you shall marry me; if you like mine better than his, I
will marry you in spite of your teeth. So, commending
my best parts to you, I rest. Yours upwards and   30
downwards, or you may choose, Bergetto.'

BERGETTO   Aha! here's stuff, uncle!

DONADO   Here's stuff indeed to shame us all. Pray,
whose advice did you take in this learnèd letter?

POGGIO   None, upon my word, but mine own.   35

BERGETTO   And mine, uncle, believe it, nobody's else;
'twas mine own brain, I thank a good wit for't.

DONADO   Get you home sir, and look you keep within
doors till I return.

BERGETTO   How! That were a jest indeed; I scorn it i'faith.   40
DONADO   What! You do not?
BERGETTO   Judge me, but I do now.
POGGIO   Indeed, sir, 'tis very unhealthy.
DONADO   Well, sir, if I hear any of your apish running
   to motions and fopperies till I come back, you were as   45
   good no; look to't.
      Exit [Donado]
BERGETTO   Poggio, shall's steal to see this horse with
   the head in's tail?
POGGIO   Ay, but you must take heed of whipping.
BERGETTO   Dost take me for a child, Poggio? Come,   50
   honest Poggio.
      Exeunt

Act II Scene V

Enter Friar and Giovanni
FRIAR   Peace! Thou hast told a tale whose every word
   Threatens eternal slaughter to the soul.
   I'm sorry I have heard it; would mine ears
   Had been one minute deaf, before the hour
   That thou cam'st to me. O young man, cast away   5
   By the religious number of mine order,
   I day and night have waked my agèd eyes
   Above my strength, to weep on thy behalf.
   But Heaven is angry, and be thou resolved,
   Thou art a man remarked to taste a mischief.   10
   Look for't; though it come late, it will come sure.
GIOVANNI   Father, in this you are uncharitable;
   What I have done, I'll prove both fit and good.
   It is a principle (which you have taught
   When I was yet your scholar) that the frame   15

And composition of the mind doth follow
The frame and composition of the body.
So where the body's furniture is beauty,
The mind's must needs be virtue, which allowed,
Virtue itself is reason but refined,   20
And love the quintessence of that. This proves
My sister's beauty, being rarely fair,
Is rarely virtuous; chiefly in her love,
And chiefly in that love, her love to me.
If hers to me, then so is mine to her;   25
Since in like causes are effects alike.

FRIAR   O ignorance in knowledge! Long ago,
How often have I warned thee this before!
Indeed, if we were sure there were no Deity,
Nor Heaven nor Hell, then to be led alone   30
By Nature's light (as were philosophers
Of elder times), might instance some defence.
But 'tis not so. Then, madman, thou wilt find
That Nature is in Heaven's positions blind.

GIOVANNI   Your age o'errules you; had you youth like
    mine,   35
You'd make her love your heaven, and her divine.

FRIAR   Nay, then I see th'art too far sold to Hell,
It lies not in the compass of my prayers
To call thee back; yet let me counsel thee:
Persuade thy sister to some marriage.   40

GIOVANNI   Marriage? Why, that's to damn her! That's
    to prove
Her greedy of variety of lust.

FRIAR   O fearful! If thou wilt not, give me leave
To shrive her, lest she should die unabsolved.

GIOVANNI   At your best leisure, father; then she'll tell you   45
How dearly she doth prize my matchless love;
Then you will know what pity 'twere we two

Should have been sundered from each other's arms.
View well her face, and in that little round
You may observe a world of variety: 50
For colour, lips; for sweet perfumes, her breath;
For jewels, eyes; for threads of purest gold,
Hair; for delicious choice of flowers, cheeks;
Wonder in every portion of that throne.
Hear her but speak, and you will swear the spheres   55
Make music to the citizens in Heaven;
But father, what is else for pleasure framed,
Lest I offend your ears, shall go unnamed.
FRIAR   The more I hear, I pity thee the more,
That one so excellent should give those parts   60
All to a second death. What I can do
Is but to pray; and yet I could advise thee,
Wouldst thou be ruled.
GIOVANNI   In what?
FRIAR   Why, leave her yet,
The throne of mercy is above your trespass;
Yet time is left you both –
GIOVANNI   To embrace each other,   65
Else let all time be struck quite out of number.
She is, like me, and I like her, resolved.
FRIAR   No more! I'll visit her. This grieves me most,
Things being thus, a pair of souls are lost.
        Exeunt

Act II Scene VI

Enter Florio, Donado, Annabella, [and] Putana
FLORIO   Where's Giovanni?
ANNABELLA   Newly walked abroad,
And, as I heard him say, gone to the friar,

His reverend tutor.
FLORIO That's a blessed man,
A man made up of holiness; I hope
He'll teach him how to gain another world.   5
DONADO   Fair gentlewoman, here's a letter sent
    [*He offers a letter to Annabella*]
To you from my young cousin. I dare swear
He loves you in his soul: would you could hear
Sometimes, what I see daily, sighs and tears,
As if his breast were prison to his heart.   10
FLORIO   Receive it, Annabella.
ANNABELLA   Alas, good man!
    [*She takes the letter*]
DONADO   What's that she said?
PUTANA   And please you, sir, she said 'Alas, good man!'
    [*Aside to Donado*] Truly, I do commend him to her
    every night before her first sleep, because I would have   15
    her dream of him, and she hearkens to that most
    religiously.
DONADO   [*aside to Putana*] Say'st so? Godamercy,
    Putana, there's something for thee [*gives her money*]
    and prithee do what thou canst on his behalf; sha'not   20
    be lost labour, take my word for't.
PUTANA [*aside to Donado*]   Thank you most heartily, sir,
    now I have a feeling of your mind, let me alone to work.
ANNABELLA   Guardian!
PUTANA   Did you call?   25
ANNABELLA   Keep this letter.
DONADO   Signior Florio, in any case bid her read it
    instantly.
FLORIO   Keep it for what? Pray read it me here right.
ANNABELLA   I shall, sir.   30
    She reads
DONADO   How d'ee find her inclined, Signior?

FLORIO   Troth, sir, I know not how; not all so well
As I could wish.

ANNABELLA   Sir, I am bound to rest your cousin's debtor.
The jewel I'll return, for if he love,   35
I'll count that love a jewel.

DONADO   Mark you that?
Nay, keep them both, sweet maid.

ANNABELLA   You must excuse me;
Indeed I will not keep it.

FLORIO   Where's the ring,
That which your mother in her will bequeathed,
And charged you on her blessing not to give't   40
To any but your husband? Send back that.

ANNABELLA   I have it not.

FLORIO   Ha, have it not! Where is't?

ANNABELLA   My brother in the morning took it from me,
Said he would wear't today.

FLORIO   Well, what do you say
To young Bergetto's love? Are you content   45
To match with him? Speak.

DONADO   There's the point indeed.

ANNABELLA   [*aside*] What shall I do? I must say
something now.

FLORIO   What say? Why d'ee not speak?

ANNABELLA   Sir, with your leave,
Please you to give me freedom.

FLORIO   Yes, you have't.

ANNABELLA   Signior Donado, if your nephew mean   50
To raise his better fortunes in his match,
The hope of me will hinder such a hope.
Sir, if you love him, as I know you do,
Find one more worthy of his choice than me.
In short, I'm sure I sha'not be his wife.   55

DONADO   Why, here's plain dealing, I commend thee for't,

And all the worst I wish thee, is Heaven bless thee!
Your father yet and I will still be friends,
Shall we not, Signior Florio?

FLORIO   Yes, why not?
Look, here your cousin comes.   60
    Enter Bergetto and Poggio

DONADO [*aside*]   O coxcomb, what doth he make here?

BERGETTO   Where's my uncle, sirs?

DONADO   What's the news now?

BERGETTO   Save you, uncle, save you! You must not
think I come for nothing, masters. And how, and how   65
is't? What, you have read my letter? Ah, there I –
tickled you i'faith!

POGGIO [*aside*]   But 'twere better you had tickled her in
another place.

BERGETTO   Sirrah sweetheart, I'll tell thee a good jest,   70
and riddle what 'tis.

ANNABELLA   You say you'd tell me.

BERGETTO   As I was walking just now in the street, I
met a swaggering fellow would needs take the wall of
me; and because he did thrust me, I very valiantly   75
called him rogue. He hereupon bade me draw. I told
him I had more wit than so; but when he saw that I
would not, he did so maul me with the hilts of his
rapier that my head sung whilst my feet capered in the
kennel.   80

DONADO [*aside*]   Was ever the like ass seen?

ANNABELLA   And what did you all this while?

BERGETTO   Laugh at him for a gull, till I see the blood run
about mine ears, and then I could not choose but find
in my heart to cry; till a fellow with a broad beard –   85
they say he is a new-come doctor – called me into this
house and gave me a plaster – look you, here 'tis; and
sir, there was a young wench washed my face and hands

most excellently, i'faith I shall love her as long as I live
for't – did she not, Poggio?   90
POGGIO   Yes, and kissed him too.
BERGETTO   Why la now, you think I tell a lie, uncle, I
warrant.
DONADO   Would he that beat thy blood out of thy head,
had beaten some wit into it; for I fear thou never wilt   95
have any.
BERGETTO   O uncle, but there was a wench would have
done a man's heart good to have looked on her; by
this light, she had a face methinks worth twenty of
you, Mistress Annabella.   100
DONADO [aside]   Was ever such a fool born?
ANNABELLA   I am glad she liked you, sir.
BERGETTO   Are you so? By my troth, I thank you forsooth.
FLORIO   Sure 'twas the doctor's niece, that was last day
with us here.   105
BERGETTO   'Twas she, 'twas she!
DONADO   How do you know that, simplicity?
BERGETTO   Why, does not he say so? If I should have
said no, I should have given him the lie, uncle, and
so have deserved a dry beating again; I'll none of   110
that.
FLORIO   A very modest, well-behaved young maid as I
have seen.
DONADO   Is she indeed?
FLORIO   Indeed she is, if I have any judgement.   115
DONADO   Well, sir, now you are free, you need not care for
sending letters: now you are dismissed; your mistress
here will none of you.
BERGETTO   No? Why, what care I for that; I can have
wenches enough in Parma for half-a-crown apiece,   120
cannot I, Poggio?
POGGIO   I'll warrant you, sir.

DONADO Signior Florio, I thank you for your free
  recourse you gave for my admittance; and to you, fair
  maid, that jewel I will give you 'gainst your marriage. 125
  Come, will you go, sir?
BERGETTO Ay, marry will I. Mistress, farewell mistress;
  I'll come again tomorrow. Farewell mistress.
    Exeunt Donado, Bergetto, and Poggio. Enter Giovanni
FLORIO Son, where have you been? What, alone, alone
    still, still?
  I would not have it so; you must forsake 130
  This over-bookish humour. Well, your sister
  Hath shook the fool off.
GIOVANNI   'Twas no match for her.
FLORIO 'Twas not indeed, I meant it nothing less;
  Soranzo is the man I only like –
  Look on him, Annabella. Come, 'tis supper-time, 135
  And it grows late.
    Exit [Florio]
GIOVANNI   Whose jewel's that?
ANNABELLA   Some sweetheart's.
GIOVANNI So I think.
ANNABELLA   A lusty youth –
  Signior Donado gave it me to wear
  Against my marriage.
GIOVANNI   But you shall not wear it:
  Send it him back again.
ANNABELLA   What, you are jealous? 140
GIOVANNI That you shall know anon, at better leisure.
  Welcome, sweet night! The evening crowns the day.
    Exeunt

Act III Scene I

Enter Bergetto and Poggio

BERGETTO   Does my uncle think to make me a baby still? No, Poggio, he shall know I have a sconce now.

POGGIO   Ay, let him not bob you off like an ape with an apple.

BERGETTO   'Sfoot, I will have the wench, if he were ten 5 uncles, in despite of his nose, Poggio.

POGGIO   Hold him to the grindstone, and give not a jot of ground. She hath, in a manner, promised you already.

BERGETTO   True, Poggio, and her uncle the doctor 10 swore I should marry her.

POGGIO   He swore, I remember.

BERGETTO   And I will have her, that's more; didst see the codpiece-point she gave me, and the box of marmalade? 15

POGGIO   Very well; and kissed you that my chops watered at the sight on't. There's no way but to clap up a marriage in hugger-mugger.

BERGETTO   I will do't, for I tell thee, Poggio, I begin to grow valiant methinks, and my courage begins to rise. 20

POGGIO   Should you be afraid of your uncle?

BERGETTO   Hang him, old doting rascal! No, I say I will have her.

POGGIO   Lose no time then.

BERGETTO   I will beget a race of wise men and 25 constables, that shall cart whores at their own charges, and break the Duke's peace ere I have done myself. Come away!

Exeunt

Act III Scene II

Enter Florio, Giovanni, Soranzo, Annabella, Putana,
and Vasques

FLORIO   My lord Soranzo, though I must confess
The proffers that are made me have been great
In marriage of my daughter, yet the hope
Of your still rising honours have prevailed
Above all other jointures. Here she is,   5
She knows my mind, speak for yourself to her;
And hear you, daughter, see you use him nobly.
For any private speech I'll give you time.
Come son, and you [*to Putana*]; the rest, let them alone;
Agree as they may.

SORANZO   I thank you, sir.   10

GIOVANNI [*aside*]   Sister, be not all woman: think on me.

SORANZO   Vasques?

VASQUES   My lord.

SORANZO   Attend me without.

Exeunt all but Soranzo and Annabella

ANNABELLA   Sir, what's your will with me?

SORANZO   Do you not know
What I should tell you?

ANNABELLA   Yes, you'll say you love me.

SORANZO   And I'll swear it too; will you believe it?   15

ANNABELLA   'Tis not point of faith.

Enter Giovanni above

SORANZO   Have you not will to love?

ANNABELLA   Not you.

SORANZO   Whom then?

ANNABELLA   That's as the fates infer.

GIOVANNI [*aside*]   Of those I'm regent now.

SORANZO   What mean you, sweet?

ANNABELLA   To live and die a maid.
SORANZO   O, that's unfit.
GIOVANNI [*aside*]   Here's one can say that's but a woman's
    note.   20
SORANZO   Did you but see my heart, then would you
    swear –
ANNABELLA   That you were dead.
GIOVANNI   [*aside*]   That's true, or somewhat near it.
SORANZO   See you these true love's tears?
ANNABELLA   No.
GIOVANNI   [*aside*]   Now she winks.
SORANZO   They plead to you for grace.
ANNABELLA   Yet nothing speak.
SORANZO   O, grant my suit!
ANNABELLA   What is't?
SORANZO   To let me live –   25
ANNABELLA   Take it.
SORANZO   – still yours.
ANNABELLA   That is not mine to give.
GIOVANNI [*aside*]   One such another word would kill
    his hopes.
SORANZO   Mistress, to leave those fruitless strifes of wit,
    I know I have loved you long, and loved you truly;
    Not hope of what you have, but what you are   30
    Have drawn me on: then let me not in vain
    Still feel the rigour of your chaste disdain.
    I'm sick, and sick to th'heart.
ANNABELLA   Help! Aqua-vitae!
SORANZO   What mean you?
ANNABELLA   Why, I thought you had been sick.
SORANZO   Do you mock my love?
GIOVANNI   [*aside*]   There, sir, she was too nimble.   35
SORANZO [*aside*]   'Tis plain, she laughs at me! [*To her*]
    These scornful taunts

Neither become your modesty or years.
ANNABELLA   You are no looking-glass; or if you were,
   I'd dress my language by you.
GIOVANNI   *[aside]*   I'm confirmed.
ANNABELLA   To put you out of doubt, my lord, methinks   40
   Your common sense should make you understand
   That if I loved you, or desired your love,
   Some way I should have given you better taste;
   But since you are a nobleman, and one
   I would not wish should spend his youth in hopes,   45
   Let me advise you here to forbear your suit,
   And think I wish you well; I tell you this.
SORANZO   Is't you speak this?
ANNABELLA   Yes, I myself; yet know –
   Thus far I give you comfort – if mine eyes
   Could have picked out a man (amongst all those   50
   That sued to me) to make a husband of,
   You should have been that man. Let this suffice;
   Be noble in your secrecy, and wise.
GIOVANNI *[aside]*   Why now I see she loves me.
ANNABELLA   One word more.
   As ever virtue lived within your mind,   55
   As ever noble courses were your guide,
   As ever you would have me know you loved me,
   Let not my father know hereof by you:
   If I hereafter find that I must marry,
   It shall be you or none.
SORANZO   I take that promise.   60
ANNABELLA   O, O my head!
SORANZO   What's the matter? Not well?
ANNABELLA   O, I begin to sicken.
GIOVANNI   *[aside]*   Heaven forbid!
    Exit [Giovanni] from above
SORANZO   Help, help, within there, ho!

65

Look to your daughter, Signior Florio!
Enter Florio, Giovanni, [and] Putana
FLORIO   Hold her up; she swoons.   65
GIOVANNI   Sister, how d'ee?
ANNABELLA   Sick, brother, are you there?
FLORIO   Convey her to bed instantly, whilst I send for a
physician; quickly, I say.
PUTANA   Alas, poor child!
Exeunt. Soranzo [remains]. Enter Vasques
VASQUES   My lord.   70
SORANZO   O Vasques, now I doubly am undone,
Both in my present and my future hopes:
She plainly told me that she could not love,
And thereupon soon sickened, and I fear
Her life's in danger.   75
VASQUES *[aside]*   By'r Lady, sir, and so is yours, if you
knew all. *[To him]* 'Las sir, I am sorry for that; may be
'tis but the maid's sickness, an overflux of youth – and
then, sir, there is no such present remedy as present
marriage. But hath she given you an absolute denial?   80
SORANZO   She hath and she hath not, I'm full of grief,
But what she said I'll tell thee as we go.
Exeunt

Act III Scene III

Enter Giovanni and Putana
PUTANA   Oh sir, we are all undone, quite undone, utterly
undone, and shamed forever; your sister, O your sister!
GIOVANNI   What of her? For Heaven's sake speak; how
does she?
PUTANA   Oh that ever I was born to see this day!   5
GIOVANNI   She is not dead, ha, is she?

PUTANA Dead? No, she is quick; 'tis worse, she is with
child. You know what you have done, Heaven forgive
'ee. 'Tis too late to repent, now Heaven help us!

GIOVANNI With child? How dost thou know't? 10

PUTANA How do I know't? Am I at these years
ignorant what the meanings of qualms and water-
pangs be? Of changing of colours, queasiness of
stomachs, pukings, and another thing that I could
name? Do not (for her and your credit's sake) spend 15
the time in asking how, and which way; 'tis so. She is
quick, upon my word; if you let a physician see her
water y'are undone.

GIOVANNI But in what case is she?

PUTANA Prettily amended; 'twas but a fit which I soon 20
espied, and she must look for often henceforward.

GIOVANNI Commend me to her; bid her take no care.
Let not the doctor visit her, I charge you,
Make some excuse till I return – O me,
I have a world of business in my head. 25
Do not discomfort her. –
How does this news perplex me! If my father
Come to her, tell him she's recovered well.
Say 'twas but some ill diet; d'ee hear woman?
Look you to't. 30

PUTANA I will, sir.

Exeunt

Act III Scene IV

Enter Florio and Richardetto

FLORIO And how d'ee find her, sir?

RICHARDETTO   Indifferent well:

I see no danger, scarce perceive she's sick,
But that she told me she had lately eaten
Melons, and as she thought, those disagreed
With her young stomach.

FLORIO   Did you give her aught?   5

RICHARDETTO   An easy surfeit-water, nothing else.
   You need not doubt her health; I rather think
   Her sickness is a fullness of her blood –
   You understand me?

FLORIO   I do; you counsel well,
   And once within these few days, will so order't   10
   She shall be married, ere she know the time.

RICHARDETTO   Yet let not haste, sir, make unworthy
      choice;
   That were dishonour.

FLORIO   Master doctor, no,
   I will not do so neither; in plain words,
   My lord Soranzo is the man I mean.   15

RICHARDETTO   A noble and a virtuous gentleman.

FLORIO   As any is in Parma. Not far hence
   Dwells Father Bonaventure, a grave friar,
   Once tutor to my son; now at his cell
   I'll have 'em married.

RICHARDETTO   You have plotted wisely.   20

FLORIO   I'll send one straight to speak with him tonight.

RICHARDETTO   Soranzo's wise, he will delay no time.

FLORIO   It shall be so.
      Enter Friar and Giovanni

FRIAR   Good peace be here and love.

FLORIO   Welcome, religious friar, you are one
   That still bring blessing to the place you come to.   25

GIOVANNI   Sir, with what speed I could, I did my best
   To draw this holy man from forth his cell

To visit my sick sister, that with words
Of ghostly comfort in this time of need,
He might absolve her, whether she live or die.　　30
FLORIO　'Twas well done Giovanni; thou herein
　　Hast showed a Christian's care, a brother's love.
　　Come, father, I'll conduct you to her chamber,
　　And one thing would entreat you.
FRIAR　　　　　　　　　　　　Say on, sir.
FLORIO　I have a father's dear impression,　　35
　　And wish, before I fall into my grave,
　　That I might see her married, as 'tis fit;
　　A word from you, grave man, will win her more
　　Than all our best persuasions.
FRIAR　　　　　　　　　　Gentle sir,
　　All this I'll say, that Heaven may prosper her.　　40
　　　　Exeunt

Act III Scene V

　　Enter Grimaldi
GRIMALDI　Now if the doctor keep his word, Soranzo,
　　Twenty to one you miss your bride. I know
　　'Tis an unnoble act, and not becomes
　　A soldier's valour; but in terms of love,
　　Where merit cannot sway, policy must.　　5
　　I am resolved; if this physician
　　Play not on both hands, then Soranzo falls.
　　　　Enter Richardetto
RICHARDETTO　You are come as I could wish; this very
　　　　night
　　Soranzo, 'tis ordained, must be affied

To Annabella; and for aught I know,   10
  Married.
GRIMALDI How!
RICHARDETTO Yet your patience.
  The place, 'tis Friar Bonaventure's cell.
  Now I would wish you to bestow this night
  In watching thereabouts. 'Tis but a night;
  If you miss now, tomorrow I'll know all.   15
GRIMALDI Have you the poison?
RICHARDETTO   Here 'tis in this box.
  Doubt nothing, this will do't; in any case,
  As you respect your life, be quick and sure.
GRIMALDI I'll speed him.
RICHARDETTO   Do. Away, for 'tis not safe
  You should be seen much here. – Ever my love!   20
GRIMALDI And mine to you.
        Exit Grimaldi
RICHARDETTO So, if this hit, I'll laugh and hug revenge;
  And they that now dream of a wedding-feast
  May chance to mourn the lusty bridegroom's ruin.
  But to my other business. – Niece Philotis!   25
        Enter Philotis
PHILOTIS Uncle.
RICHARDETTO My lovely niece, you have bethought 'ee?
PHILOTIS Yes, and as you counselled,
  Fashioned my heart to love him; but he swears
  He will tonight be married, for he fears
  His uncle else, if he should know the drift,   30
  Will hinder all, and call his coz to shrift.
RICHARDETTO Tonight? Why, best of all! But let me see,
  Ay – ha – yes, – so it shall be; in disguise
  We'll early to the friar's, I have thought on't.
        Enter Bergetto and Poggio
PHILOTIS Uncle, he comes!

RICHARDETTO   Welcome, my worthy coz.   35
BERGETTO   Lass, pretty lass, come buss, lass! [*Kisses her*]
    Aha, Poggio!
PHILOTIS   There's hope of this yet.
RICHARDETTO   You shall have time enough; withdraw a
    little,
We must confer at large.   40
BERGETTO   Have you not sweetmeats or dainty devices
    for me?
PHILOTIS   You shall have enough, sweetheart.
BERGETTO   Sweetheart! Mark that, Poggio; by my troth
    I cannot choose but kiss thee once more for that word   45
    'sweetheart'. [*Kisses her*] Poggio, I have a monstrous
    swelling about my stomach, whatsoever the matter be.
POGGIO   You shall have physic for't, sir.
RICHARDETTO   Time runs apace.
BERGETTO   Time's a blockhead.   50
RICHARDETTO   Be ruled; when we have done what's fit
    to do,
Then you may kiss your fill, and bed her too.
    Exeunt

Act III Scene VI

*Enter the Friar in his study, sitting in a chair, Annabella
kneeling and whispering to him, a table before them and
wax-lights; she weeps, and wrings her hands*
FRIAR   I am glad to see this penance; for believe me,
You have unripped a soul so foul and guilty,
As I must tell you true, I marvel how
The earth hath borne you up. But weep, weep on,
These tears may do you good; weep faster yet,   5
Whiles I do read a lecture.

ANNABELLA   Wretched creature!

FRIAR   Ay, you are wretched, miserably wretched,
    Almost condemned alive. There is a place –
    List, daughter – in a black and hollow vault,
    Where day is never seen; there shines no sun,   10
    But flaming horror of consuming fires;
    A lightless sulphur, choked with smoky fogs
    Of an infected darkness. In this place
    Dwell many thousand thousand sundry sorts
    Of never-dying deaths: there, damnèd souls   15
    Roar without pity; there, are gluttons fed
    With toads and adders; there, is burning oil
    Poured down the drunkard's throat; the usurer
    Is forced to sup whole draughts of molten gold;
    There is the murderer forever stabbed,   20
    Yet can he never die; there lies the wanton
    On racks of burning steel, whiles in his soul
    He feels the torment of his raging lust.

ANNABELLA   Mercy, oh mercy!

FRIAR   There stands these wretched things
    Who have dreamt out whole years in lawless sheets   25
    And secret incests, cursing one another.
    Then you will wish each kiss your brother gave
    Had been a dagger's point; then you shall hear
    How he will cry, 'O, would my wicked sister
    Had first been damned, when she did yield to lust!'   30
    But soft, methinks I see repentance work
    New motions in your heart; say, how is't with you?

ANNABELLA   Is there no way left to redeem my miseries?

FRIAR   There is, despair not: Heaven is merciful,
    And offers grace even now. 'Tis thus agreed,   35
    First, for your honour's safety, that you marry
    The Lord Soranzo; next, to save your soul,
    Leave off this life, and henceforth live to him.

ANNABELLA Ay me!
FRIAR   Sigh not; I know the baits of sin
Are hard to leave – O, 'tis a death to do't.   40
Remember what must come! Are you content?
ANNABELLA I am.
FRIAR   I like it well; we'll take the time.
Who's near us there?
    Enter Florio [and] Giovanni
FLORIO   Did you call, father?
FRIAR Is Lord Soranzo come?
FLORIO   He stays below.
FRIAR Have you acquainted him at full?
FLORIO   I have,   45
And he is overjoyed.
FRIAR   And so are we;
Bid him come near.
GIOVANNI [*aside*] My sister weeping, ha?
I fear this friar's falsehood. [*To them*] I will call him.
    Exit [Giovanni]
FLORIO Daughter, are you resolved?
ANNABELLA   Father, I am.
    Enter Giovanni, Soranzo, and Vasques
FLORIO My lord Soranzo, here   50
Give me your hand; for that I give you this.
    [*He joins their hands*]
SORANZO Lady, say you so too?
ANNABELLA   I do, and vow
To live with you and yours.
FRIAR   Timely resolved:
My blessing rest on both. More to be done,
You may perform it on the morning sun.   55
    Exeunt

Act III Scene VII

Enter Grimaldi with his rapier drawn, and a dark lantern

GRIMALDI 'Tis early night as yet, and yet too soon
To finish such a work. Here I will lie
To listen who comes next.
He lies down
Enter Bergetto and Philotis disguised, and after,
Richardetto and Poggio

BERGETTO We are almost at the place, I hope, sweetheart.

GRIMALDI [*aside*] I hear them near, and heard one say
'sweetheart'. 5
'Tis he; now guide my hand, some angry Justice,
Home to his bosom. [*Aloud*] Now have at you, sir!
Strikes Bergetto and exit[s]

BERGETTO O help, help! Here's a stitch fallen in my
guts. O for a flesh-tailor quickly! – Poggio!

PHILOTIS What ails my love? 10

BERGETTO I am sure I cannot piss forward and
backward, and yet I am wet before and behind. Lights,
lights, ho, lights!

PHILOTIS Alas, some villain here has slain my love!

RICHARDETTO O, Heaven forbid it! – Raise up the next
neighbours 15
Instantly, Poggio, and bring lights.
Exit Poggio
How is't, Bergetto? Slain? It cannot be!
Are you sure y'are hurt?

BERGETTO O, my belly seethes like a porridge-pot:
some cold water, I shall boil over else. My whole body 20
is in a sweat, that you may wring my shirt; feel here –
why, Poggio!

Enter Poggio with officers, and lights and halberts
POGGIO   Here! Alas, how do you?
RICHARDETTO   Give me a light – what's here? All blood!
    O sirs,
Signior Donado's nephew now is slain!   25
Follow the murderer with all thy haste
Up to the city; he cannot be far hence.
Follow, I beseech you!
OFFICERS   Follow, follow, follow!
    Exeunt officers
RICHARDETTO   Tear off thy linen, coz, to stop his
    wounds;
Be of good comfort, man.   30
BERGETTO   Is all this mine own blood? Nay, then good-
    night with me. Poggio, commend me to my uncle, dost
    hear? Bid him, for my sake, make much of this wench.
    O – I am going the wrong way sure, my belly aches so.
    – O, farewell, Poggio! – O! – O! –   35
    Dies
PHILOTIS   O, he is dead!
POGGIO   How! Dead!
RICHARDETTO   He's dead indeed.
    'Tis now too late to weep; let's have him home,
And with what speed we may, find out the murderer.
POGGIO   O my master, my master, my master!
    Exeunt

Act III Scene VIII

    Enter Vasques and Hippolita
HIPPOLITA   Betrothed?
VASQUES   I saw it.

HIPPOLITA   And when's the marriage-day?

VASQUES   Some two days hence.

HIPPOLITA   Two days? Why, man, I would but wish
    two hours   5
  To send him to his last and lasting sleep.
  And Vasques, thou shalt see, I'll do it bravely.

VASQUES   I do not doubt your wisdom, nor (I trust)
  you my secrecy; I am infinitely yours.

HIPPOLITA   I will be thine in spite of my disgrace.   10
  So soon? O wicked man, I durst be sworn
  He'd laugh to see me weep.

VASQUES   And that's a villainous fault in him.

HIPPOLITA   No, let him laugh; I'm armed in my
    resolves,
  Be thou still true.   15

VASQUES   I should get little by treachery against so
  hopeful a preferment as I am like to climb to.

HIPPOLITA   Even to my bosom, Vasques. Let my youth
  Revel in these new pleasures. If we thrive,
  He now hath but a pair of days to live.   20
    Exeunt

Act III Scene IX

*Enter Florio, Donado [weeping], Richardetto, Poggio,
and officers*

FLORIO   'Tis bootless now to show yourself a child,
  Signior Donado; what is done, is done.
  Spend not the time in tears, but seek for justice.

RICHARDETTO   I must confess, somewhat I was in fault,
  That had not first acquainted you what love   5

Passed 'twixt him and my niece; but as I live,
His fortune grieves me as it were mine own.
DONADO   Alas, poor creature, he meant no man harm,
That I am sure of.
FLORIO   I believe that too.
But stay, my masters, are you sure you saw   10
The murderer pass here?
OFFICER   And it please you sir, we are sure we saw a
ruffian with a naked weapon in his hand, all bloody,
get into my lord Cardinal's grace's gate – that, we are
sure of; but for fear of his grace (bless us!) we durst go   15
no further.
DONADO   Know you what manner of man he was?
OFFICER   Yes, sure I know the man; they say 'a is a
soldier – he that loved your daughter, sir, an't please
ye, 'twas he for certain.   20
FLORIO   Grimaldi, on my life!
OFFICER   Ay, ay, the same.
RICHARDETTO   The Cardinal is noble; he no doubt
Will give true justice.
DONADO   Knock someone at the gate.
POGGIO   I'll knock, sir.   25
     Poggio knocks
SERVANT (*within*)   What would 'ee?
FLORIO   We require speech with the lord Cardinal
About some present business; pray inform
His grace that we are here.
     Enter Cardinal and Grimaldi
CARDINAL   Why, how now, friends! What saucy mates
     are you   30
That know nor duty nor civility?
Are we a person fit to be your host?
Or is our house become your common inn,
To beat our doors at pleasure? What such haste

77

Is yours, as that it cannot wait fit times?   35
Are you the masters of this commonwealth,
And know no more discretion? O, your news
Is here before you; you have lost a nephew,
Donado, last night by Grimaldi slain:
Is that your business? Well, sir, we have knowledge on't.   40
Let that suffice.
GRIMALDI   In presence of your grace,
In thought I never meant Bergetto harm;
But Florio, you can tell with how much scorn
Soranzo, backed with his confederates,
Hath often wronged me. I, to be revenged,   45
(For that I could not win him else to fight)
Had thought by way of ambush to have killed him,
But was unluckily therein mistook;
Else he had felt what late Bergetto did.
And though my fault to him were merely chance,   50
Yet humbly I submit me to your grace, [*kneels*]
To do with me as you please.
CARDINAL   Rise up, Grimaldi.
      [*He rises*]
You citizens of Parma, if you seek
For justice, know, as nuncio from the Pope,
For this offence I here receive Grimaldi   55
Into his Holiness' protection.
He is no common man, but nobly born;
Of princes' blood, though you, Sir Florio,
Thought him too mean a husband for your daughter.
If more you seek for, you must go to Rome,   60
For he shall thither; learn more wit, for shame.
Bury your dead. – Away, Grimaldi – leave 'em!
      Exeunt Cardinal and Grimaldi
DONADO   Is this a churchman's voice? Dwells Justice
      here?

FLORIO   Justice is fled to Heaven and comes no nearer.
　　Soranzo! Was't for him? O impudence!　　　　　　65
　　Had he the face to speak it, and not blush?
　　Come, come Donado, there's no help in this,
　　When cardinals think murder's not amiss.
　　Great men may do their wills; we must obey,
　　But Heaven will judge them for't another day.　　70
　　　　Exeunt

Act IV Scene I

A banquet. Hautboys.
Enter the Friar, Giovanni, Annabella, Philotis, Soranzo,
Donado, Florio, Richardetto, Putana, and Vasques

FRIAR   These holy rites performed, now take your times,
To spend the remnant of the day in feast;
Such fit repasts are pleasing to the saints
Who are your guests, though not with mortal eyes
To be beheld. Long prosper in this day,   5
You happy couple, to each other's joy!

SORANZO   Father, your prayer is heard. The hand of
    goodness
Hath been a shield for me against my death;
And, more to bless me, hath enriched my life
With this most precious jewel; such a prize   10
As earth hath not another like to this.
Cheer up, my love; and gentlemen, my friends,
Rejoice with me in mirth: this day we'll crown
With lusty cups to Annabella's health.

GIOVANNI (*aside*)   O, torture! Were the marriage yet
    undone,   15
Ere I'd endure this sight, to see my love
Clipped by another, I would dare confusion,
And stand the horror of ten thousand deaths.

VASQUES   Are you not well, sir?

GIOVANNI   Prithee, fellow, wait;
I need not thy officious diligence.   20

FLORIO   Signior Donado, come, you must forget
Your late mishaps, and drown your cares in wine.

SORANZO   Vasques!

VASQUES   My lord.

SORANZO   Reach me that weighty bowl.

Here, brother Giovanni, here's to you;
Your turn comes next, though now a bachelor: 25
Here's to your sister's happiness and mine!
    [*Drinks, and offers him the bowl*]
GIOVANNI   I cannot drink.
SORANZO   What?
GIOVANNI   'Twill indeed offend me.
ANNABELLA   Pray, do not urge him if he be not willing.
    Hautboys
FLORIO   How now, what noise is this?
VASQUES   O sir, I had forgot to tell you; certain young   30
    maidens of Parma, in honour to Madam Annabella's
    marriage, have sent their loves to her in a masque, for
    which they humbly crave your patience and silence.
SORANZO   We are much bound to them, so much the
    more
    As it comes unexpected; guide them in.   35
    Enter Hippolita and ladies [masked,] in white robes
    with garlands of willows. Music and a dance
SORANZO   Thanks, lovely virgins; now might we but
    know
    To whom we have been beholding for this love,
    We shall acknowledge it.
HIPPOLITA   Yes, you shall know.
    [*Unmasks*]
    What think you now?
ALL   Hippolita!
HIPPOLITA   'Tis she.
    Be not amazed; nor blush, young lovely bride.   40
    I come not to defraud you of your man.
    [*To Soranzo*] 'Tis now no time to reckon up the talk
    What Parma long hath rumoured of us both.
    Let rash report run on; the breath that vents it
    Will, like a bubble, break itself at last.   45

[*To Annabella*] But now to you, sweet creature; lend's
    your hand.
Perhaps it hath been said that I would claim
Some interest in Soranzo, now your lord.
What I have right to do, his soul knows best:
But in my duty to your noble worth,   50
Sweet Annabella, and my care of you,
Here take Soranzo; take this hand from me.
    [*She joins their hands*]
I'll once more join what by the holy Church
Is finished and allowed: have I done well?
SORANZO   You have too much engaged us.
HIPPOLITA   One thing more.   55
That you may know my single charity,
Freely I here remit all interest
I e'er could claim, and give you back your vows;
And to confirm't – reach me a cup of wine –
My Lord Soranzo, in this draught I drink   60
Long rest t'ee! [*Aside*] Look to it, Vasques.
VASQUES [*aside*]   Fear nothing.
    He gives her a poisoned cup; she drinks
SORANZO   Hippolita, I thank you, and will pledge
This happy union as another life. –
Wine there!   65
VASQUES   You shall have none, neither shall you pledge
her.
HIPPOLITA   How!
VASQUES   Know now, mistress she-devil, your own
mischievous treachery hath killed you. I must not   70
marry you.
HIPPOLITA   Villain!
ALL   What's the matter?
VASQUES   Foolish woman, thou art now like a
firebrand, that hath kindled others and burnt thyself.   75

Troppo sperare inganna; thy vain hope hath deceived
thee. Thou art but dead; if thou hast any grace, pray.

HIPPOLITA   Monster!

VASQUES   Die in charity, for shame! – This thing of
malice, this woman, had privately corrupted me with   80
promise of marriage, under this politic reconciliation
to poison my lord, whiles she might laugh at his
confusion on his marriage-day. I promised her fair, but
I knew what my reward should have been; and would
willingly have spared her life, but that I was   85
acquainted with the danger of her disposition – and
now have fitted her a just payment in her own coin.
There she is, she hath yet – and end thy days in peace,
vile woman; as for life there's no hope, think not on't.

ALL   Wonderful justice!

RICHARDETTO   Heaven, thou art righteous.   90

HIPPOLITA   O, 'tis true,
I feel my minute coming. Had that slave
Kept promise – O, my torment! – thou this hour
Hadst died, Soranzo. – Heat above hell-fire! –
Yet ere I pass away – cruel, cruel flames! –   95
Take here my curse amongst you: may thy bed
Of marriage be a rack unto thy heart;
Burn, blood, and boil in vengeance. – O my heart,
My flame's intolerable! – Mayst thou live
To father bastards, may her womb bring forth   100
Monsters, and die together in your sins,
Hated, scorned, and unpitied! – O! – O! –
   Dies

FLORIO   Was e'er so vile a creature?

RICHARDETTO   Here's the end
Of lust and pride.

ANNABELLA   It is a fearful sight.

SORANZO   Vasques, I know thee now a trusty servant,   105

And never will forget thee. – Come, my love,
We'll home, and thank the heavens for this escape.
Father and friends, we must break up this mirth;
It is too sad a feast.

DONADO   Bear hence the body.

FRIAR [*aside to Giovanni*]   Here's an ominous change;   110
Mark this, my Giovanni, and take heed.
I fear the event; that marriage seldom's good,
Where the bride-banquet so begins in blood.
    Exeunt [*with Hippolita's body*]

Act IV Scene II

Enter Richardetto and Philotis

RICHARDETTO   My wretched wife, more wretched in
    her shame
Than in her wrongs to me, hath paid too soon
The forfeit of her modesty and life.
And I am sure, my niece, though vengeance hover,
Keeping aloof yet from Soranzo's fall,   5
Yet he will fall, and sink with his own weight.
I need not – now my heart persuades me so –
To further his confusion. There is One
Above begins to work, for, as I hear,
Debates already 'twixt his wife and him   10
Thicken and run to head; she (as 'tis said)
Slightens his love, and he abandons hers.
Much talk I hear. Since things go thus, my niece,
In tender love and pity of your youth,
My counsel is that you should free your years   15
From hazard of these woes, by flying hence
To fair Cremona, there to vow your soul

In holiness a holy votaress.
Leave me to see the end of these extremes.
All human worldly courses are uneven;   20
No life is blessed but the way to Heaven.
PHILOTIS   Uncle, shall I resolve to be a nun?
RICHARDETTO   Ay, gentle niece, and in your hourly
    prayers
Remember me, your poor unhappy uncle.
Hie to Cremona now, as fortune leads,   25
Your home your cloister, your best friends your beads.
Your chaste and single life shall crown your birth;
Who dies a virgin lives a saint on earth.
PHILOTIS   Then farewell, world, and worldly thoughts
    adieu!
Welcome, chaste vows; myself I yield to you.   30
    Exeunt

Act IV Scene III

Enter Soranzo unbraced, and Annabella dragged in
SORANZO   Come, strumpet, famous whore! Were every
    drop
Of blood that runs in thy adulterous veins
A life, this sword – dost see't? – should in one blow
Confound them all. Harlot, rare, notable harlot,
That with thy brazen face maintain'st thy sin,   5
Was there no man in Parma to be bawd
To your loose cunning whoredom else but I?
Must your hot itch and pleurisy of lust,
The heyday of your luxury, be fed
Up to a surfeit, and could none but I   10
Be picked out to be cloak to your close tricks,

Your belly-sports? Now I must be the dad
To all that gallimaufry that's stuffed
In thy corrupted bastard-bearing womb!
Why must I?

ANNABELLA   Beastly man, why, 'tis thy fate.   15
I sued not to thee, for, but that I thought
Your over-loving lordship would have run
Mad on denial, had ye lent me time,
I would have told 'ee in what case I was.
But you would needs be doing.

SORANZO   Whore of whores!   20
Dar'st thou tell me this?

ANNABELLA   O yes, why not?
You were deceived in me: 'twas not for love
I chose you, but for honour. Yet know this,
Would you be patient yet, and hide your shame,
I'd see whether I could love you.

SORANZO   Excellent quean!   25
Why, art thou not with child?

ANNABELLA   What needs all this,
When 'tis superfluous? I confess I am.

SORANZO   Tell me by whom.

ANNABELLA   Soft, sir, 'twas not in my bargain.
Yet somewhat, sir, to stay your longing stomach,
I'm content t'acquaint you with. The man,   30
The more than man that got this sprightly boy –
For 'tis a boy; that for your glory, sir;
Your heir shall be a son.

SORANZO   Damnable monster!

ANNABELLA   Nay, and you will not hear, I'll speak no
        more.

SORANZO   Yes, speak, and speak thy last.

ANNABELLA   A match, a match!   35

This noble creature was in every part
So angel-like, so glorious, that a woman
Who had not been but human, as was I,
Would have kneeled to him, and have begged for love.
You, why you are not worthy once to name   40
His name without true worship, or indeed,
Unless you kneeled, to hear another name him.
SORANZO   What was he called?
ANNABELLA   We are not come to that;
Let it suffice that you shall have the glory
To father what so brave a father got.   45
In brief, had not this chance fall'n out as't doth,
I never had been troubled with a thought
That you had been a creature. But for marriage,
I scarce dream yet of that.
SORANZO   Tell me his name.
ANNABELLA   Alas, alas, there's all.   50
Will you believe?
SORANZO   What?
ANNABELLA   You shall never know.
SORANZO   How!
ANNABELLA   Never; if you do, let me be cursed.
SORANZO   Not know it, strumpet! I'll rip up thy heart,
And find it there.
ANNABELLA   Do, do!
SORANZO   And with my teeth
Tear the prodigious lecher joint by joint.   55
ANNABELLA   Ha, ha, ha, the man's merry!
SORANZO   Dost thou laugh?
Come, whore, tell me your lover, or by truth
I'll hew thy flesh to shreds! Who is't?
ANNABELLA (*sings*)   *Che morte più dolce che morire per
amore?*

SORANZO   Thus will I pull thy hair, and thus I'll drag   60
Thy lust-belepered body through the dust.
Yet tell his name.

ANNABELLA (*sings*)   *Morendo in grazia a lui, morirei senza*
dolore.

SORANZO   Dost thou triumph? The treasure of the earth
Shall not redeem thee; were there kneeling kings   65
Did beg thy life, or angels did come down
To plead in tears, yet should not all prevail
Against my rage. Dost thou not tremble yet?

ANNABELLA   At what? To die? No, be a gallant hangman.
I dare thee to the worst; strike, and strike home.   70
I leave revenge behind, and thou shalt feel't.

SORANZO   Yet tell me ere thou diest, and tell me truly,
Knows thy old father this?

ANNABELLA   No, by my life.

SORANZO   Wilt thou confess, and I will spare thy life?

ANNABELLA   My life! I will not buy my life so dear.   75

SORANZO   I will not slack my vengeance. [*Draws his sword*]
        Enter Vasques

VASQUES   What d'ee mean, sir?

SORANZO   Forbear, Vasques; such a damnèd whore
Deserves no pity.

VASQUES   Now the gods forfend!
And would you be her executioner, and kill her in your
rage too? O, 'twere most unmanlike! She is your wife;   80
what faults hath been done by her before she married
you, were not against you; alas, poor lady, what hath
she committed which any lady in Italy in the like case
would not? Sir, you must be ruled by your reason, and
not by your fury; that were unhuman and beastly.   85

SORANZO   She shall not live.

VASQUES   Come, she must. You would have her confess
the author of her present misfortunes, I warrant 'ee;

'tis an unconscionable demand, and she should lose
the estimation that I, for my part, hold of her worth,   90
if she had done it. Why sir, you ought not of all men
living to know it. Good sir, be reconciled; alas, good
gentlewoman!

ANNABELLA   Pish, do not beg for me; I prize my life
As nothing. If the man will needs be mad,   95
Why let him take it.

SORANZO   Vasques, hear'st thou this?

VASQUES   Yes, and commend her for it. In this she shows
the nobleness of a gallant spirit, and beshrew my heart
but it becomes her rarely. [*Aside to Soranzo*] Sir, in any
case smother your revenge; leave the scenting-out your   100
wrongs to me. Be ruled, as you respect your honour, or
you mar all. [*Aloud*] Sir, if ever my service were of any
credit with you, be not so violent in your distractions.
You are married now; what a triumph might the report
of this give to other neglected suitors! 'Tis as manlike   105
to bear extremities, as godlike to forgive.

SORANZO   O Vasques, Vasques, in this piece of flesh,
This faithless face of hers, had I laid up
The treasure of my heart! – Hadst thou been virtuous,
Fair, wicked woman, not the matchless joys   110
Of life itself had made me wish to live
With any saint but thee. Deceitful creature,
How hast thou mocked my hopes, and in the shame
Of thy lewd womb, even buried me alive!
I did too dearly love thee.   115

VASQUES [*aside*] (*to Soranzo*)   This is well. Follow this
temper with some passion. Be brief and moving; 'tis
for the purpose.

SORANZO   Be witness to my words thy soul and
        thoughts,
And tell me, didst not think that in my heart   120

I did too superstitiously adore thee?
ANNABELLA   I must confess, I know you loved me well.
SORANZO   And wouldst thou use me thus? O Annabella,
Be thou assured, whatsoe'er the villain was
That thus hath tempted thee to this disgrace,   125
Well he might lust, but never loved like me.
He doted on the picture that hung out
Upon thy cheeks, to please his humorous eye;
Not on the part I loved, which was thy heart,
And, as I thought, thy virtues.
ANNABELLA   O my lord!   130
These words wound deeper than your sword could do.
VASQUES   Let me not ever take comfort, but I begin to
weep myself, so much I pity him; why, madam, I knew
when his rage was overpassed what it would come to.
SORANZO   Forgive me, Annabella. Though thy youth   135
Hath tempted thee above thy strength to folly,
Yet will not I forget what I should be,
And what I am, a husband; in that name
Is hid divinity. If I do find
That thou wilt yet be true, here I remit   140
All former faults, and take thee to my bosom.
VASQUES   By my troth, and that's a point of noble charity.
ANNABELLA   Sir, on my knees –
SORANZO   Rise up; you shall not kneel.
Get you to your chamber, see you make no show
Of alteration; I'll be with you straight.   145
My reason tells me now that 'tis as common
To err in frailty as to be a woman.
Go to your chamber.
      Exit Annabella
VASQUES   So, this was somewhat to the matter; what do
you think of your heaven of happiness now, sir?   150

SORANZO I carry Hell about me; all my blood
  Is fired in swift revenge.
VASQUES That may be, but know you how, or on
  whom? Alas, to marry a great woman, being made
  great in the stock to your hand, is a usual sport in 155
  these days; but to know what ferret it was that
  haunted your cony-berry, there's the cunning.
SORANZO I'll make her tell herself, or –
VASQUES Or what? You must not do so. Let me yet
  persuade your sufferance a little while. Go to her, use 160
  her mildly, win her if it be possible to a voluntary, to
  a weeping tune; for the rest, if all hit, I will not miss
  my mark. Pray, sir, go in; the next news I tell you shall
  be wonders.
SORANZO Delay in vengeance gives a heavier blow. 165
    Exit [Soranzo]
VASQUES Ah, sirrah, here's work for the nonce! I had a
  suspicion of a bad matter in my head a pretty whiles
  ago; but after my madam's scurvy looks here at home,
  her waspish perverseness and loud fault-finding, then
  I remembered the proverb, that where hens crow and 170
  cocks hold their peace there are sorry houses. 'Sfoot,
  if the lower parts of a she-tailor's cunning can cover
  such a swelling in the stomach, I'll never blame a false
  stitch in a shoe whiles I live again. Up, and up so
  quick? And so quickly too? 'Twere a fine policy to 175
  learn by whom. This must be known; and I have
  thought on't.
    [Enter Putana in tears]
  Here's the way, or none. – What, crying, old mistress?
  Alas, alas, I cannot blame 'ee; we have a lord, Heaven
  help us, is so mad as the devil himself, the more shame 180
  for him.

PUTANA   O Vasques, that ever I was born to see this
day! Doth he use thee so too, sometimes, Vasques?

VASQUES   Me? Why, he makes a dog of me; but if some
were of my mind, I know what we would do. As sure as   185
I am an honest man, he will go near to kill my lady with
unkindness. Say she be with child, is that such a matter
for a young woman of her years to be blamed for?

PUTANA   Alas, good heart, it is against her will full sore.

VASQUES   I durst be sworn, all his madness is for that   190
she will not confess whose 'tis; which he will know,
and when he doth know it, I am so well acquainted
with his humour, that he will forget all straight. Well I
could wish she would in plain terms tell all, for that's
the way indeed.   195

PUTANA   Do you think so?

VASQUES   Foh, I know't; provided that he did not win
her to't by force. He was once in a mind that you
could tell, and meant to have wrung it out of you, but
I somewhat pacified him for that; yet sure you know a   200
great deal.

PUTANA   Heaven forgive us all, I know a little, Vasques.

VASQUES   Why should you not? Who else should?
Upon my conscience, she loves you dearly, and you
would not betray her to any affliction for the world.   205

PUTANA   Not for all the world, by my faith and troth,
Vasques.

VASQUES   'Twere pity of your life if you should; but in
this you should both relieve her present discomforts,
pacify my lord, and gain yourself everlasting love and   210
preferment.

PUTANA   Dost think so, Vasques?

VASQUES   Nay, I know't. Sure 'twas some near and entire
friend.

PUTANA 'Twas a dear friend indeed; but –   215

VASQUES But what? Fear not to name him; my life between you and danger. Faith, I think 'twas no base fellow.

PUTANA Thou wilt stand between me and harm?

VASQUES Ud's pity, what else? You shall be rewarded   220
too; trust me.

PUTANA 'Twas even no worse than her own brother.

VASQUES Her brother Giovanni, I warrant 'ee?

PUTANA Even he, Vasques; as brave a gentleman as
ever kissed fair lady. O, they love most perpetually.   225

VASQUES A brave gentleman indeed; why, therein I commend her choice. [*Aside*] Better and better! [*To her*] – You are sure 'twas he?

PUTANA Sure; and you shall see he will not be long from her too.   230

VASQUES He were to blame if he would; but may I believe thee?

PUTANA Believe me! Why, dost think I am a Turk or a Jew? No, Vasques, I have known their dealings too long to belie them now.   235

VASQUES Where are you? There within, sirs!
    Enter Banditti

PUTANA How now, what are these?

VASQUES You shall know presently. Come sirs, take me this old damnable hag, gag her instantly, and put out her eyes. Quickly, quickly!   240

PUTANA Vasques, Vasques!

VASQUES Gag her I say. 'Sfoot, d'ee suffer her to prate? What d'ee fumble about? Let me come to her. – I'll help your old gums, you toad-bellied bitch! [*He gags Putana*] – Sirs, carry her closely into the coal-house   245

and put out her eyes instantly. If she roars, slit her
nose; d'ee hear, be speedy and sure.

Exeunt [Banditti] with Putana

Why, this is excellent and above expectation. Her own
brother? O horrible! To what a height of liberty in
damnation hath the devil trained our age. Her brother, 250
well! There's yet but a beginning; I must to my lord, and
tutor him better in his points of vengeance. Now I see
how a smooth tale goes beyond a smooth tail. But soft –
What thing comes next?

Enter Giovanni

Giovanni! As I would wish. My belief is strengthened; 255
'tis as firm as winter and summer.

GIOVANNI   Where's my sister?

VASQUES   Troubled with a new sickness, my lord; she's
somewhat ill.

GIOVANNI   Took too much of the flesh, I believe. 260

VASQUES   Troth, sir, and you I think have e'en hit it;
but my virtuous lady –

GIOVANNI   Where's she?

VASQUES   In her chamber. Please you visit her; she is
alone. [*Giovanni gives him money*] Your liberality hath 265
doubly made me your servant, and ever shall, ever –

Exit Giovanni. Enter Soranzo

Sir, I am made a man, I have plied my cue with cunning
and success; I beseech you, let's be private.

SORANZO   My lady's brother's come; now he'll know all.

VASQUES   Let him know't; I have made some of them 270
fast enough. How have you dealt with my lady?

SORANZO   Gently, as thou hast counselled. O, my soul
Runs circular in sorrow for revenge!
But Vasques, thou shalt know –

VASQUES   Nay, I will know no more, for now comes your 275
turn to know. I would not talk so openly with you. Let

my young master take time enough, and go at pleasure;
he is sold to death, and the devil shall not ransom him.
Sir, I beseech you, your privacy.

SORANZO   No conquest can gain glory of my fear.   280

   [*Exeunt*]

Act V Scene I

Enter Annabella above [with a letter written in blood]

ANNABELLA   Pleasures farewell, and all ye thriftless
    minutes
Wherein false joys have spun a weary life;
To these my fortunes now I take my leave.
Thou precious Time, that swiftly rid'st in post
Over the world, to finish up the race   5
Of my last fate; here stay thy restless course,
And bear to ages that are yet unborn
A wretched woeful woman's tragedy.
My conscience now stands up against my lust
With depositions charactered in guilt,   10
    Enter Friar [below]
And tells me I am lost. Now I confess
Beauty that clothes the outside of the face
Is cursèd if it be not clothed with grace.
Here like a turtle, mewed up in a cage
Unmated, I converse with air and walls,   15
And descant on my vile unhappiness.
O Giovanni, that hast had the spoil
Of thine own virtues and my modest fame,
Would thou hadst been less subject to those stars
That luckless reigned at my nativity!   20
O, would the scourge due to my black offence
Might pass from thee, that I alone might feel
The torment of an uncontrollèd flame!
FRIAR [*aside*]   What's this I hear?
ANNABELLA   That man, that blessed friar,
Who joined in ceremonial knot my hand   25
To him whose wife I now am, told me oft
I trod the path to death, and showed me how.

But they who sleep in lethargies of lust
Hug their confusion, making Heaven unjust,
And so did I.
FRIAR [*aside*]   Here's music to the soul!   30
ANNABELLA   Forgive me, my good genius, and this once
   Be helpful to my ends. Let some good man
   Pass this way, to whose trust I may commit
   This paper double-lined with tears and blood;
   Which being granted, here I sadly vow   35
   Repentance, and a leaving of that life
   I long have died in.
FRIAR   Lady, Heaven hath heard you,
   And hath by providence ordained that I
   Should be his minister for your behoof.
ANNABELLA   Ha, what are you?
FRIAR   Your brother's friend, the friar;   40
   Glad in my soul that I have lived to hear
   This free confession 'twixt your peace and you.
   What would you, or to whom? Fear not to speak.
ANNABELLA   Is Heaven so bountiful? Then I have found
   More favour than I hoped. Here, holy man –   45
      (*Throws a letter*)
   Commend me to my brother, give him that,
   That letter; bid him read it and repent.
   Tell him that I – imprisoned in my chamber,
   Barred of all company, even of my guardian,
   Who gives me cause of much suspect – have time   50
   To blush at what hath passed; bid him be wise,
   And not believe the friendship of my lord.
   I fear much more than I can speak. Good father,
   The place is dangerous, and spies are busy;
   I must break off – you'll do't?
FRIAR   Be sure I will,   55
   And fly with speed. My blessing ever rest

With thee, my daughter; live to die more blessed!
   Exit [Friar]
ANNABELLA   Thanks to the Heavens, who have
   prolonged my breath
To this good use. Now I can welcome death.
   Exit

Act V Scene II

Enter Soranzo and Vasques

VASQUES   Am I to be believed now? First marry a
   strumpet that cast herself away upon you but to laugh
   at your horns? To feast on your disgrace, riot in your
   vexations, cuckold you in your bride-bed, waste your
   estate upon panders and bawds? 5
SORANZO   No more, I say, no more!
VASQUES   A cuckold is a goodly tame beast, my lord.
SORANZO   I am resolved; urge not another word.
   My thoughts are great, and all as resolute
   As thunder. In mean time I'll cause our lady 10
   To deck herself in all her bridal robes,
   Kiss her, and fold her gently in my arms.
   Begone – yet hear you, are the banditti ready
   To wait in ambush?
VASQUES   Good sir, trouble not yourself about other 15
   business than your own resolution; remember that
   time lost cannot be recalled.
SORANZO   With all the cunning words thou canst, invite
   The states of Parma to my birthday's feast;
   Haste to my brother rival and his father, 20
   Entreat them gently, bid them not to fail.
   Be speedy and return.

VASQUES   Let not your pity betray you. Till my coming
   back, think upon incest and cuckoldry.
SORANZO   Revenge is all the ambition I aspire;   25
   To that I'll climb or fall: my blood's on fire.
      Exeunt

Act V Scene III

   Enter Giovanni
GIOVANNI   Busy opinion is an idle fool,
   That, as a school-rod keeps a child in awe,
   Frights the unexperienced temper of the mind.
   So did it me; who, ere my precious sister
   Was married, thought all taste of love would die   5
   In such a contract. But I find no change
   Of pleasure in this formal law of sports.
   She is still one to me, and every kiss
   As sweet and as delicious as the first
   I reaped, when yet the privilege of youth   10
   Entitled her a virgin. O, the glory
   Of two united hearts like hers and mine!
   Let poring book-men dream of other worlds,
   My world, and all of happiness, is here,
   And I'd not change it for the best to come: 15
   A life of pleasure is Elysium.
      Enter Friar
   Father, you enter on the jubilee
   Of my retired delights. Now I can tell you,
   The Hell you oft have prompted is nought else
   But slavish and fond superstitious fear;   20
   And I could prove it, too –
FRIAR   Thy blindness slays thee.

Look there, 'tis writ to thee.
    (*Gives the letter*)
GIOVANNI   From whom?
FRIAR   Unrip the seals and see.
  The blood's yet seething hot, that will anon   25
  Be frozen harder than congealed coral.
  Why d'ee change colour, son?
GIOVANNI   'Fore Heaven, you make
  Some petty devil factor 'twixt my love
  And your religion-maskèd sorceries.
  Where had you this?
FRIAR   Thy conscience, youth, is seared,   30
  Else thou wouldst stoop to warning.
GIOVANNI   'Tis her hand,
  I know't; and 'tis all written in her blood.
  She writes I know not what. Death? I'll not fear
  An armèd thunderbolt aimed at my heart.
  She writes we are discovered – pox on dreams   35
  Of low faint-hearted cowardice! Discovered?
  The devil we are! Which way is't possible?
  Are we grown traitors to our own delights?
  Confusion take such dotage; 'tis but forged!
  This is your peevish chattering, weak old man.   40
     Enter Vasques
  Now, sir, what news bring you?
VASQUES   My lord, according to his yearly custom
  keeping this day a feast in honour of his birthday, by
  me invites you thither. Your worthy father, with the
  Pope's reverend nuncio, and other magnificoes of   45
  Parma, have promised their presence, will't please you
  to be of the number?
GIOVANNI   Yes, tell them I dare come.
VASQUES   Dare come?
GIOVANNI   So I said; and tell him more, I will come.   50

VASQUES   These words are strange to me.
GIOVANNI   Say I will come.
VASQUES   You will not miss?
GIOVANNI   Yet more? I'll come! Sir, are you answered?
VASQUES   So I'll say. – My service to you.   55
    Exit Vasques
FRIAR   You will not go, I trust.
GIOVANNI   Not go! For what?
FRIAR   O do not go! This feast, I'll gage my life,
  Is but a plot to train you to your ruin;
  Be ruled, you sha'not go.
GIOVANNI   Not go! Stood Death
  Threat'ning his armies of confounding plagues,   60
  With hosts of dangers hot as blazing stars,
  I would be there. Not go! Yes; and resolve
  To strike as deep in slaughter as they all.
  For I will go.
FRIAR   Go where thou wilt; I see
  The wildness of thy fate draws to an end,   65
  To a bad, fearful end. I must not stay
  To know thy fall; back to Bologna I
  With speed will haste, and shun this coming blow.
  Parma farewell; would I had never known thee,
  Or aught of thine! Well, youngman, since no prayer   70
  Can make thee safe, I leave thee to despair.
    Exit Friar
GIOVANNI   Despair, or tortures of a thousand hells,
  All's one to me; I have set up my rest.
  Now, now, work serious thoughts on baneful plots.
  Be all a man, my soul; let not the curse   75
  Of old prescription rend from me the gall
  Of courage, which enrols a glorious death.
  If I must totter like a well-grown oak,
  Some under-shrubs shall in my weighty fall

Be crushed to splits: with me they all shall perish.   80
    Exit

Act V Scene IV

Enter Soranzo, Vasques, and Banditti

SORANZO   You will not fail, or shrink in the attempt?

VASQUES   I will undertake for their parts. [*To Banditti*] –
Be sure, my masters, to be bloody enough, and as
unmerciful as if you were preying upon a rich booty
on the very mountains of Liguria. For your pardons,   5
trust to my lord; but for reward you shall trust none
but your own pockets.

BANDITTI   We'll make a murder.

SORANZO   Here's gold, here's more; want nothing. What
    you do
Is noble, and an act of brave revenge.   10
I'll make ye rich banditti, and all free.

BANDITTI   Liberty, liberty!

VASQUES   Hold, take every man a vizard. When ye are
withdrawn, keep as much silence as you can possibly.
You know the watch-word, till which be spoken, move   15
not, but when you hear that, rush in like a stormy
flood; I need not instruct ye in your own profession.

BANDITTI   No, no, no.

VASQUES   In, then; your ends are profit and preferment –
    away!
    [*Exeunt*] *Banditti*

SORANZO   The guests will all come, Vasques?   20

VASQUES   Yes, sir, and now let me a little edge your
resolution; you see nothing is unready to this great

work, but a great mind in you. Call to your remembrance your disgraces, your loss of honour, Hippolita's blood, and arm your courage in your own   25
wrongs; so shall you best right those wrongs in vengeance which you may truly call your own.

SORANZO   'Tis well; the less I speak, the more I burn,
And blood shall quench that flame.

VASQUES   Now you begin to turn Italian! This beside;   30
when my young incest-monger comes, he will be sharp set on his old bit. Give him time enough, let him have your chamber and bed at liberty; let my hot hare have law ere he be hunted to his death, that if it be possible he may post to Hell in the very act of his   35
damnation.

Enter Giovanni

SORANZO   It shall be so; and see, as we would wish,
He comes himself first. – Welcome, my much-loved
    brother,
Now I perceive you honour me; y'are welcome.
But where's my father?

GIOVANNI   With the other states,   40
Attending on the nuncio of the Pope
To wait upon him hither. How's my sister?

SORANZO   Like a good housewife, scarcely ready yet;
Y'are best walk to her chamber.

GIOVANNI   If you will.

SORANZO   I must expect my honourable friends;   45
Good brother, get her forth.

GIOVANNI   You are busy, sir.

Exit Giovanni

VASQUES   Even as the great devil himself would have it!
Let him go and glut himself in his own destruction.

Flourish

Hark, the nuncio is at hand; good sir, be ready to
receive him.   50
    Enter Cardinal, Florio, Donado, Richardetto, and
    attendants
SORANZO   Most reverend lord, this grace hath made me
    proud
That you vouchsafe my house; I ever rest
Your humble servant for this noble favour.
CARDINAL   You are our friend, my lord; his holiness
Shall understand how zealously you honour   55
Saint Peter's vicar in his substitute.
Our special love to you.
SORANZO   Signiors, to you
My welcome, and my ever best of thanks
For this so memorable courtesy.
Pleaseth your grace to walk near?
CARDINAL   My lord, we come   60
To celebrate your feast with civil mirth,
As ancient custom teacheth; we will go.
SORANZO   Attend his grace there! Signiors, keep your
    way.
    Exeunt

Act V Scene V

    Enter Giovanni and Annabella [in her wedding dress]
    lying on a bed
GIOVANNI   What, changed so soon? Hath your new
    sprightly lord
Found out a trick in night-games more than we
Could know in our simplicity? Ha, is't so?
Or does the fit come on you, to prove treacherous

To your past vows and oaths?
ANNABELLA   Why should you jest   5
At my calamity, without all sense
Of the approaching dangers you are in?
GIOVANNI   What danger's half so great as thy revolt?
Thou art a faithless sister, else, thou know'st,
Malice, or any treachery beside,   10
Would stoop to my bent brows. Why, I hold fate
Clasped in my fist, and could command the course
Of time's eternal motion, hadst thou been
One thought more steady than an ebbing sea.
And what? You'll now be honest, that's resolved?   15
ANNABELLA   Brother, dear brother, know what I have
      been,
And know that now there's but a dining-time
'Twixt us and our confusion. Let's not waste
These precious hours in vain and useless speech.
Alas, these gay attires were not put on   20
But to some end; this sudden solemn feast
Was not ordained to riot in expense;
I that have now been chambered here alone,
Barred of my guardian, or of any else,
Am not for nothing at an instant freed   25
To fresh access. Be not deceived, my brother,
This banquet is an harbinger of death
To you and me; resolve yourself it is,
And be prepared to welcome it.
GIOVANNI   Well then,
The schoolmen teach that all this globe of earth   30
Shall be consumed to ashes in a minute.
ANNABELLA   So I have read too.
GIOVANNI   But 'twere somewhat strange
To see the waters burn; could I believe
This might be true, I could believe as well

There might be Hell or Heaven.
ANNABELLA   That's most certain.   35
GIOVANNI   A dream, a dream; else in this other world
  We should know one another.
ANNABELLA   So we shall.
GIOVANNI   Have you heard so?
ANNABELLA   For certain.
GIOVANNI   But d'ee think
  That I shall see you there, you look on me?
  May we kiss one another, prate or laugh,   40
  Or do as we do here?
ANNABELLA   I know not that,
  But good, for the present, what d'ee mean
  To free yourself from danger? Some way, think
  How to escape; I'm sure the guests are come.
GIOVANNI   Look up, look here; what see you in my
  face?   45
ANNABELLA   Distraction and a troubled countenance.
GIOVANNI   Death, and a swift repining wrath – yet look,
  What see you in mine eyes?
ANNABELLA   Methinks you weep.
GIOVANNI   I do indeed. These are the funeral tears
  Shed on your grave; these furrowed up my cheeks   50
  When first I loved and knew not how to woo.
  Fair Annabella, should I here repeat
  The story of my life, we might lose time.
  Be record, all the spirits of the air,
  And all things else that are, that day and night,   55
  Early and late, the tribute which my heart
  Hath paid to Annabella's sacred love
  Hath been these tears, which are her mourners now.
  Never till now did Nature do her best
  To show a matchless beauty to the world,   60

Which, in an instant, ere it scarce was seen,
The jealous Destinies required again.
Pray, Annabella, pray. Since we must part,
Go thou, white in thy soul, to fill a throne
Of innocence and sanctity in Heaven.   65
Pray, pray, my sister.
ANNABELLA   Then I see your drift;
  Ye blessèd angels, guard me!
GIOVANNI   So say I.
  Kiss me. If ever after-times should hear
  Of our fast-knit affections, though perhaps
  The laws of conscience and of civil use   70
  May justly blame us, yet when they but know
  Our loves, that love will wipe away that rigour
  Which would in other incests be abhorred.
  Give me your hand. How sweetly life doth run
  In these well-coloured veins; how constantly   75
  These palms do promise health! But I could chide
  With Nature for this cunning flattery.
  Kiss me again – forgive me.
ANNABELLA   With my heart.
GIOVANNI   Farewell.
ANNABELLA   Will you be gone?
GIOVANNI   Be dark, bright sun,
  And make this midday night, that thy gilt rays   80
  May not behold a deed will turn their splendour
  More sooty than the poets feign their Styx!
  One other kiss, my sister.
ANNABELLA   What means this?
GIOVANNI   To save thy fame, and kill thee in a kiss.
    Stabs her
  Thus die, and die by me, and by my hand.   85
  Revenge is mine; honour doth love command.

ANNABELLA   O brother, by your hand?
GIOVANNI   When thou art dead
    I'll give my reasons for't; for to dispute
    With thy (even in thy death) most lovely beauty,
    Would make me stagger to perform this act   90
    Which I most glory in.
ANNABELLA   Forgive him, Heaven – and me my sins;
        farewell,
    Brother unkind, unkind. – Mercy, great Heaven! – O!
        – O! –
        Dies
GIOVANNI   She's dead, alas, good soul; the hapless fruit
    That in her womb received its life from me,   95
    Hath had from me a cradle and a grave.
    I must not dally. This sad marriage-bed,
    In all her best, bore her alive and dead.
    Soranzo, thou hast missed thy aim in this;
    I have prevented now thy reaching plots,   100
    And killed a love for whose each drop of blood
    I would have pawned my heart. Fair Annabella,
    How over-glorious art thou in thy wounds,
    Triumphing over infamy and hate!
    Shrink not, courageous hand; stand up, my heart,   105
    And boldly act my last and greater part!
        Exit with the body

Act V Scene VI

*A banquet. Enter Cardinal, Florio, Donado, Soranzo,
Richardetto, Vasques, and attendants; they take their
places.*
VASQUES [*aside to Soranzo*]   Remember, sir, what you
    have to do; be wise and resolute.

SORANZO [*aside to Vasques*]   Enough, my heart is fixed.
   [*To the Cardinal*] Pleaseth your grace
  To taste these coarse confections? Though the use   5
  Of such set entertainments more consists
  In custom than in cause, yet, reverend sir,
  I am still made your servant by your presence.
CARDINAL   And we your friend.
SORANZO   But where's my brother Giovanni?   10
   Enter Giovanni with a heart upon his dagger
GIOVANNI   Here, here, Soranzo! trimmed in reeking blood
  That triumphs over death; proud in the spoil
  Of love and vengeance! Fate, or all the powers
  That guide the motions of immortal souls,
  Could not prevent me.
CARDINAL   What means this?   15
FLORIO   Son Giovanni!
SORANZO   [*aside*]   Shall I be forestalled?
GIOVANNI   Be not amazed. If your misgiving hearts
  Shrink at an idle sight, what bloodless fear
  Of coward passion would have seized your senses
  Had you beheld the rape of life and beauty   20
  Which I have acted? My sister, O my sister!
FLORIO   Ha! What of her?
GIOVANNI   The glory of my deed
  Darkened the midday sun, made noon as night.
  You came to feast, my lords, with dainty fare.
  I came to feast too, but I digged for food   25
  In a much richer mine than gold or stone
  Of any value balanced; 'tis a heart,
  A heart, my lords, in which is mine entombed.
  Look well upon't; d'ee know't?
VASQUES   What strange riddle's this?   30
GIOVANNI   'Tis Annabella's heart, 'tis; why d'ee startle?
  I vow 'tis hers; this dagger's point ploughed up

Her fruitful womb, and left to me the fame
Of a most glorious executioner.
FLORIO   Why, madman, art thyself?   35
GIOVANNI   Yes, father, and that times to come may know
How as my fate I honoured my revenge,
List, father; to your ears I will yield up
How much I have deserved to be your son.
FLORIO   What is't thou say'st?
GIOVANNI   Nine moons have had their changes   40
Since I first throughly viewed and truly loved
Your daughter and my sister.
FLORIO   How! Alas,
My lords, he's a frantic madman!
GIOVANNI   Father, no.
For nine months' space, in secret I enjoyed
Sweet Annabella's sheets; nine months I lived   45
A happy monarch of her heart and her.
Soranzo, thou know'st this; thy paler cheek
Bears the confounding print of thy disgrace,
For her too fruitful womb too soon bewrayed
The happy passage of our stol'n delights,   50
And made her mother to a child unborn.
CARDINAL   Incestuous villain!
FLORIO   O, his rage belies him!
GIOVANNI   It does not, 'tis the oracle of truth;
I vow it is so.
SORANZO   I shall burst with fury;
Bring the strumpet forth!   55
VASQUES   I shall, sir.
     Exit Vasques
GIOVANNI   Do sir; have you all no faith
To credit yet my triumphs? Here I swear
By all that you call sacred, by the love
I bore my Annabella whilst she lived,

These hands have from her bosom ripped this heart.　60
　　Enter Vasques
Is't true or no, sir?
VASQUES　　　　　　　　'Tis most strangely true.
FLORIO　Cursed man! – Have I lived to –
　　Dies
CARDINAL　　　　　　　　　　Hold up Florio;
　Monster of children, see what thou hast done,
　Broke thy old father's heart! Is none of you
　Dares venture on him?
GIOVANNI　　　　　　Let 'em. O, my father,　65
　How well his death becomes him in his griefs!
　Why, this was done with courage; now survives
　None of our house but I, gilt in the blood
　Of a fair sister and a hapless father.
SORANZO　Inhuman scorn of men, hast thou a thought　70
　T'outlive thy murders?
GIOVANNI　　　　　　　Yes, I tell thee, yes;
　For in my fists I bear the twists of life.
　Soranzo, see this heart which was thy wife's;
　Thus I exchange it royally for thine,
　　[*Stabs him*]
　And thus, and thus; now brave revenge is mine.　75
　　[*Soranzo falls*]
VASQUES　I cannot hold any longer. You, sir, are you
　grown insolent in your butcheries? Have at you!
　　Fight
GIOVANNI　Come, I am armed to meet thee.
VASQUES　No, will it not be yet? [*Thrusting at him*] If this
　will not, another shall. Not yet? I shall fit you anon. –　80
　Vengeance!
　　Enter Banditti
GIOVANNI　Welcome! Come more of you, whate'er you
　be;

111

I dare your worst –
    [*They surround and wound him*]
O, I can stand no longer; feeble arms,
Have you so soon lost strength?   85
    [*He falls*]
VASQUES   Now you are welcome, sir! – Away, my
    masters, all is done. Shift for yourselves, your reward
    is your own; shift for yourselves.
BANDITTI   Away, away!
    Exeunt Banditti
VASQUES   How d'ee, my lord? See you this? How is't?   90
SORANZO   Dead; but in death well pleased that I have
    lived
    To see my wrongs revenged on that black devil.
    O Vasques, to thy bosom let me give
    My last of breath; let not that lecher live – O! –
    Dies
VASQUES   The reward of peace and rest be with him,   95
    my ever dearest lord and master.
GIOVANNI   Whose hand gave me this wound?
VASQUES   Mine, sir, I was your first man; have you
    enough?
GIOVANNI   I thank thee; thou hast done for me but what   100
    I would have else done on myself. Art sure
    Thy lord is dead?
VASQUES   O impudent slave! As sure as I am sure to see
    thee die.
CARDINAL   Think on thy life and end, and call for mercy.   105
GIOVANNI   Mercy? Why, I have found it in this justice.
CARDINAL   Strive yet to cry to Heaven.
GIOVANNI   O, I bleed fast!
    Death, thou art a guest long looked-for; I embrace
    Thee and thy wounds. O, my last minute comes!
    Where'er I go, let me enjoy this grace,   110

Freely to view my Annabella's face.
 Dies
DONADO Strange miracle of justice!
CARDINAL Raise up the city; we shall be murdered all!
VASQUES You need not fear, you shall not. This strange
 task being ended, I have paid the duty to the son 115
 which I have vowed to the father.
CARDINAL Speak, wretched villain, what incarnate fiend
 Hath led thee on to this?
VASQUES Honesty, and pity of my master's wrongs.
 For know, my lord, I am by birth a Spaniard, brought 120
 forth my country in my youth by Lord Soranzo's
 father; whom, whilst he lived, I served faithfully; since
 whose death I have been to this man, as I was to him.
 What I have done was duty, and I repent nothing but
 that the loss of my life had not ransomed his. 125
CARDINAL Say, fellow, know'st thou any yet unnamed
 Of counsel in this incest?
VASQUES Yes, an old woman, sometimes guardian to
 this murdered lady.
CARDINAL And what's become of her? 130
VASQUES Within this room she is; whose eyes, after her
 confession, I caused to be put out, but kept alive, to
 confirm what from Giovanni's own mouth you have
 heard. Now, my lord, what I have done you may judge
 of, and let your own wisdom be a judge in your own 135
 reason.
CARDINAL Peace! First this woman, chief in these effects;
 My sentence is that forthwith she be ta'en
 Out of the city, for example's sake,
 There to be burnt to ashes.
DONADO   'Tis most just. 140
CARDINAL Be it your charge, Donado, see it done.
DONADO I shall.

VASQUES   What for me? If death, 'tis welcome. I have
  been honest to the son, as I was to the father.
CARDINAL   Fellow, for thee, since what thou didst was
      done   145
  Not for thyself, being no Italian,
  We banish thee for ever, to depart
  Within three days; in this we do dispense
  With grounds of reason, not of thine offence.
VASQUES   'Tis well; this conquest is mine, and I rejoice 150
  that a Spaniard outwent an Italian in revenge.
    Exit Vasques
CARDINAL   Take up these slaughtered bodies; see them
      buried;
  And all the gold and jewels, or whatsoever,
  Confiscate by the canons of the Church,
  We seize upon to the Pope's proper use.   155
RICHARDETTO [*discovers himself*]   Your grace's pardon.
      Thus long I lived disguised,
  To see the effect of pride and lust at once
  Brought both to shameful ends.
CARDINAL   What? Richardetto, whom we thought for
      dead?
DONADO   Sir, was it you –
RICHARDETTO   Your friend.
CARDINAL   We shall have time 160
  To talk at large of all; but never yet
  Incest and murder have so strangely met.
  Of one so young, so rich in Nature's store,
  Who could not say, '*Tis pity she's a whore?*
    Exeunt [*with the bodies*]

Notes

sd = stage direction

Act I Scene I

Openings often signal a play's themes and chief dramatic business; *'Tis Pity She's a Whore* starts with intellectual debate. The language of the two disputants is significantly different. Giovanni argues his case for incest as if it were a philosophical exercise; by contrast, the Friar refuses to reason, but insists on the immorality of Giovanni's ideas. This intellectual struggle is a feature of the play. Throughout, the Friar is staunchly Christian both in his theology (9–11) and his spiritual counsel (43–5). Giovanni, by contrast, owes more to contemporary culture: he speaks of *beauty* (21) and *nature* (31), and his 'theology' has a distinctly pagan or classical (Greek or Roman) flavour: *the gods/ Would make a god of* (21–2). See Interpretations page 202.

Another indication of the kind of play Ford has written is that it starts with Giovanni imparting the secret of his incestuous desires. Martin Wiggins (see Further Reading page 257) observes that 'The central dynamic of the play's plot is the discovery of secrets'. See Note to line 13. Much of the business to come will involve concealment and disclosure (see V.iii.36).

Ford also introduces what might be called the play's thematic plot line; that is, themes that are embodied in the actions of the characters. The Friar warns Giovanni that *death waits on thy lust* (59). Already, the ghastly climax of the last two scenes is present: the lust of Giovanni and Annabella leads to death.

The opening scene is also anticipatory in that the upholders of moral authority compromise themselves. The Friar is correct in saying that promiscuity is a lesser sin than incest, but that is morally different from advising Giovanni to *take thy choice* (62). In his defence, it should be said that he adds that promiscuity is a game in which *they lose that win* (63). *'Tis Pity* does not present a

character in which the moral standards of the play are
completely embodied (see Interpretations page 230).

The play opens, as do many of Shakespeare's, in the middle of
a conversation. It is up to the audience to work out from the tone
of the Friar's first speech what Giovanni has been saying and how
he might have said it.

1 **Dispute**   As the word *dispute* was (and is) used of matters over
which disagreement is possible, the Friar is firmly denying that
Giovanni's incestuous desires can be a matter of discussion.
The word may have the resonances that Shakespeare gave to it
of physical struggle, of striving and resistance. See
Interpretations page 199.
young man   The name Giovanni means *young man*.

2 **school-points**   matters that belong to the formal business of a
school (university) disputation rather than, in the Friar's view, a
real moral issue.
nice   This word has a number of connotations: detailed,
subtle, exact and over-particular. All of them support the
Friar's belief that Giovanni's language is out of place in serious
moral debate.

3 **unlikely**   improbable.

4 **Heaven**   God.
jest   This word is often used of frolicking or merrymaking,
but here means an idea taken up for the amusement of seeing
where the argument leads.

4–5 **wits... too much**   intellectuals (*wits*) who put excessive trust
(*presumed*) upon the agility of their own thinking.

6 **art**   This word implies cunning contrivance.

9 **fond**   foolish.

11 **he**   God.

13 **unclasped**   The opening of a book becomes an image of
disclosing a secret. Books often had locks.

15–17 Giovanni is probably talking about all that he has ever (*All what
I ever*) told the Friar, rather than just his incestuous desires.

18 As this is a question, Giovanni is reproachfully asking: 'Is this
all the consolation you are going to give me?'

19 **love**   Giovanni does not say here what or whom is the object
of his love. See I.ii.246–7.

20–23 **Must I not... kneel to them**   Giovanni imagines that if the classical gods (the gods of Greece and Rome) could see the one he loves, they would kneel to her just as Giovanni kneels to them. It is not clear at this point whether this is a poetic comparison or whether he is saying that he does not believe in the Christian God.

24 **peevish**   senseless, with the implication of perversity. See Interpretations page 245.

25 Giovanni is asserting that the ban on incest is merely a human convention and not a divine prohibition. The idea that deeply held moral beliefs are mere conventions is a feature of his thinking; see V.iii.1–3. See Interpretations page 202.

32 **blood**   This is the first appearance of an important word in the play. See Interpretations page 194.

33 **one**   This word is frequently used in religious texts such as teachings about marriage: 'and they twain shall be one flesh' (Matthew 19:5).

35 **unhappy**   This could mean mischievous and provocative. If it also means fatal, the Friar is saying that Giovanni's views will lead to his destruction.

36 **for that**   because.

38–9 The combination of *eyes* with *pity and compassion* might indicate that Giovanni can see tears in the Friar's eyes. See Interpretations page 229.

40 **distils**   The primary meaning is 'extracts the essence of a substance'. Distilling, therefore, becomes an image of how his life of spiritual advice – *The life of counsel* – produces *pity and compassion*. As *distils* also meant falling in minute drops, the word can also indicate the Friar's tears. Given the image of the *sacred oracle*, is there the hint of tears as a sacred stream, water being associated with sacred places?

42 **cure**   Is Giovanni aware of the irony that in using the word *cure* he recognizes that his incestuous desires are a disease?

45 This line can be performed to show the Friar reaching for words. He calls *sin* (43) *unrangèd* (unlimited), and then his thinking stutters before he says that what Giovanni wants is *almost blasphemy*. The result is that *almost* could refer either to *unrangèd* or *blasphemy*.

47 **wit**   mind, intellectual acuity.

49–52   Giovanni was the outstanding scholar of his generation at *Bologna*, one of the leading universities of Europe. The Friar praises him as an ideal young man, renowned for *government* (self-discipline), *behaviour* (manner of life), *learning* (academic prowess), *speech* (cultivated language) and *Sweetness* (gracious poise) – *all that could make up a man*. See Interpretations page 238.

    53   **tutelage**   guardianship and moral guidance, as well as academic formation.

 53–4   The Friar abandoned his own life of scholarship at Bologna rather than *part with* Giovanni. What possibilities for characterization does this give to the actor playing the part? As the Friar returns there at the end of the play, Bologna marks its opening and close.

    57   **schools**   This was a common name for university education.

    58   **death**   The Friar sees the death as spiritual, and the audience might later see this as anticipating Giovanni's murder in the last scene.

    62   **choice**   The Friar seems to be saying that Giovanni can choose any woman to gratify his sexual desires. The meaning of *'tis much less sin* is that promiscuity is not as grave a sin as incest. See I.ii.77.

    65   **floats and ebbs**   high and low tides. See V.v.14.
            vows   wishes, desires.

    66   **wilful**   impulsive and unreasoning.

69–71   Ford's audiences would probably recognize the similarity between the Friar's counsel and the words of the Sermon on the Mount on prayer (Matthew 6:5–6).

    74   **leprosy**   Martin Wiggins (see Further Reading) points out that *leprosy* was used as a metaphor for sexual corruption.

    76   **worm**   In religious texts, *worm* refers to the utter worthlessness of a person, as in 'I am a worm, and no man' (Psalm 22:6).

    84   **my fate's my god**   See Interpretations page 233.

Act I Scene II

The second scene consists of three pieces of action: a duel, a 'parade' of suitors and the 'love duet' of Giovanni and Annabella.

Duelling corresponds to the intellectual debate of the first scene. As Putana says, it is a scene of *threatening, challenging, quarrelling, and fighting* (68–9). Vasques is shown to be more aggressive than Grimaldi, because he has already drawn his sword. For Grimaldi there is a social dimension: he tries to avoid fighting with someone who is not his social *equal* (3). Grimaldi only draws his sword after a series of insults. His *Provoke me not, for if thou dost* (23) appears to be the point at which his patience runs out.

The parade of suitors establishes Ford's presentation of Italy as a place of public rituals (see page 9). Because Putana's remarks come very early in the play, we might be persuaded to accept her judgements. It is, however, up to us – audiences and readers – to decide whether we agree with her.

The 'wooing' passage, the most important in the scene, presents a number of interesting problems. How it is understood will shape our interpretation of the whole play. There is the matter of Annabella's first sight of Giovanni. When she sees him, he is unaware of her presence. It may therefore be assumed that he is not consciously playing the role of the forlorn lover: he *Walks careless of himself* (140). That he is distracted is evident from Annabella's remark: *I trust he be not frantic* (189). A difficulty is that although he has been at home in Parma for three months (I.i.48), Annabella does not recognize him. Perhaps a production should show that Giovanni's strict life of prayer and fasting (158–60) has altered his appearance and manner. Another possibility is that Ford is trying to present the scene as a wonderful discovery, as in the scene in Shakespeare's *The Tempest* (I.ii.412) in which Miranda, on first seeing Ferdinand, thinks he is a spirit. If, however, Annabella is telling the truth when she declares she has long desired him (249–51), this can hardly be the 'Romeo and Juliet' moment of first love.

Giovanni is given the first soliloquy of the play. Ford probably learned from Shakespeare how a soliloquy can be used to show a character reaching after what he desires. (*Macbeth* is a wonderful example.) Giovanni struggles to discard religion and the moral constraints associated with it (150–68). Do his struggles sound realistic?

Ford gives to Annabella the line that sums up the problem of the play: *You are my brother Giovanni* (237). This may be the first sign that she, unlike him, can view life in moral terms. His reply is interesting. He does not dodge the nature of the relationship: *You,/ My sister Annabella* (237–8). Onstage, the crucial matter is the tone in which this is delivered. Does he convey the wonder of mutual love, and does this exclude the recognition of a moral bar? And what should Annabella's tone be?

1   **stand to your tackling**   be prepared to *stand* (fight), so draw your *tackling* (weapon). *Stand* is used several times in the opening dialogue of *Romeo and Juliet*, when servants talk of fighting in the street.

4–8   Vasques says that he is not a man who boasts of his military exploits in order to get good dinners from those who want to hear tales of the battlefield; he implies that this is what Grimaldi does. A *mountebank* was a travelling seller of medicines; they had a reputation for speaking eloquently but untruthfully about their wares. His *grey hairs* represent Vasques' long years of military service. Is there any evidence for this? The term *gear* means what they have to do – fight.

10   **cast-suit**   Servants commonly wore the cast-off clothing of those who had previously served.

12   **cot-quean**   an insulting term meaning a man who is concerned with matters that properly belong to a housewife.

12–13   **your profession**   the type of man you are.

13–15   **Thou poor shadow… performance**   See Putana's equally derogatory remarks about Grimaldi's impotence at 84–6.

15   **quality and performance**   social class and skill with the sword.

19   **expense**   shedding.

24 sd   *They fight*   In the late sixteenth century, several manuals on the art of fencing were translated from the Italian (see page 7). The duel is puzzling, because it is not exactly clear why Vasques is challenging Grimaldi. Might Florio's *haunted still* (28) indicate that they have fought in public before? Donado's *you are ever*

forward/ In seconding contentions (32–3) shows that Vasques has a reputation for starting quarrels.

25 **sudden** impetuous, rash and violent.

26 **other places** Duelling often took place in remote parts of a town.

27 **spleen** It was believed that anger and violence were generated in the *spleen*.

30 **naught** wrong.

33 **ground** reason.

34 **resolve** explain, make clear, sort out. This word will become particularly important at the end of the play. See Interpretations page 241.

35 **fame** reputation.

38 **prefers** presses. As is made explicit in *to disparage me* (40), in doing so he questions the worthiness of Soranzo.

42 **bewrays** shows up. This implies the laying bare of Grimaldi's dishonest scheming.

43–7 Soranzo indicates the class basis of his antagonism to Grimaldi.

48–51 Vasques' first image is of a doctor who, to ease a patient's over-excited condition, will *let* (draw) *blood* from the *gills* (the flesh beneath the chin.) There is an enjoyable comic disparity in Vasques calling Grimaldi a *gentleman* while wanting to cut his throat. The second image is of controlling a rabid dog, which is *wormed* (has part of its tongue cut out) to prevent it *running mad*. A performer must decide how Grimaldi responds.

52 **revenged** This is the first mention of revenge in the play.

53–4 **On a dish... stomach** Vasques continues to use the language of medicine, this time suggesting that *warm broth* would *stay* (quell) Grimaldi's weak appetite and uncontrollable aggression. Both meanings are present in *stomach*.

55 **Spanish blade** Spain was famous for manufacturing steel for swords. In the closing scene, Vasques reveals that he is *a Spaniard* (V.vi.120).

57–60 This speech must be delivered privately to Soranzo, for otherwise Donado would know that Florio has no intention of marrying Annabella off to Bergetto.

59 **Owing** owning. Soranzo, he says, already owns Annabella's *heart*.

60 A proverb, meaning roughly that it is those who have lost who talk a great deal.

62 **unspleened dove**   Vasques says that Grimaldi would even outrage a *dove* (the epitome of gentleness) without a *spleen* (the organ that produces anger). See Note to line 27.

67 **put up**   As this means 'put your sword back in its scabbard', Vasques must have had his sword drawn since the start of the scene.

68 **child**   Putana's language is sadly at odds with her conduct. She may call Annabella *child* and *charge* (71, 76, 83), yet treats her as a young woman ripe for sexual activity. It is also inappropriate for Annabella to call Putana *tutoress* (72).

72–3 This is one of those signals by which dramatic irony works. We are to wonder what *other ends* (other matters) Annabella is thinking about. If we are to believe her confession to Giovanni that her desires are the same as his (249–51), then *such a life*, a phrase that sounds like a renunciation of worldly pleasure, is actually an expression of incestuous desire.

75–6 **leave me no leaving**   don't talk to me about leaving.

76 **love outright**   This is the big question of the play: is it?

77 **fit**   fitting, suitable, appropriate.

80 **well-timbered**   solidly built (as in a wooden house).

81–3 **a Roman... the Milanese**   This is an indication that the action is set in the sixteenth century. Grimaldi is *Roman* but, as was common, he did military service for another city. *Monferrato* was a strategically important city state in north-west Italy, which was at war with Milan over the control of Parma in 1551–2. See page 8.

85–6 **some privy... upright**   Putana says that soldiers often sustain an injury that renders them sexually incapable – *mars their standing upright*. A character in Cyril Tourneur's *The Atheist's Tragedy* (1611) speaks of a soldier who will return from the wars 'lame and impotent' (I.iv.97).

87–8 **crinkles so much... might serve**   Putana thinks Grimaldi is given to bowing (*hams* means thighs) and implies that he shrinks from his sexual duties, though she adds that he may be able to *serve* (father children).

91 **Signior**   Soranzo's title should be 'Lord'. Florio always gets this right.

97 **wholesome**   healthy, with the strong implication that he does not suffer from venereal disease.

98 **liberal** generous. It is clear that Putana has taken bribes from him. For her taking bribes, see also II.vi.18–21.

100 **good name with Hippolita** i.e. Hippolita obviously found him attractive and desirable.

lusty The usual meaning is vigorous, but here it could also mean lustful.

101 **but** only. Putana asserts that the affair with Hippolita proves Soranzo is *a man sure*.

103–4 **plain-sufficient, naked man** Putana's idea of a husband is one who sexually satisfies his wife.

106 Annabella wonders if Putana has drunk too much.

108 **ciphers** nonentities.

109 **brave old ape in a silken coat** This proverb means that *brave* (fine) clothes cannot conceal the stupidity of the wearer. As no performers are obliged to follow what any character says, actors have to decide whether Bergetto deserves more sympathy than Putana gives him.

110–11 Bergetto indicates that he was challenged to a *fight* but refused.

114 **coxcomb** either a simpleton or, perhaps more interestingly, a conceited person. Does Bergetto prove to be either?

120–21 **another purchase in hand** It looks as if Bergetto has agreed to be a suitor to Annabella, and that his motive is financial.

123 sd *Walks affectedly* The audience's estimation of Bergetto's character depends on whether he deliberately behaves in a ridiculous manner. See Interpretations page 222.

125 **Spanish pavan** a grave and courtly dance, often performed in elaborate costumes.

130–32 **to make... a right Israelite** Putana is alluding to the story in the Bible (Exodus 32) of the Israelites worshipping a calf made of gold. She thinks that Donado expects Annabella to be attracted by Bergetto's wealth and to overlook his stupidity. A *cousin* is a close relative.

133–4 **fool's bauble** the carved stick (sometimes called a coxcomb) of a jester. In the context it also means a penis.

135 **dearth** lack. Annabella has plenty of potential husbands and, therefore, in Putana's terms, there are many men who might have sex with her.

139 **aspect** appearance, manner.

141 **your brother**   Ford dwells on the relationship between the brother and sister. Annabella first addresses him as *Brother* (169). **Ha!**   How might this be spoken?

142–5   Giovanni shows many of the signs of the forlorn lover.

146 **partake**   learn.

148 **partage**   a share.

150–52   See Interpretations pages 192–3.

152 **hope**   This is a theologically important word. *Hope* was the prospect of salvation and heaven, so to lose hope is to lose faith in God.

154 **wounds**   This is a reference to the injuries inflicted by Cupid's dart of love.

155 **examined**   This word has the force of a practical as well as a mental activity, so here it means *throughly* (thoroughly) investigated. See also *practised* (161).

157   To make *love a god* would be idolatry and therefore a *sin*.

160 **fasts**   The Friar did not counsel Giovanni to fast.

162–3   This is the first time that Giovanni dismisses the claims of religion as fantasies devised by the old to control the young.

164 **Or... or**   either... or.

166   Giovanni interprets respect for religious morality as being the mentality of *slaves*. It is another step in his abandonment of religious belief. See Interpretations page 201.

168 **rated**   valued or judged.

170 **ye heavenly powers**   not God, but the classical gods – Venus, Cupid.

171 **virtue**   power, force, life (not morality).

177 **private**   alone. But given what follows, an audience might dwell on the other meaning of the word, intimate.

180–81 **office of some credit**   Were the meeting not between a brother and sister, Putana would expect to be paid for her absence.

183 **blush**   A modest young woman would not be seen walking with a young man who was not related to her.

184   See page 19.

189 **frantic**   mentally distracted.

190 **Trust me**   believe me.

196 **merry**   amusing but also, in Shakespeare, sexually playful.

197–200 **The poets feign… did theirs** Giovanni follows the convention of claiming that the ancient *poets* were not telling the truth, for Annabella's beauty exceeds that of *Juno*, the most beautiful of all the goddesses. See Interpretations page 215.

202 **Promethean fire** Prometheus formed people out of clay and breathed life into them with the fire he had stolen from heaven.

205 **strange** different, opposed.

206 **change** i.e. Annabella's colour is changing from the white of astonishment to the red of blushes.

208 **anchorite** hermit who lives a solitary life of religious contemplation.

210 **exact** perfect.

212 **glass** mirror.

213 **trim** This is a compliment (though perhaps intended humorously) meaning 'in full sail'. See Interpretations page 192.

214 sd *dagger* Ford may be thinking of the scene in Shakespeare's *Richard III* (I.ii) in which Richard, courting Lady Anne, offers her the chance to kill him. See V.v.84.

215 **Rip** This is a frequently used word in the play. See Interpretations page 195.

216 The image of truth written in the heart was conventional.

219 **death** His sufferings are so intense that he might die.

222–3 **untuned… and life** The idea of harmony *untuned* was a common way of expressing disorder. The word *rest* can mean earthly and heavenly peace, and perhaps a *rest* (silence) in music.

224 **just fears** true apprehensions.

232 The advice that would be given by the young, who have no experience of adult passion. As we know the only person who has advised him is the Friar, Giovanni might be making this up.

233 **bootless** pointless.

235 **in sadness** in earnest, sincerely.

241–2 See Interpretations page 202.

246–7 This is a lie. See I.i.19–20. See also Interpretations page 239.

247 **just** fitting, appropriate.

249–50 **won/The field** Love was frequently written about in terms of warfare, so *field* means battlefield. See Interpretations page 210.

251 **long ago** Is it worthwhile asking how long ago?

255 **for that**   because.

257 **music**   i.e. this is not an *untuned... harmony* (222–3).

262 **my mother's dust**   Annabella said *our mother's dust* (259). See Interpretations page 251.

265 **good sooth**   She wants to know that Giovanni really means what he says. His reply offering *good troth* means the same. A marriage vow is: 'I plight (pledge) thee my troth.' Uneasiness about sincerity is a feature of this scene.

267 **kiss**   A kiss was often a feature of the marriage service.

269 **Elysium**   the home of the gods, an earthly paradise.

272 **kiss and sleep**   This is a restrained description of love-making.

Act I Scene III

The actor playing Florio has an opportunity to establish his character more fully than in the brief exchange in I.ii. He can be played as a confident, civil man who is open about what he wants for his daughter. His character is in his language; he speaks insistently and unambiguously in firm monosyllables. He accords with the views of most audiences in his insistence that he *would not have her marry wealth, but love* (11). Is there any good reason why we should not take him at his word? One reason why we might hesitate to believe him is that he talks to Donado as if he is interested in marrying Annabella to Bergetto, when we know he has virtually promised her to Soranzo (I.ii.58–9) – perhaps he can be played as sincerely believing that Annabella can find love with Soranzo. See Interpretations page 221.

The success of the scene depends upon how Bergetto is played. One issue is his relation to Poggio. Poggio's *Answer for yourself, master* (49) might be played as indicating that if Bergetto is to grow up he should indeed start answering for himself. This would be consistent with playing Bergetto as a young man in the charge of an older guardian figure. Alternatively, Poggio and Bergetto might be played as two young men new to adult society. In that case, Poggio could simply be afraid of Donado. How the relationship is performed will have a strong bearing on Poggio's response to Bergetto's death (III.vii). See Interpretations page 222.

Is one of the pleasing effects of the scene that Bergetto is not abashed by his failure to speak appropriately to Donado? A performance might bring out the contrast between the serious exasperation of Donado and the blithe unconcern of his ever-cheerful nephew. It might also indicate that Bergetto, in spite of his remarks in I.ii.120–23, is not really interested in Annabella. He may see that Annabella will turn him down.

2 **but**   only.

5 **book**   studies.

6 **doubt**   fear for.

7 **miscarry**   die.

16 **presently**   at this moment.

17–18   Donado promises that Bergetto will have an annual income of about £300 and, upon his death, the whole of his estate. As masons and carpenters earned about £30 a year, Bergetto's income would have made him very comfortable, though not exceedingly rich. We must assume that Donado's estate would have made him much richer.

20 **suit**   courtship, wooing.

27 **in good time**   at the right time.

29 **whither away so fast?**   Bergetto's haste indicates that he does not think wooing Annabella is an urgent matter.

31 **out of the mint**   This is a colloquial phrase meaning fresh (newly-minted).

34 **Why look ye uncle?**   Bergetto is responding to the look – surprise? disapproval? anger? – on Donado's face.
   barber   As has often been the case, barbers were regarded as a good source of gossip.

36–7 **undertakes to… with sandbags**   The *mill* that works on sandbags was probably an attempt at perpetual motion. Renaissance scientists pondered whether it was possible to construct a machine that worked on its own without running out of power.

38–41 **a strange horse… his tail is**   This was a fairground 'scam'. A horse's tail was tied to a manger, so its tail was where its head was expected to be. At this point, Ford's play has stepped into the dramatic world of Ben Jonson, with its cast of fraudsters deceiving the unwary at the big London fairs.

46–7 **more mind... the business**   i.e. Bergetto is more concerned with a side-show at a fair than wooing Annabella.

48 **May-game**   object of derisive laughter.

51 **gallants**   rich and fashionable young men. It seems Bergetto wants to live up to the public image of the *gallant*.

52 **hobby-horses**   A *hobby-horse* was one of the members of a morris dancing team. Donado means that Bergetto wants to waste his time on frivolities. In *The Witch of Edmonton*, partly written by Ford, there is a morris team with one character playing the hobby-horse.

55–7 Bergetto's colloquial speech hardly has the tone of the *wise talk* (52) Donado hopes he has enjoyed with Annabella. Are the sexual connotations of *tickled* and *belly* intended by Bergetto?

61 **parmesan**   the highly celebrated cheese of Parma. See page 8.

72–3 Does Donado's approval of the question about wealth show that he has as little idea of wooing as his nephew?

77 **glory**   It seems that Bergetto means 'shame'.

78 **white boy**   favourite child.

79 **fit**   This probably means 'to respond in a suitable way to', though the meaning 'to engage in sexual intercourse with' was also current.

80–81 **no changing of nature**   This idea might express one of the main themes of the play.

85–7 **write to her... the letter**   The letter will be styled in the *courtly* (elevated) *manner*, and the paper on which it is written will *enclose some rich jewel*. See Interpretations page 198.

91 **'tis but the fortune of a fool**   This is a way of saying: what else can be expected from a fool?

Act II Scene I

The audience's reaction to the opening of this scene depends upon how the actor playing Giovanni delivers the first two speeches. If he says *love, a name more gracious* (2) tenderly, and *Beauty's sweet wonder* (3) with awe, then the mood will be one of fresh delight awakened by first love. His second speech, however, comes close to the type of male boasting that lightly dismisses female anxieties about the loss of virginity. Is it possible to play the part as a young man new to love, who is enjoying using such language for the first time? And could even the indecent wordplay on *nothing* (11, see Note) be performed with youthful innocence?

Annabella is also merry and witty. Indeed, she is more consistently so than Giovanni. It is possible to deliver her line *'Tis well for you* (12) playfully, and later when Giovanni is afflicted by the thought that she must marry another, she continues to joke bawdily: to his disconsolate *Someone must have you*, she replies, in the manner of sexual wordplay, with *You must* (23). When Giovanni persists in his seriousness, she says: *do not speak so without jesting* (24).

Ford is alert to the dramatic possibilities of the scene. As in I.ii there is still an anxiety about mutual faithfulness, which might give a disturbing colouring to the tone of an otherwise happy scene. Giovanni, having received Annabella's heart-felt profession of true love, immediately says *Remember what thou vow'st* (32). Annabella is aware of the dangerous position she is in, so, anxiously and wisely, says she would not want news of what they have done *known for all the world* (47), and almost immediately her father calls: *Daughter Annabella!* (50). How might she deliver the line *O me, my father!* (51)?

The audience might also be alive to the ironic possibilities of the scene. Is it true that Annabella is *no more sister now* (1)? Music has figured in the language of Annabella and Giovanni as an indication of mood and also as an image of love-making. Towards the end of the scene Richardetto, apparently a doctor, comes to the house to offer the services of Philotis, a musician. When the audience later come to know who Richardetto is, it might be seen as ironic that after Giovanni's anxieties about faithfulness there should enter a man whose life has been blighted by an unfaithful wife.

2 **blush** Think about the associations of blushing – desire and modesty. The word is important in the early part of the play. See I.ii.183.

4–5 **inflamed... thy brother's life** This is a verbal anticipation of a later action. The *tribute* is not only the life of a brother.

10 **pretty toy** trivial matter.

11 **nothing** There is a play on different meanings here. First, loss of virginity is *nothing* because it is of no account, and, second, because it leads to sexual indulgence. The vagina is *nothing*, because it is 'no thing' – 'thing' meaning penis.

13–14 **Music as well... the playing** Giovanni is assuring his sister that it is possible to understand something – such as, in this case, loss of virginity – without experiencing it. *Music* could be used as an image for love-making.

14 **wanton** lascivious, sexy. The tone is playful.

16 **thus hung Jove on Leda's neck** Giovanni is comparing himself to *Jove* (Jupiter) who, in the form of a swan, impregnated *Leda*, the wife of a king of Sparta. The child born to her was Helen of Troy. How far should the details of this story be applied to Giovanni and Annabella?

17 **ambrosia** the unimaginably delightful food of the gods.

18–20 See Interpretations page 218.

21 Perhaps there is something convincing about this sudden disquiet. Being in love can make people more conscious of the changes that time brings.

23 **have** both sexually possess and take in marriage. In the wordplay of the dialogue it is the opposite of *lose* (21).

25 **you will not** Giovanni wonders whether she will refuse to marry.

27 It is worth asking whether throughout the play Annabella heeds Giovanni's *live to me*.

34 **Look you do** make sure you do.

38 **Child** What, in the context, is the force of this term of endearment?

39 **paradise** In the sixteenth and seventeenth centuries, religiously charged words were often used in passages about love. See I.ii.269 and Interpretations page 212.

40–42 **passed over... passed under** Annabella means that she has *passed* into a new world – a *paradise*. Putana simply means that she has been physically *under* her brother. What is the importance of the differences between these two prepositions?

45 **fit**   sexual desire, with the strong implication that it is barely controllable and possibly the result of lunacy. The word occurs several times in the play, but not always with this meaning.

48 **speech of the people**   gossip.

55 **Padua**   The University of Padua was well known for the teaching of medicine.

57 **sickly**   The audience are in a position to know that she has probably been sick with longing for Giovanni.

58 **reverend**   respected, worthy.

60 There is no reason why the audience should doubt that there is *large report* (widespread and fulsome speech) in Annabella's *praise*.

61 If *virtue* is of the soul and *perfection* of the body, these are close to the terms that Giovanni has used to persuade Annabella to commit incest.

64 **content**   The audience might understand this ironically.

65 **parts**   accomplishments.

67 **make not strange**   do not behave like a stranger.

70 **bind me**   The bonds are those of gratitude.

74 **cunning**   artistic skill.

76 Unintentionally, Florio's language has sexual connotations: *instrument* (penis) and *done't* (had sex).

Act II Scene II

As characters in Renaissance drama usually tell the truth in soliloquy, the audience might accept that here Soranzo reveals the true state of his soul. It might be said that, like Giovanni, he is dependent upon the conventional love language of his day – such as *her diviner cheeks* (17) – but people do express themselves in the terms available to them, so such borrowing cannot be regarded as evidence of insincerity. In several scenes of the play (including the middle sections of this one), Soranzo is a character who is easy to condemn. Yet in his opening soliloquy, Ford encourages us to think of him as a sincere and distraught young man. Soranzo certainly finds it difficult (perhaps comically so) to cope with Hippolita's anger.

Hippolita's story of the fatal journey her husband makes to *Leghorn* (76) comes after we have met the man who turns out to be that husband – Richardetto. It is possible that an audience might connect the doctor accompanied by a *kinswoman* (II.i.63) with the story Hippolita tells, but there is no confirmation of that in this scene. Richardetto's identity is not revealed until the next scene.

The tone of the scene changes with the exit of Soranzo. The angry accusations and recriminations cease, but the moral atmosphere is still poisoned. When in an aside Hippolita addresses *opportunity* (126), the audience can see that she is scheming. What the later plot movement reveals is that the apparently concerned Vasques is doing the same – but not, as he claims, in her interest. She shows a bold independence in her offer of marriage (or is it just sex?) when she makes her bid to recruit him (134–8). Should an audience admire her enterprise, or remember that this is a scene in which the breaking of promises has been a central matter? See Interpretations page 193.

1 sd **in his study**   See page 19 for how this scene might have been staged.

1–18   Soranzo is reading the Italian love poet Jacopo Sannazaro (1458–1530). Ford clearly knew two things about Sannazaro: his poetry, in particular his *Arcadia* (completed 1489), has a wistful and melancholic tone, and he wrote a poem in praise of Venice (12–15), for which he was rewarded by the Venetian authorities. However, as the lines 'quoted' at 1–2 do not appear in Sannazaro's work, it is unlikely that Ford read him. Instead, Ford imagines him as a poet who dealt in the paradoxes and polarities – *measure/extreme, comfort/pain* – of the kind of love poetry made popular by the Italian poet Petrarch (1304–74). Perhaps the important point is that it is conventional for a young man uncertain of success in love to read and write poetry. What Soranzo writes (10–11) contradicts the imagined lines from Sannazaro. See Interpretations page 196.

1 **measure**   middle way, the normal or expected course. The word also meant the rhythmical aspect of poetry.

4 **smooth licentious**   These terms probably refer to Sannazaro being a love poet. *Smooth* might carry the meanings it has in Shakespeare: using flattery and glossing over. These meanings are certainly present in line 47.

5 **liest**   Soranzo is being conventional here: a poet would often claim that other poets did not really know what it is to love because they had not seen his beloved.

7 **kissed the rod**   willingly submitted to the *smart* (pains) of love.

8–9 Soranzo asks the *Muse* to help him *contradict* what Sannazaro has written in ill-will or *envy* (malice).

10 **the mean**   what is normal or average. See line 1 and Note.

13 **encomium**   elaborate and formal expression of praise.

17 **cheeks**   The *cheeks* of a beloved were a conventional object of praise in love poetry.

20 **taxed of**   blamed for.

25 sd **in mourning clothes**   We learn in line 40 that Hippolita is in mourning for her husband.

26–8 Is her entrance and unveiling (*Do you know me now?*) too melodramatic and self-regarding (*'Tis I*)? She also unveils herself at IV.i.38.

28 **distracted**   The word was stronger in Ford's day, having implications of madness. Again, we might ask: is she wrong?

31 **foil**   the setting for a jewel. Hippolita is asking whether Soranzo wants her to set off (form a suitable contrast to) his new, and still unsatisfied, lust for Annabella.

32 **modest fame**   reputation for living a good life.

36 Does the anguish of Soranzo in 1–18 strengthen her accusation that he was a lover pleading for sexual favours with *tears* and *oaths*?

39–42 Hippolita rhetorically asks whether she who has lost so much – her husband, her reputation – is to be rewarded with *hatred and contempt*. But after what she has said, would she want him to marry her?

49 **Your goodly Madam Merchant**   For the class basis of this sneer, see page 8.

52 **double** two-faced, deceiving.

53 **dissimulation** pretence.

54 **habit, weeds** clothes.

57 She is a *widow* in her *widowhood*, because Soranzo will not marry her.

61 He accuses her of being beyond *sense* (reason), and she counters by saying he is beyond the saving *grace* of God.

62–7 Vasques speaks first to Hippolita and then to Soranzo. It is the first time he plays the role of the go-between and the first time, the audience later discover, that he sets out to deceive a character who stands in Soranzo's way.

64 **unedge** make blunt.

65 **perplex** trouble.

70–72 See Interpretations page 217.

70–83 Perhaps the detailed nature of this story prompts us to wonder whether Ford had a reason for making Hippolita recount it. Might it be a parable of the play – the story of a character who embarks on a journey never to return? Put in those terms, it could be said to be the story of Hippolita and Soranzo as well as Annabella and Giovanni.

74 **protests** vows, as in a promise to marry.

75–6 **to counsel him… voyage** Might Hippolita have persuaded her husband to make this journey in the hope that he would not return, or did she simply want him out of the way so she could engage in an adulterous affair with Soranzo?

76 **Leghorn** a port on the western coast of Italy at the mouth of the river Arno (the present day Livorno). Travelling was still an uncertain business in the seventeenth century, so to embark on a journey involved risks. Moreover, Leghorn was near marshy land, where fevers could breed. As a port, Leghorn would be known to the English. Sir Robert Dudley (1574–1649), son of the Earl of Leicester, acted as engineer for a massive breakwater, administered the port and supervised the draining of the marshy land between Leghorn and Pisa.

78 **unfriended** without the support of friends or family.

86–8 **The vows… to break them** What is to be made of Soranzo's argument? Is keeping a promise one should not have made a *sin*? See Interpretations page 240.

89 **mask** hide.

90 **digressed from honest shame**   become shameless through departing from virtuous living.

93 **quality**   high social status.
condition   This could mean either his wealth or his personal virtues.

94 **entertainment**   generosity, hospitality.

95 **braver**   finer, more outstanding.

96 Vasques' plan of deceiving Hippolita into thinking he is assisting her requires that she hears this line said to Soranzo.

99 **corse**   dead body, corpse.

103 Soranzo recklessly ignores his approaching *fate*. He is not the only one. See Interpretations page 232.

106 **his woe**   the sorrow he has caused.

112 **moved**   i.e. to anger.

118 **shrewd**   angrily outspoken.

122 **hearty**   sincere.

128 **spleen**   bitterness.

130–2 The servant abandoned after a lifetime's service is a familiar figure in sixteenth- and seventeenth-century literature. See line 143.

135 **honest**   genuine and sincere.

137 **acquittance**   repayment.

138 **myself**   This implies an offer either of marriage or of sexual favours.

139 This might be either an expression of gratitude for a generous offer, or a modest declaration that he does not deserve such an elevated person.

140 **feed**   Scenes involving food and feasting are a feature of the play. See lines 168–9 and Interpretations page 199.

145 **private to me**   in on my secrets.
designs   plots, plans, schemes.

147 **dispose**   disposal.

148–9 The aside, as so often in this play, is indicative of deception.

148 **mole**   A *mole* works purposefully but blindly.

150 **compass**   range or reach.

155 **but**   only.

157–8 These lines may be influenced by the scene in Webster's *The Duchess of Malfi* (I.i) in which the Duchess, a person of high rank, proposes marriage to a social inferior.

159 **merry** merely play-acting.
162–5 Is this a plain lie, or is the language so diplomatic that Vasques
could claim that he does not reveal the secret until *it be effected*?
166 Hippolita regards what he has said as a betrothal – a promise to
marry.
168 **bane** poison.

Act II Scene III

Hippolita's betrayal of her husband was mentioned by Putana in
I.ii.99–101. From the wording – *her husband's lifetime* – the
audience learn that her husband is dead, and the story of his
supposed death is recounted by her in II.ii.74–80. A secret is now
disclosed: Richardetto is Hippolita's husband, and Philotis is his
niece.

It is also disclosed that Richardetto as well as Hippolita are
revengers. She has spoken of *a plot I have* (II.ii.156), and now
Philotis sees that her uncle has *some strange revenge* (15) in mind.
Later in the scene Richardetto provides the frustrated and angry
Grimaldi (also bent on revenge) with a scheme and the means to
carry it out. It is the first time in the play that a specific revenge
plot is given in detail. Ford is working in the tradition of creating
a scene in which poison is purchased. This happens in *Romeo and
Juliet* (V.i), and in Chaucer's *The Pardoner's Tale* there is a grimly
humorous scene in which a treacherous young man buys poison
on the excuse that a polecat is troubling his chickens.

Richardetto has one characteristic in common with many
revengers. This is that he awaits his opportunity (see II.ii.126). He
does not go to Grimaldi, but when Grimaldi comes to him he
persuades him to act against Soranzo. This was clearly why he
offered Philotis's services to Florio. He asks her whether she has
learned that *Signior Florio means to give his daughter/ In marriage to
Soranzo* (17–19).

1 **niece**   Before this scene, Richardetto has used the less specific term *kinswoman* (II.i.63) to describe Philotis.

3–4 See page 10.

5 **borrowed shape**   i.e. his disguise as a doctor. A production must decide whether Philotis indicates what he is wearing – probably a beard, cap and gown – or whether she points to a disguise that he has taken off.

6 **content**   The word was used by Richardetto in his previous scene (II.i.64). Several of the characters are seeking *content*.

8 **secure**   unsuspicious and free from fears.

10 **rumoured**   Richardetto, who has suffered from the rumours of Hippolita's infidelity, now uses rumour to keep a watch on Hippolita.

13 Richardetto wants to know how people regard Hippolita's behaviour.

16 **ignorance**   See Interpretations page 227.

23 **mystery**   No one other than Richardetto and Philotis has noticed that there is something strange in Annabella's behaviour with regard to her suitors.

24 **used you kindly**   received you in a friendly manner.

31 **nuncio**   The Cardinal is the *nuncio* – official representative – *of the Pope*.

40 **receipts**   recipes, formulae for medical preparations.

41 **move**   incline (to love).

48 **bar**   In Renaissance comedies, lovers often encountered a *bar* which prevented them from fulfilling their desires. Here the bar to Grimaldi's love is the life of another suitor.

49 Richardetto has in fact just learned that Soranzo is not *the man that hath her heart*.

50 **speed**   go further, prosper (in your pursuit of Annabella).

53 **confusion**   This could mean destruction, damnation or mental affliction. It occurs several times in the play. See Interpretations page 195.

60 **Hydra**   a many-headed, poisonous water-snake in classical mythology which grew two new heads whenever one was cut off. One of the labours of Hercules was to fight the Hydra.

Act II Scene IV

Bergetto's letter with its ill-advised frankness, its potentially bawdy innuendoes and its blunt references to Annabella's appearance has all the usual comedy of language in an inappropriate register. And, as in I.iii, the agitated frustrations of Donado can prompt laughter. Furthermore, his criticism of Bergetto is comically inept. Donado's scheme is not going to be furthered by telling Bergetto in rather hectoring terms that he is a fool. Ford is also concerned to keep the Bergetto plot going. It is because he disobeys his uncle's order to stay *within doors* (38–9) that, as he recounts in II.vi, he meets Philotis.

   2 **secretary**   It was the job of a *secretary* to write letters for his employer. Here Donado is stressing how much he is helping Bergetto by disclosing that he has written the letter himself.

   8 **fool's head**   This is a reference to the watermark on writing paper depicting a fool wearing the cap of his profession. We still speak of 'foolscap' paper.

12–14 **if she will not... another's handwriting**   Donado might call Bergetto a fool, but here Bergetto makes a sound point.

  15 **indited**   Because *indited* is an elevated way of saying 'written', Bergetto may be trying to show that he can speak like a well-educated gentleman.

  19 **hand**   handwriting. Does this mean that Bergetto has difficulty reading?

  23 **lie**   This is a word with unfortunate implications.

  25 **the colour of his beard**   Donado's beard must be grey.

  26 **board**   The literal meaning of this word is to go aboard a ship, but it also meant to tackle, and to mount as in sexual intercourse.

  32 **stuff**   The usual meaning is the real matter or substance of something. It could also mean, as it still does, to have sex.

  45 **motions and fopperies**   i.e. the side-shows at a fair.

47–8 See Note to I.iii.38–41.

Act II Scene V

An interesting feature of the plot is that once he has committed incest, Giovanni still talks to the Friar. If *before the hour/ That thou cam'st to me* (4–5) refers to the present (though it is possible that he is referring to their first meeting in Bologna), then Giovanni actually sought out the Friar to talk about his failure to resist.

From the impatient first word of the Friar, the audience assume that they have been arguing about Giovanni's behaviour. The scene might also be played to indicate that Giovanni has been very full in his accounts of what passed between him and his sister. For Giovanni's argument, see Interpretations pages 208–210.

What Ford creates in this scene is the human context in which morality is debated. It has been costly for the Friar to follow Giovanni to Parma; he has been *cast away/ By the religious number of mine order* (5–6). There is also a glimpse into the relationship between teacher and pupil when the Friar says *How often have I warned thee this before!* (28). The audience might understand that the Friar followed Giovanni to Parma because he was worried about the intellectual (and moral) errors into which the young man might fall. Another aspect of their relationship is the disparity in age. Giovanni accuses the Friar of not understanding him simply because the Friar is old (35–6).

> 2 **eternal slaughter** The punishments of hell are endless.
> 5–6 **cast away... of mine order** This passage is not clear. It looks as if in following Giovanni to Parma, the Friar has been *cast away* (cut off) from his *number* (companions) in his religious *order* (the Franciscans).
> 10 **mischief** disaster, misfortune, grief.
> 12 **uncharitable** Charity was equivalent to Christian love. It may be that one of the meanings it had in the late Middle Ages is present here: the bond that unites people seeking to live the good life. Giovanni might be picking up the Friar's expression *cast away* to indicate that his behaviour is not loving. An ironic interpretation might ask whether it is Giovanni who is unloving.

13 **fit and good**   This is the basis of Giovanni's justification and of his whole philosophy. See Interpretations page 209.

15, 17 **frame**   the shape or form of a structure, with the strong implication that this is a matter of how it has been designed. Giovanni used the word in his conversation with Annabella (I.ii.211).

16, 17 **composition**   how something is made or constituted. Again, there is a strong sense of design.

16 **follow**   be in accordance with, resemble, match.

18 **furniture**   This usually refers to trappings or embellishments, but here focuses on the physical appearance of *the body*.

19 **virtue**   This is a matter of correspondences. Moral goodness (*virtue*) is to the mind what physical beauty is to the body.
allowed   accepted as true, for the purpose of the argument.

20 **refined**   in a purer state.

21 **quintessence**   literally the fifth essence, but here the real or purest nature of something.

22, 23 **rarely**   outstandingly.

26 A philosophical tag (pithy statement) which means when causes are the same the effects will be also.

27 **knowledge**   The difference between Giovanni and the Friar is that Giovanni tries to argue, while the Friar talks of *knowledge* of what is right and wrong.

29–34 Medieval thinkers held that without the benefit of revelation (God showing his nature and purposes in actions and the words of scripture), it was possible to live a good life by following nature. As God was the creator of nature, *Nature's light* (its order and pattern) was a guide to what is right. The ancient Greek philosophers, therefore, could live good lives and might be saved. Once we know what God wants, however, there is no excuse for only looking to nature for guidance.

29 **Deity**   God.

32 **instance**   provide.

34 **blind**   i.e. *Nature* cannot see God's specific moral *positions* (purposes).

37 **sold to**   possessed or owned by.

38 **compass**   scope and power.

40 The Friar might be criticized for suggesting that Annabella enter into what would no doubt be a loveless marriage. Yet what is the alternative for her?

42 **lust**   Giovanni seems to have no idea of marriage other than
sexual activity.

44 **shrive**   give the sacrament of penance (or shriving) in which,
after sins have been confessed, forgiveness is pronounced.
unabsolved   Those who had committed mortal sins (sins that
merited damnation) could only escape hell by being absolved
(shriven) of their sins.

45 **At your best leisure**   whenever you like.

48 **sundered**   Giovanni uses the language of the marriage service –
'Those whom God hath joined together, let no man put
asunder' – to describe their union. See I.i.34.

49–58 Giovanni describes Annabella in terms of the poetic
convention of praising the beauty of the beloved, starting with
the face and ending with the more intimate parts of the body:
what is else for pleasure framed.

50 **variety**   It was customary to think of the beauty of a face as
consisting in a *variety* of tones, forms and textures, as in 51–3.

54 **throne**   The image is of the face, which, like the *throne* in a
court, is adorned and embellished by beautiful things.

55–6 This is a reference to the music of the spheres – the idea that as
the stars revolve they make beautiful music, which people on
earth cannot hear. Love poets often praised their beloved's
voice by comparing it with the music of the spheres.

60 **parts**   intellectual and poetic abilities.

61 **second death**   the death of the soul (damnation).

62 **but**   only.

63 **yet**   still.

64 **throne of mercy**   God's throne, from which forgiveness
comes. He is playing on Giovanni's praise of Annabella – *that
throne* (54).

66 **number**   order.

Act II Scene VI

Courtship is again the occasion for comedy. Once more Donado,
as much as Bergetto, is a figure of fun. His words about

Bergetto's *sighs and tears* (9) are so wrong as to expose yet again the folly of Donado's marriage scheme. Putana is clearly misrepresenting Annabella's supposed interest in Bergetto, but Donado's gift of money (and his promise of more) shows that bribery is a way of life and a source of income. But if we think badly of her we should also think pretty much the same of Donado.

As in other scenes, the audience are invited to feel for Annabella. She has to negotiate her first proposal soon after committing incest. We may also admire her, because she is more adept and more sensitive than the older generation. When she declines the gift of the jewel (34–6) she is kind and tactful. By contrast, Donado is too eager (27–8), Putana lies (14–17), and Florio does not quite know what to do (29). However, an attractive feature of the scene is the understanding and generosity Donado shows when Annabella refuses the inept Bergetto (56–9).

The dialogue about the mother's ring (38–44) might have been a dangerous moment for the brother and sister, but the fact that no one thinks it significant shows how inconceivable incest is. (The audience would know that the word *ring* also meant vagina.)

The ordering of events is characteristic of comedy. A moment after Annabella has declined to marry Bergetto, Bergetto himself enters. But Ford avoids the possible pathos of his disappointment by making him recount with all the gleeful excitement of first love his meeting with *a young wench* (88). Bergetto's account of this meeting is comically enriched by his lack of social tact. He makes unfortunate comparisons between the beauty of Philotis and Annabella, and his account of the street brawl makes it clear that he was unable to defend himself.

There are delightful comic passages between the two older men. Florio, no doubt to smooth things over, calls *the doctor's niece* (104) *modest* and *well-behaved* (112). Donado, however, is sceptical: *Is she indeed?* (114).

This is the first time that Florio makes public his desire that Annabella marry Soranzo (134). For the business of the jewel, see Interpretations page 198.

5 The audience might reflect that Giovanni has gained *another world*.

11 **Alas, good man** Is Annabella referring to Bergetto or Donado? What would be the different dramatic effects?

15 **first sleep** Martin Wiggins (see Further Reading) refers to the belief that it was the *first sleep* of the night that was filled with dreams and, in the case of young women, dreams of sexual delight.

16–17 **most religiously** There is dramatic irony here: Putana's (quite insincere) meaning is that Annabella regards Bergetto's attentions with the utmost seriousness. Later, we see Annabella take her plight seriously with a real religious intent (III.vi).

23 Donado might take Putana's words as gratitude, but the audience might see that she now knows what to do to acquire more money.

35 **if** Consider the weight of this possibly important word.

41 **Send back that** Which jewel is Florio speaking about?

43 **took it from me** The audience can read more into this than the other characters. Can Annabella be aware of the corrosive irony?

48 **Why d'ee not speak** The silence gives the audience opportunity to pity Annabella's plight.

49 **freedom** This might mean the freedom to speak, the freedom to choose for herself, or the freedom to think further.

51 **his better fortunes** As Annabella is wealthy, *fortunes* must mean social rather than economic status here. The word *worthy* (54) should be interpreted in the same way.

61 **what doth he make here** what's he up to here.

66–7 **I – tickled you** Martin Wiggins (see Further Reading) points out that the dash might indicate that Bergetto is searching for something to say. What comes out has the immediate meaning of to please by flattery, but the audience would no doubt have picked up the probably unintended meaning, pointed out by Poggio in his bawdy aside (68–9), of amorous touching.

70 **Sirrah sweetheart** As *Sirrah* means 'Sir', this is either Bergetto being confused about how to address people or, if a comma is inserted between the two words, Bergetto telling Poggio to be quiet so he can address Annabella. As the word *sweetheart* often occurs in lower-class speech, Bergetto may be getting his language wrong again.

143

73–80 Streets in towns and cities had an open drain running down the middle (*the kennel*). Pedestrians avoided this by trying to walk on the outer edge of the street (*take the wall*). Their heads would then be protected by the overhang of the upper storeys from anything thrown out of the windows. It was also expected that a person of lower rank would step away from the wall to allow a superior to pass. See page 7. There may be echoes of the beginning of *Romeo and Juliet*, in which a servant talks of forcing 'Montague's men from the wall' (I.i.16).

76 **draw**   i.e. prepare to use his sword. This is another case of fighting with swords and an anticipation of Bergetto's own death (III.vii). A later line – *till I see the blood run* (83) – has the same function.

78 **hilts**   Although Bergetto speaks of *hilts* he probably means that the *swaggering fellow* (74) beat him about the head with a sword's hilt.

83 **gull**   stupid, easily deceived person.

95 **wit**   intelligence.

109 **given him the lie**   accused him of lying.

120 **half-a-crown**   As scholars point out that this is about twice the price for a prostitute, we may assume that either Bergetto has been cheated or that he is making it up to annoy Donado.

125 **'gainst**   for, in anticipation of.

129 **alone, alone still, still?**   Increasingly alone. Though Florio puts Giovanni's behaviour down to his *over-bookish humour* (deep devotion to learning, 131), the audience know better.

140 **jealous**   Jealousy will become an increasingly important feature of Giovanni's behaviour. See Interpretations page 241.

Act III Scene I

As Bergetto's new-found love for the doctor's niece was only introduced half-way through the last scene, the exchange here between the young master and his man might be appropriately played with the zest of newly found love. Bergetto's language has been briskly youthful in his previous scenes, and here there is added the proverbial and colloquial tangs of the street: *in despite of his nose* (6) and *clap up* (17–18).

The reference to the *codpiece* (14) is another indication that Ford is consciously setting his play in the sixteenth century. The fashion for wearing them had passed by the 1630s, though presumably the term was still familiar from literature.

    2 **I have a sconce**   The chief meaning is that now he has a mind, he is not to be treated as *a baby* (1). As another contemporary meaning of *sconce* was a small fort, perhaps Bergetto is saying that he can defend himself – look after himself.

    3 **bob you off**   In the light of the above, this colloquial phrase can mean either 'cheat you' or 'assault you'. If this is wordplay in which both meanings are present, then Bergetto need not be presented as a complete fool.

    8 **promised**   To make a verbal promise to marry was a significant step from which it was difficult to retreat. The point here is that Poggio asserts that Philotis has all but promised herself to Bergetto.

13–15 Bergetto feels encouraged by the rather intimate present Philotis has given him. A *codpiece-point* was the lace that tied up the end of a codpiece – a prominent ornamental pouch that men wore over their penises. The gift of *the box of marmalade* is quite innocent. Oranges grew in Italy. The *box* is a small pot.

16–17 **my chops watered**   Poggio is saying that he drooled over the sight of Philotis kissing Bergetto.

17–18 **clap up a marriage in hugger-mugger**   marry secretly and in haste (*hugger-mugger*). The phrase *in hugger-mugger* is used in *Hamlet* (IV.v.84) and in Middleton's *The Revenger's Tragedy* (V.i.19).

   20 Both *courage* and *rise* have sexual implications. If Bergetto intends these, he can hardly be the *innocent* that Donado and Putana call him (I.ii.136 and I.iii.89). But see III.v.46–7.

25–7 This is a rather strange outburst. Prostitutes (*whores*) were sometimes punished by being paraded in or whipped at the tail of a *cart*. It looks as if Bergetto imagines making the prostitutes pay for this punishment (*at their own charges*). This is to be done before he breaches public order. It is probably best to take the speech as not-too-carefully-worded bragging.

Act III Scene II

Florio can be played as the shrewd merchant, who has been conducting delicate negotiations with a number of people but now drops the merchant mode and presents Annabella – *Here she is* (5). The scene is not a betrothal (see Interpretations page 216), though the ritual of bringing his daughter to her suitor might be understood (at least by Florio and Soranzo) as a prelude to the actual ceremony in which the pair promise themselves to each other. It is up to a director and actors to decide whether Florio is forcing the issue. In what tone does he say *She knows my mind* (6)?

Giovanni has conventional doubts about the reliability of women under pressure from powerful men, so warns Annabella to be faithful: *think on me* (11). The scene that follows, however, shows that Annabella does not display the supposed female characteristics of being meek and easily manipulated.

It is possible to play this scene so as to arouse some sympathy for Soranzo. This may be the first time he has proposed marriage (though he probably gave hints to Hippolita), and we should not forget that he is young. On the other hand, it does seem to take rather a long time for him to realize *she laughs at me* (36).

The scene might be regarded as Annabella's triumph because, perhaps for the first time, she is fully herself. When Soranzo asks whether she is really speaking for herself, she replies: *Yes, I myself* (48). And speaking as and for herself (she does not know that Giovanni is watching the scene) she is eloquent and lucid. Soranzo's attempts to woo her have failed and, the wordplay over, she makes her views known firmly (40–47). Her rejection of him is unambiguous, but she avoids being abrasive or scornful, even to the point of saying that of all her suitors, he would have been her choice (49–52). Furthermore, she trusts him to keep what she has said secret (55–8). For Giovanni's presence, see Interpretations page 198.

A production might make something of the fact that when Annabella falls ill, the dialogue is between her and Giovanni. In the family crisis, Soranzo is effectively excluded; he remains onstage and is joined by Vasques.

1 As in I.ii.57, Florio respectfully addresses Soranzo as *My lord*.

2 **proffers** offers (of marriage). We know of one offer – Donado's on behalf of Bergetto (I.iii.14–18). Annabella speaks of *all those/ That sued to me* (50–51).

4 **your still rising honours** It is not clear what Florio means by Soranzo's *rising honours*. Can it be the prospect of an elevated position in society (in government or the army), even though nothing else in the play supports this? An audience might have an uneasy memory of Putana's words about Soranzo's *good name with Hippolita, the lusty widow, in her husband's lifetime* (I.ii.100–101).

5 **jointures** property offered as part of a marriage proposal.

11 **all woman** As women were thought of as unstable, Giovanni is saying: don't go back on what we have sworn.

16 **point of faith** doctrine that members of the Church must believe. Annabella, therefore, is saying that she is not obliged to believe what Soranzo says.

17 **fates** How much weight should be placed on this word?
    infer cause or determine.

18 **What mean you** what do you intend, mean to do.

20 **note** Giovanni, who knows that Annabella is not a *maid* (virgin), dismisses what she says with the smug confidence of one who knows that that's the sort of thing women say.

23 **winks** closes her eyes.

26 **That is not mine to give** What senses does this sentence have?

28 **wit** The word had several meanings in Ford's day. Here it is close to our modern sense of clever and entertaining speech.

30 **what you have** This is clearly a delicate matter, in view of Annabella's wealth through her father.

32 **rigour of your chaste disdain** In contemporary love poetry, the beloved was often presented as unyielding and disdainful.

The word *rigour* meant severity and also carried the association of stiffness, as in rigor mortis – the stiffening of a body after death. Perhaps the association is not inappropriate in a scene that has played with conventional notions of failure in love being like death.

33 **sick**   This recalls another convention of contemporary love poetry: the unsuccessful lover falls ill with unsatisfied longing. In mockery, Annabella calls for *Aqua-vitae* (the water of life) to restore him.

35 **nimble**   quick-witted.

38–9 **You are no… by you**   The imagery, drawn from the idea of dressing oneself in front of a *looking-glass* (mirror), carries with it the critical sting that Soranzo is not a model of *modesty*. Annabella knows about his seduction of Hippolita (I.ii.100–101).

45 **hopes**   mere expectations (rather than the satisfaction of what he wants).

46 **forbear**   give up, abandon.

55–7 This is an example of anaphora – the repetition, usually at the beginning of a line, of a sequence of words. The effect of anaphora is usually of a lulling insistence.

59–60 **If I hereafter… you or none**   Why does Annabella say she might marry Soranzo? Does she need an offer to rely on, or is she indicating that Soranzo is an attractive figure (as at lines 49–53)? It might just be that Ford is preparing us for the plot development.

62 **Heaven forbid**   *Heaven forbid* what? See III.iii.9.

64 The appeal *Look to your daughter* was sometimes a warning to a father that his daughter was in moral danger. See *Hamlet* II.ii.185–6.

76 **and so is yours**   Vasques keeps the audience guessing as to whose side he is on.

78 **the maid's sickness**   Most editors interpret this as chlorosis, or green-sickness (anaemia). There is no consistent picture of medicine in the play. Chlorosis was thought to be a lack of blood, but Vasques says it is caused by *an overflux of youth* (excess of sexual desire caused by excess of blood). The debate continues with Richardetto's diagnosis in III.iv.8. Perhaps Ford

intended the characters to seem confused. The audience, of course, know the cause of Annabella's illness.

Act III Scene III

Putana's tone has changed from the coarse language of II.i.43–6. Language such as *Heaven forgive 'ee* (8–9) has been absent, except in the mouth of the Friar. Does its presence indicate desperation or repentance?

How should Giovanni receive the news of Annabella's pregnancy? Marion Lomax (in the Oxford World's Classics edition, see Further Reading) points out that in the 1991–2 production by the Royal Shakespeare Company, the actor (Jonathan Cullen) delivered *With child? How dost thou know't?* (10) 'as excited questions which showed his delight and immediately identified him as a proud, would-be father' (page xix). Such a performance would set up a contrast between his pride and Putana's very graphic description of the symptoms of early pregnancy.

In performance, players might bring out the differing responses of the two characters. Putana may be so distressed that she is incapable of action (see Giovanni's agitated *d'ee hear woman?*, line 29). By contrast, Giovanni is decisive. But is his strong sense of what to do an indication that he does not see, as Putana might, the implications of Annabella's plight?

1 **undone** The word is often used of loss of virginity rather than, as here, pregnancy.

7 **quick** alive; also pregnant.

12–15 **qualms and water-pangs... I could name** Putana runs though the signs of pregnancy: *qualms* (feeling faint), *water-pangs* (frequent need to urinate), *changing of colours* (looking pale), *queasiness of stomachs* (nausea), *pukings* (vomiting), *and another thing* (her periods have stopped).

15 **credit** reputation.

17–18 **if you let... y'are undone** A doctor would be able to tell from her urine (*water*) that she is pregnant.

20 **Prettily amended**   much improved.

22 **care**   worry.

25 **a world of business**   many things to deal with.

27 **perplex**   trouble, disturb.

29 **ill diet**   food that disagreed with her.

Act III Scene IV

This is a scene full of ironies: as the audience know, Richardetto is not a doctor, so Annabella's pregnancy, known to Putana and Giovanni, is not diagnosed. His diagnosis, however, unexpectedly works against Giovanni and in favour of Florio and the Friar. Richardetto agrees with Vasques (*an overflux of youth*, III.ii.78) in saying that Annabella is suffering from *a fullness of her blood* (8), the cure for which is marriage. Giovanni will therefore lose Annabella, Florio's hopes will be fulfilled, and the Friar has a solution to the moral plight of the brother and sister. The situation is also advantageous to Richardetto. He must see that if he suggests that Annabella marry – *You understand me?* (9) – then Grimaldi will be incited to carry out his revenge. He is also fortunate in hearing the actual marriage plans.

There is another possibility: perhaps Richardetto does realize that Annabella is pregnant, but gives a diagnosis that will help him pursue his revenge against Soranzo.

1 **Indifferent well**   tolerably well.

3–5 **she told me... young stomach**   Giovanni had suggested they say that Annabella is suffering from an *ill diet* (III.iii.29).

6 **easy surfeit-water**   mild medicine to settle the stomach. Many illnesses were thought to result from surfeits – excesses of particular foods.

7 **doubt**   fear for.

8 **fullness of her blood**   excess of blood, a condition for which marriage – that is, sexual activity – was thought to be the cure. See III.ii.78–80. The audience can see the irony.

10–11 Florio says that *once* (at some time soon), Annabella will be married *ere she know the time* (before she comes to the crisis of the illness). The crisis would be a deep melancholy. There is irony against Florio in that her *time* would also refer to the birth of her child.

17 **As any is in Parma** As we can hardly believe that Florio is unaware of Soranzo's seduction of Hippolita, this is a strange thing to say.

18 **Bonaventure** His name indicates that the Friar is a Franciscan – a follower of St Francis of Assisi. Bonaventure was the head of the Franciscan order. He was also a considerable philosopher.

20 **plotted wisely** Might Richardetto make the same point about himself?

21 **straight** immediately.

26–30 Giovanni must be an accomplished actor to deliver these lines.

29 **ghostly** spiritual.

32 **a brother's love** Again the irony works against Florio.

36 **before I fall into my grave** Florio can hardly think it likely he will die before Annabella marries. However, there is more irony as his actions here do lead to his death.

37 **fit** appropriate.

40 The closing line also turns out to be ironical.

Act III Scene V

This scene might come across as uncomfortable and perhaps even unpleasant. The audience have seen an arrangement for a hurried marriage, and witness Richardetto planning the murder of the intended bridegroom. Does he show any signs of guilt? In his slightly troubled soliloquy, Grimaldi at least acknowledges that he is acting ignobly for a soldier, though that does not stop him. Does Ford show that feelings of guilt rarely prevent characters from doing wrong?

Ford is clearly interested in the workings of his characters' minds. He presents the precise moment when Richardetto decides that a marriage that very night is the best course for Philotis and Bergetto: *Ay – ha – yes* (33). Perhaps Ford signals his thought processes so the audience are prepared for the dramatic irony when the plan turns out to be a bad one.

The final mood of the scene is established by the lovers. Are our responses mixed? Bergetto's inept courtship, talking openly of his erection – *monstrous swelling* (46–7) – might amuse or embarrass. In terms of the actors' performance, Philotis is quite a challenge. She has not been onstage since Bergetto has reported meeting her (II.vi.88–90). When she appears, Richardetto asks whether she has *bethought* herself, and she replies *Yes, and as you counselled,/ Fashioned my heart to love him* (27–8). She must now show that love. Ford gives her the line (delivered in an intimate whisper?): *There's hope of this yet* (38).

Do the rhyming couplets contribute anything to the scene?

2 **Twenty to one** This is a term from gambling.

5 **policy** scheming, cunning.

6 **resolved** Tragic figures often use this word to express their determination.

7 **Play not on both hands** isn't engaged in double-dealing. This is another irony: the audience know that Richardetto is helping Grimaldi in order to revenge himself on Soranzo. There is a further irony in our knowing that Richardetto's playing *on both hands* will actually assist Grimaldi.

9 **ordained** arranged, perhaps with a hint that fate is in control.
 affied betrothed (a binding form of engagement). Richardetto goes on to say Annabella might also soon be *Married* (11).

11 **Yet your patience** keep calm and listen.

13 **bestow** spend (your) time.

16 **box** This is another *box* from Richardetto's household (see III.i.14–15).

19 **speed** despatch, send (to death).

22 **if this hit** if this plan comes off.

31 **shrift** confession and absolution. Here the meaning is probably closer to having to own up to, and be told off by, his uncle.

40 **at large**   at length or in detail.
41 **sweetmeats**   sweet food, such as candied fruit or preserves. The adjective *sweet* was often used of sexual pleasure. Philotis's reply – *You shall have enough* (43) – might confirm this.
43 **sweetheart**   See Note to II.vi.70.
46–7 **monstrous swelling**   Bergetto's sexual innocence (he does not realize he is having an erection) is a source of humour. It is worth asking whether Bergetto is consistently presented as unaware of sexual matters.
48 **physic**   a cure, remedy.
51 **fit**   appropriate, fitting. That is, when the marriage has taken place.

Act III Scene VI

This scene offers a parallel to III.iii, in which Giovanni is alert and in control. Here, Annabella confesses her sins. Should we emphasize the differences between an active man of the world and a woman who has succumbed to the prevailing morality of her day, or should we see Annabella taking her behaviour seriously, while Giovanni is only concerned to escape from a difficult situation? See Interpretations pages 210 and 230.

An audience today might feel hostile to the Friar's speech about hell (8–23). It is very long, in a play of few long speeches, and it dwells in disturbing detail on the pains of the damned. The idea that the punishments of hell are grotesque parodies of the sins that have brought about the damnation of the sinner goes back at least to Dante's *Inferno*, the first part of his epic fourteenth-century poem *Divine Comedy*. Martin Wiggins (see Further Reading) helpfully points out that the direct source is Thomas Nashe's *Pierce Penniless*: 'the usurer to swallow molten gold, the glutton to eat nothing but toads, and the murderer to be still stabbed with daggers, but never die'. See Interpretations page 197.

Notes

1 sd   **kneeling... weeps, and wrings her hands**   These are the actions of a penitent woman who is sorry for her sins.

    1   **penance**   There are two very closely related meanings of this word: the sacrament of *penance* in which a person confesses sins and receives absolution, and the state of mind in which a sinner seeks forgiveness. See Interpretations page 246.

    2   **unripped**   brought into the open. See I.ii.215 and V.vi.60.

5–6   Tears were a sign that one was truly sorry for one's sins (see Interpretations page 229). Annabella should weep *Whiles* (while) he proceeds to *read a lecture* (speak sternly about her sins). Though Annabella calls herself a *Wretched creature* (6), it might be thought that Giovanni is more wretched than she is.

    9   **hollow vault**   vast, cavernous space, like a dungeon.

  11   **horror**   Derek Roper (in the Revels edition of the play, see Further Reading) makes the point that the original meaning of *horror* involves the idea of something bristling. There is, therefore, an unpleasantly physical dimension to the *consuming fires*.

  13   **infected darkness**   The *darkness* itself is contaminated.

  14   **sundry**   This is a chilling thought – there are many different types of persons in hell.

  16   **without pity**   Is *pity* absent from this scene?

  21   **wanton**   loose, sexually unrestrained person. In the seventeenth century this term was frequently applied to women, though here it is to a man.

  22   **racks**   instruments of torture, which stretched limbs. (Later, Giovanni describes the agony of seeing Annabella married as *torture* – IV.i.15.) See also IV.i.97.

  25   **dreamt**   i.e. they have not woken up to their sins.
        lawless   lacking in the laws of morality.

  28   **dagger's point**   This echoes I.ii.214–16 and anticipates V.vi.83–5.

  32   **motions**   feelings of regret and remorse.

  34   **despair**   This is the worst of all spiritual states, because the one who despairs no longer hopes to be saved.

  37   **next**   the next thing you must do.

  38   **live to him**   be faithful to him (Soranzo). See V.iii.6–11.

  41   **what must come**   i.e. the pains of hell, unless she repents.

  44   **stays**   waits.

48 **falsehood** betrayal.
49 **resolved** See Interpretations page 241.
50–1 This is a betrothal. The publicly witnessed joining of hands
indicates the couple have mutually promised themselves to
each other.

Act III Scene VII

If the stage were darkened (see page 21) the sinister and
accidental nature of the action would be uncomfortably realistic.
Bergetto's call *Lights, lights, ho, lights* (12–13) might indicate that
some of the candles that lit the stage have been extinguished to
create a night scene.

The death of Bergetto is not only a ghastly accident but is also
horribly botched. Should the actor playing Bergetto resist the
opportunity for presenting a man grotesquely cavorting in the
death-throes of a wound in an unmentionable place? (Grimaldi
did not drive his sword *Home to his bosom*, 7.) And Bergetto is not
only wounded: the presence of Richardetto reminds us that
Grimaldi's sword was tipped with poison. The homely
comparison *my belly seethes like a porridge-pot* (19) is Bergetto's
moving though inelegant attempt to describe the effect of venom
poisoning his blood stream.

Yet Bergetto's death can be played to bring out a rare pathos.
The puzzled anguish of *I cannot piss forward and backward* (11–12)
is the kind of thing a child would say, and as T.S. Eliot, who did
not appreciate Ford's low comedy, admitted, *Is all this mine own
blood?* (31) 'is almost pathetic'. (Eliot was using 'pathetic'
positively, to mean arousing the helpless pity an audience feel for
a suffering character.)

Bergetto's death raises two questions. The first is a matter of
critical terminology: is it helpful to call his death 'tragic', and
what are the reasons for using or withholding that term? The
second is whether the mood of the play changes after his death.

It might be said that the audience are not distracted by folly from the high drama of the play's ending. Alternatively, it might be said that the play loses an innocent character, whose happiness would have tempered the anguish and blood which the final struggle between Giovanni and Soranzo releases.

It is noticeable that once he has been stabbed, all Bergetto's words are addressed to Poggio, and the scene concludes with Poggio's grief. See Interpretations page 232. In the design of the play, their bond might be compared with that between Soranzo and Vasques.

Although he does not address her directly, Bergetto does think of Philotis. His request that Donado *make much of this wench* (33) shows that he has grown up sufficiently to be concerned for her future welfare.

1 sd **dark lantern** lantern with a shutter.
2 **Here I will lie** As indicated in the stage direction that follows, Grimaldi puts his ear to the ground to hear whether anyone is approaching. He strikes at Bergetto from this position.
6 **angry Justice** Grimaldi is certainly angry, but where is the *Justice* in what he is doing?
8–9 Bergetto, perhaps unexpectedly, speaks of his wound in terms of a conceit – a striking extended metaphor. The wound in his flesh is like *a stitch fallen*, so he needs *a flesh-tailor*.
15 **next** nearest.
22 sd **halberts** semi-ceremonial weapons carried by the city watch (night guards) which combined a spear and axe head. It is usually spelt 'halberds'.
26 **with all thy haste** as quickly as you can.
27 **Up to the city** Ford is correct in imagining that Franciscans would have established a cell on the outskirts rather than in the centre of a city.
32 **uncle** Although his uncle has been impatient and insulting, Bergetto remembers him.
34 **the wrong way** i.e. towards death.

Act III Scene VIII

The scene is something of a 'filler' between the death of Bergetto and the hopeless appeal to the Cardinal for justice, but it advances the Hippolita plot. Like the previous scene it is about revenge. It could be played hurriedly and, given that it is also a night scene, with an air of secrecy. The darkness continues.

The scene starts mid-way through a conversation. Hippolita is still raw from Soranzo's desertion of her. She speaks of *my disgrace* (10) and, in the manner of an actor in a high passion – although her emotion must be real – she denounces him: *O wicked man* (11). When she says that he would *laugh to see* her *weep* (12), the line could only have dramatic force if she were weeping while she delivered it.

Is Vasques' devotion to her cause too intensely voiced (*I am infinitely yours*, 9)?

    1 **Betrothed**   Betrothals – mutual promises to marry – were public events.
    7 **bravely**   with bravado. See Interpretations page 242.
16–17 **so hopeful**   so full of promise.
   18 **my youth**   The context indicates that Soranzo is the *youth*.

Act III Scene IX

This scene is about justice. Florio advises Donado to *seek for justice* (3), and Richardetto is sure that they will receive it. The Cardinal, he says confidently, *Will give true justice* (23). The Cardinal's refusal is greeted at the end with a bitter rhetorical question by the grieving Donado: *Dwells Justice here?* (63). The officers have already indicated the fear that the Cardinal's power arouses: *for fear of his grace* (15).

Language indicates social class. The Cardinal's servant speaks colloquially – *What would 'ee?* (26) – and Florio replies with civility: *pray inform/ His grace that we are here* (28–9). There is a further contrast in the haughty sneer of the Cardinal, who calls them *saucy mates* and accuses them of lacking the very qualities they have shown: *you/ That know nor duty nor civility* (30–31). He even sneers at Florio for not favouring Grimaldi as a suitor to his daughter. The Cardinal has no moral language: the word *duty* means people's duty to him, not moral duty. Florio gets him right when he says *there's no help in this,/ When cardinals think murder's not amiss* (67–8). The Cardinal also lacks a language for the feelings: no regret is expressed for Bergetto's death. See Interpretations page 231.

It is worth asking whether Grimaldi's 'confession' has too much about it of the prepared speech.

1 **bootless** pointless.
  child Donado is weeping.
2 **what is done, is done** This is a characteristically Italian summary of the ancient idea that there is no point in regretting the past, because the past cannot be changed.
4 **somewhat** This is something of an understatement.
7 **fortune** Bergetto's death is his *fortune*, because whatever is apparently arbitrary or random is put down to fate or fortune.
10 **stay** Perhaps the officers were signalling that they were going to leave.
13 **naked** i.e. drawn rather than in its sheath.
28 **present** urgent.
30 **saucy mates** This is an insulting term, meaning rude and presumptuous fellows.
32 **we** He uses the 'royal we' when talking about himself.
36 **commonwealth** This is possibly a recognition that the well being and prosperity of Parma depend upon the administrative and mercantile activity of people such as Florio.
42 **In thought** Martin Wiggins (see Further Reading) interestingly points out that English courts would not have accepted the defence that he did not intend kill Bergetto.
44 **confederates** We only know of one *confederate* – Vasques.
57 In any system of justice the social class of the accused should

be irrelevant. In any case, what evidence is there that Grimaldi was *nobly born*?

59 **mean**   of lowly birth.

61 **wit**   intelligence; though in the context it is uncomfortably close to the political sense, that is to say, the way power is exercised.

64 Florio may be referring to the myth of Astrea, goddess of justice who, to escape the evils of the world, fled to heaven. The parallel with the Cardinal's behaviour is clear.

65 **impudence**   The word had a strong moral force; Grimaldi's behaviour is outrageous.

70 In terms of events, the Cardinal is not judged at the end of the play, unless it is in the sense that the audience recognize his blatant immorality.

Act IV Scene I

In this wedding scene, it is clear that neither Annabella nor Giovanni are at ease. Soranzo says *Cheer up, my love* (12) to his bride, and to Vasques' question *Are you not well, sir?* (19), Giovanni gives a critical and scornful reply: *I need not thy officious diligence* (20).

Onstage, Giovanni is given prominence by his asides. (Because asides are addressed to audiences, a bond is established between speaker and listeners.) He acts as a commentator on the action, so the audience can view events from his perspective. This role is touched with irony. In the opening speech, the Friar speaks of *the saints/ Who are your guests, though not with mortal eyes/ To be beheld* (3–5). Giovanni also observes the feast, but with, in two senses of the word, very *mortal eyes*: he is consumed with jealousy and says he would *stand the horror of ten thousand deaths* (18) in order to undo Annabella's marriage. Once again, we are prepared for ironies: although nothing lives up to the hyperbole of *ten thousand deaths*, Giovanni does die of multiple sword thrusts.

The drama of the scene works by a gradual undermining of the conventions and moods appropriate to a marriage feast. Giovanni is hostile to Vasques' manner, Florio has to comfort the grieving Donado, and Giovanni refuses to drink. These lead to Hippolita's outrageous defiance of morality and decorum. Vasques refuses comfort to the dying; having poisoned Hippolita, he grimly says he will not marry her (70–71).

The scene has many of the characteristics of the ending of a plot: there is an ominous performance (the masque), a bogus offer of reconciliation, a trick that goes awry, and final confessions, explanations and curses (Hippolita's dying speech can be relished by a performer). It is, of course, Hippolita who, so to speak, plots events appropriate to a closing scene, and Vasques who contrives for her *a just payment in her own coin* (87) as a moral judgement on her own terrible intentions. The audience may wonder whether even more terrible things are yet to come. The next feast (V.vi) is also troubled by an intruder and ends in death.

1 sd   **A banquet. Hautboys**   This is the grandest entry in the play. The discovery space might have been used both for the formal entrance of the characters and as the place in which the table of food stood.

1–6   The Friar's speech is the kind that could have come at the end of a play. The confusion is over, the wedding ceremony has been performed and nothing remains but the celebration. The Friar assures the people that *the saints* in heaven, though invisible, are present to bless the marriage feast. But the audience, knowing far more than most of the characters, view matters with less buoyancy.

1   **These holy rites performed**   now that the marriage ceremonies have been completed.

5   **in this day**   because of this day.

7–8   See Interpretations pages 225–6.

10   **jewel**   This word might be understood as poetic lover's talk, though an audience might see an allusion to Annabella's riches or her virginity.

14 **lusty cups**   merry and vigorous drinking.

17 **Clipped**   amorously embraced.

confusion   destruction, with a strong suggestion of damnation.

19 **wait**   The word was applied to servants, who waited on their masters.

20 **officious diligence**   The *Shorter Oxford English Dictionary* gives this definition of *officious*, dating from 1600: 'unduly forward in proffering services'. The word *diligence* was often used of the work of servants.

24 **brother**   The word has associations of which Soranzo is quite unaware.

28 sd *Hautboys*   Music offstage can evoke many feelings: pleasure, mystery, expectation, foreboding.

33 **patience and silence**   The audience are asked to allow the performance and watch it respectfully.

35 sd *garlands of willows*   The willow was a symbol for women abandoned by their lovers.

37 **beholding**   beholden, owing a debt of gratitude.

love   kind gesture.

41 **defraud**   deprive.

43 **rumoured**   gossiped about.

45 **break itself**   i.e. gossip will exhaust itself.

48 **lord**   husband.

52–4 Hippolita performs a parody of a betrothal or marriage service. It is as if she is the one who joins the couple's hands or gives the bride away, though here she presents her sometime lover to Annabella. She claims she does what the Church has already *finished* (done) and *allowed* (sanctioned) – a marriage.

55 **engaged**   In Ford's day, as in ours, this word could mean betrothed. Soranzo is saying that Hippolita has obliged them to be very grateful for her kindness.

56 **single charity**   sincere goodwill. (She is speaking to Soranzo.)

57 **remit**   cancel, relinquish.

61 **rest**   What kind of *rest* does she wish him?

61 sd *Aside*   Hippolita must walk over to a table supplied with drink to whisper this instruction to Vasques. Would the audience assume that he will do as she wishes?

64 **union**   There are several possible meanings. The *union* could be the drinks to the health (*pledge*) of his marriage, his apparent

reconciliation to Hippolita or, ironically and following *Hamlet*, it might mean something dropped into the wine.

70 **I must not** I am not destined to.

75 This is a version of 'the biter bit' – plots against others which hurt the perpetrator.

76 *Troppo sperare inganna* Italian meaning 'too much hope deceives'. Vasques provides his own translation.

77 **but** all but.

79 **Die in charity** die in a kind and loving frame of mind. The audience should think back to her apparently conciliatory lines earlier in the scene. Later in the same speech, Vasques urges her: *end thy days in peace* (88).

80 **corrupted** attempted to corrupt.

81 **politic** craftily plotting.
   reconciliation This had the quite specific meaning of submission to a proposal in order to be restored to favour.

83 **confusion** destruction, death.
   fair favourably, courteously.

86 **disposition** temperament, state of mind.

89 **vile** In Ford's day the word had connotations both of being low-born and having an evil influence. See also line 103.

90 What is to be made of the chorus of approval, and of Richardetto's *Heaven, thou art righteous*?

92 **minute** moment of death.
   slave low-born menial.

94–5 **Heat above hell-fire... cruel flames** The language of hell is appropriate to Hippolita's fate, and may pick up associations from III.vi.8–23.

96–102 What is to be made of the uncomfortable fact that Hippolita's *curse* is horribly close to what happens to the marriage of Annabella and Soranzo?

101 **Monsters** deformed children. See V.vi.63.

110–13 Does the Friar speaks for the audience here?

112 **the event** what is to come.

113 sd *Exeunt [with Hippolita's body]* Martin Wiggins (see Further Reading) makes the point that as Vasques is the only servant onstage, he will have to carry Hippolita's body. This, he says, is 'an ironic visual conclusion to their duplicitous marital arrangement'. He adds that Richardetto and Philotis are thus given time to prepare for their scene.

Act IV Scene II

Enough time has passed since the last scene for there to be rumours of unhappiness in the marriage of Annabella and Soranzo (9–13). There is a disturbing parallel between Richardetto hearing of the disputes that blight Annabella's and Soranzo's marriage and the way his own wife's infidelities were generally known. Perhaps the recognition of this parallel might be present in the manner of his delivery.

Nor does Richardetto speak directly of his own part in the death of Bergetto. Again, it is up to the actor to play this scene in a way that shows the weight of that event upon him. Does his talk about the inevitability of Soranzo's fall express a belief in fate or that God – *One/ Above* (8–9) – will frustrate the plans of the wicked? See Interpretations pages 226–7.

Richardetto is a deeply compromised figure. Perhaps he is as preoccupied with his own sorrows as Hippolita was with hers. And what of his concern for Philotis: does he send her to a convent because of his own sorrows? Philotis's acceptance is also a problem. Should this be made to feel credible, or should she indicate that she is a victim of Richardetto's responses to the fate of his wife?

Richardetto's words about seeing *the end of these extremes* (19) sums up the position of the audience, who also wait for the hideous conclusion.

   1 **wretched**   This was a very strong word in the seventeenth century, meaning miserable and loathsome.
   3 **modesty**   the moderation of a blameless reputation.
   7 **need not**   i.e. need take no further steps.
   8 **confusion**   ruin, destruction and possibly damnation.
  11 **Thicken**   increase.
  12 **Slightens**   disdains, rejects.
  14 **pity**   In the light of what has happened in the previous scenes, perhaps Richardetto's *pity* is understandable.
  16 **hazard**   dangers brought by chance.

17 **Cremona**   a small city about 30 miles from Parma which had many convents.

18 **votaress**   one who lives under a vow, as do nuns.

19 **extremes**   This word had connotations of excess and of finality. See Interpretations page 225.

20 **uneven**   The *courses* of life are hard because they are not level.

25 **Hie**   go quickly.

   fortune   Is this merely a way of saying the way things have worked out, or is there an appeal to the idea that our lives are controlled?

26 **beads**   rosary beads, used in prayer.

30 **yield**   There are two sorts of vows here: Philotis will give way to her vows of chastity rather than the sexual desires sanctioned by marriage vows.

Act IV Scene III

We now see the unhappy marriage that Richardetto spoke of in the previous scene. The drama of the opening – its pathos and its pain – might be brought out by the setting and costume. Do they enter from the discovery space, and if so, what effects would be created if a bed were visible? Soranzo is *unbraced* – his clothes unfastened. This would certainly increase the sense of domestic privacy, and we might wonder what has immediately led to his anger. The audience, even if they have some pity for his feelings of betrayal, will find it hard to forget that he drags in the heavily pregnant Annabella and threatens to kill her.

Soranzo's *rage* (68) is expressed in his insults (see Note to line 1) and his piling up of adjectives, as in *loose cunning whoredom* (7). It is not always clear what he is saying. Does he actually accuse her of prostitution? He creates a ludicrous picture of himself as a dog, which with its teeth will *Tear the prodigious lecher joint by joint* (55). And as rage and exasperation are very often funny, can we exclude laughter?

Annabella resorts to common sense. Who could deny that he *would needs be doing* (20) or *'twas not for love/ I chose you, but for honour* (22–3)? Her offer that if he would conceal his *shame,/ I'd see whether I could love you* (24–5) is bluntly practical and must have applied to many marriages made hastily or for political reasons. Perhaps, also, she is right that his *over-loving lordship would have run/ Mad on denial* (17–18). The irony, of course, is that it has run mad on her secrecy. In whatever she says, she knows she is (and perhaps enjoys?) being in control. She entices him with what might be a full confession and then exultingly tells him that the father of her child is *more than man* (28–33). Had Giovanni witnessed the scene, would he have accused her of *revolt* (V.v.8)?

The actor playing Soranzo must decide how to deliver the lines addressed to Annabella about the completeness of his love and the inconceivable depths of his disappointment (107–115 and 123–130). It may owe something to the painful regrets of Othello (for example, the latter's speech in IV.ii.48–65). The borrowings from religious language (*The treasure of my heart*, 109), the troubled oxymoron of *Fair, wicked woman* (110) and the sense of living death he suffers (*buried me alive*, 114) might be delivered with heart-wrenching anguish. But Soranzo is playing a role on the advice of Vasques. Look at his comments on Soranzo's performance in 116–18. Can these two aspects of the lines be combined?

For the role of Vasques, see Interpretations pages 230–231.

1 **strumpet** prostitute, but also sexually immoral woman. *Come* was often used as an invitation to love.
 famous infamous, notorious.
 whore As in the case of *strumpet*, the word could mean either a prostitute or an immoral woman. The title and last line of the play point to the latter meaning. See Interpretations page 247.
2 **adulterous** If Giovanni's boast in V.vi.44–6 that he *enjoyed* Annabella for *nine months* is true, then Soranzo is correct in calling her behaviour *adulterous*.

4 **notable harlot** As in the case of *strumpet* and *whore*, *harlot* meant prostitute or a sexually immoral woman, and, like *famous*, *notable* meant notorious.

5 **brazen face** The word *brazen* means like brass; that is, displaying a hard, unyielding surface. Here Soranzo probably means that Annabella's *face* is without remorse, and may indicate that her manner and looks are impudent and unabashed.

6 **bawd** He is comparing his role as her husband to that of a pimp or brothel-keeper, who supplies women for other men's sexual gratification.

7 **cunning** This word colours the scene. See also 157 and 172.
else but I other than me.

8–10 **Must your... to a surfeit** Compare this accusation with what Giovanni says to the Friar in II.v.41–2.

8 **itch** sexual urges.

9 **heyday** strong state of sexual excitement.
luxury lustfulness.

10 **surfeit** state of fullness or satiety after excessive consumption (as in *fed*, 9).

11 **cloak to your close tricks** method of concealment (as under a *cloak*) for your secret (as in a closet – private room) bouts of sexual activity, and/or schemes for meeting lovers.

12 **belly-sports** sexual acts. In Shakespeare *belly* was used to mean the female genital region.
dad This is the word children used of their fathers in Ford's day.

13 **gallimaufry** jumble, hodge-podge. This is a way of saying 'no one knows who the father is'.

15 **Beastly man** Soranzo has effectively been saying Annabella has the sexual morals of an animal, so she replies to this abuse in kind.
fate This is probably a way of saying it is his lot, what he has chosen.

16 **sued** begged.

19 **case** condition (i.e. pregnant).

24 **patient** calm, forbearing.

25 **quean** This is a term of abuse close to the ones Soranzo has already used – *strumpet, harlot, whore*.

28 **bargain** Presumably she means: I didn't promise to tell you that when I married you.

29 **longing stomach** i.e. desire to know.

32 **glory** honour and reputation. She uses the word again in 44. But who is actually doing the glorying?

33 **monster** If the *monster* is the child she is bearing, an audience might recall Hippolita's curse, IV.i.99–101.

34 **and** if.

35 **match** bargain, deal.

38 **but** only.

39 **begged for love** As Soranzo did to her.

43 **We are not come to that** Annabella is in control. See Interpretations pages 218–219.

44 **suffice** be sufficient, enough.

45 **brave** This word expressed the pride and swagger of an outstanding man.

47–8 **I had never... a creature** It would have been as if you had not even existed in my world.

52 **cursed** This is a prophetic word.

55 **prodigious** monstrous.

59 What death more sweet than to die for love? Singing in her native Italian to her Spanish husband is a way of saying she is not engaging with his concerns. She sings again in 63.

60 **Thus** He may match his actions to the words.

61 **lust-belepered** Her lust has made her body as loathsome as a leper's.

63 Dying in favour with him, I would die without pain.

64 **triumph** glory, exalt. See 104.

66 **angels** Does Soranzo taunt her with her own word *angel-like* (37)?

69 **hangman** executioner. The word *strike* (70) indicates the axe-man.

71 If you kill me, there is still someone who will exact revenge.

76 **slack** be neglectful or slow in.

78 **forfend** avert, prohibit.

88 **author** the one responsible for impregnating her.

89 **unconscionable** without conscience, unscrupulous.

90 **estimation** reputation, valuation.

97 **commend her for it** Vasques speaks for the audience here.

98 **beshrew my heart**   may evil fall on me.

99–100 **in any case**   in any way you can.

103 **distractions**   rages.

105 **other neglected suitors**   those who failed to win Annabella's hand.

105–6 **'Tis as manlike… to forgive**   it becomes a man to bear his wrongs (*extremities*) as it becomes God to forgive.

109 **treasure**   This is an echo of the teaching of Jesus on true wealth, Matthew 6:19–21.

111 **life**   i.e. the *life* of the blessed in Heaven, hence *saint* in 112.

117 **temper**   controlled emotion.
  passion   outbursts of rage.

121 **superstitiously adore**   i.e. he worshipped her as an idol.

122 Soranzo's change of tone is working on Annabella. See also 130–1.

128 **humorous**   changeable, and therefore shallow.

134 **overpassed**   over and done with.

140 **remit**   forgive.

143 Talk of kneeling will no doubt remind the audience of the 'vows' of Giovanni and Annabella (I.ii.258–64).

145 **alteration**   changes of mind and of behaviour.

149 **somewhat to the matter**   relevant to the matter in hand.

150 **heaven of happiness**   the great joy of the married state. It is not only Annabella who can mock the excessive language of poetic lovers.

154 **great woman**   This is a pun on a woman of high rank, and one who is *great* with child, pregnant.

154–5 **being made… to your hand**   Soranzo has married a woman who already has the family *stock* (the unborn child) in her. *Stock* could also mean a handle and a rabbit hole (see 157).

157 **cony-berry**   rabbit hole. There is an obscene quibble on the sound of the word, as also in *cunning*.

160 **sufferance**   patience.

161–2 **voluntary… weeping tune**   This image from music plays on the meaning of acting from free will.

162 **if all hit**   if everything goes well.

162–3 **I will not miss my mark**   This is a phrase from archery.

166–71 Is there any reason why an audience should not believe what Vasques says about the troubled married life of Soranzo and

Annabella? The proverbial tang of *hens* and *cocks* is in accordance with the contemporary idea that husbands should have authority over their wives.

166 **nonce**   now, the present time.

172–4 **if the lower... whiles I live again**   The *she-tailor* is someone (probably a man) who makes the *lower parts* of a dress full enough to conceal pregnancy (*swelling in the stomach*). The phrase *lower parts* is also a bawdy reference to the female body. Such skill in tailoring should make one hesitate to criticize any stitchwork.

174–5 **Up, and... quickly too**   This is a series of bawdy associations: the swelling of pregnancy, the creation of life (the *quick*) and how easily (*quickly*) women engage in sexual activity. He uses the words again, though in a different context, in 240.

175 **policy**   craft.

177 sd **in tears**   The audience judge from Putana's state just how distressed Annabella is.

180 **mad**   beside himself with anger.

182 **Vasques**   Putana addresses him by his Christian name.

183 **use thee so**   treat you in the same way.

186 **honest**   decent and genuine. But if audiences recall Iago in Shakespeare's *Othello* (his most popular play in the early seventeenth century), it might be seen as a word that villains use of themselves.

186–7 **kill my lady with unkindness**   This is perhaps a witty reference to a play by Thomas Heywood called *A Woman Killed with Kindness* (1607).

189 Putana knows this is not true.

190 **madness**   rage.

193 **humour**   character, nature.

211 **preferment**   promotion to a better social position.

213–14 **entire friend**   devoted acquaintance who was capable of impregnating her (*entire* also meaning uncastrated).

215 **dear**   close and, ironically, costly (to Annabella).

216–17 **my life between you and danger**   Vasques promises to protect Putana, and says she will be *rewarded* (220).

220 **Ud's pity**   God's pity.

224 **brave**   fine.

225 **perpetually**   This might just mean she will always love him or,

more exactly, her love for him has continued without a break. The latter meaning implies that she has continued to have sexual relations with Giovanni. Lines 229–30 are consistent with this meaning.

233–4 **a Turk or a Jew** Popular belief held that neither were trustworthy.

235 **belie** deny.

238 **presently** immediately.

242 **prate** prattle.

243 **Let me come to her** Does Putana fight fiercely? Are the Banditti reluctant to be very rough with a woman? Does Vasques show no hesitation in his use of violence?

245 **closely** secretly.

248–53 As Vasques is alone onstage, the audience may assume that he says what he thinks. There is glee in his *excellent* and the distaste of the malcontent in *O horrible*. He continues his jaundiced moralizing in his talk of *liberty*, *damnation* and the *devil*.

249 **liberty** the freedom to sin.

250 **trained** taught and tempted.

253 **a smooth tale... a smooth tail** His gentle coaxing (*smooth tale*) has outwitted a woman (*smooth tail*). The bawdy sense – i.e. smooth talk allows a man to enter a woman (*tail* meaning vagina) – would be an appropriate comment on Giovanni.

255–6 His suspicion is as certain as the changes in the seasons.

260 **flesh** meat; also (the unintended irony), sex.

261 **hit it** got it. Vasques picks up the unintended irony.

265 sd **gives him money** Vasques takes over Putana's role as the one who takes money for assisting men to visit Annabella.

265 **liberality** generosity.

267 **made a man** a successful man, one who has made his way in the world.
    plied my cue This is the language of acting. Vasques compares himself to an actor who has controlled a scene by delivering his lines efficiently and thereby enabled others to play their parts. See Interpretations page 230.

271 **fast** secure. That is, he has silenced Putana.

273 **Runs circular** runs round and round without getting anywhere.

277 **my young master**   Giovanni.
   pleasure   Given what Vasques now knows, this word is
   charged with significance.
280 This probably means that no matter what Vasques has to tell
   him, it cannot make him fear.

Act V Scene I

As the importance of this scene in plot terms is that Annabella
sends Giovanni a letter, it might have been short and functional.
Instead, Ford makes it her chief scene. It contains some of the
best verse in the play (see Interpretations page 247) and it shows
her recognizing her situation and seeking to warn her brother. In
a play that frequently lacks the note of charity, Annabella,
although imprisoned and estranged from a violent and
unpredictable husband, is above all concerned about the trouble
she has brought upon Giovanni. Are our feelings of admiration
affected by the thought that she is wrong to take the blame upon
herself?

   The farewell or valedictory speech has an important place in
English Renaissance literature. These usually follow a moment of
realization in which the character sees that worldly success is
either empty or over. So Othello, convinced of his wife's
faithlessness, says: O *farewell,/ Farewell the neighing steed, and the
shrill trump* (III.iii.356–7). Annabella sees the emptiness of things.
Think about the different nuances of *Pleasure* in her valediction
and Vasques' use of it in IV.iii.277.

   The problem for a production is to make convincing the
coincidence of Annabella's plaintive cry for help and the
answering presence of the Friar. It would be all too easy to play
this for laughs, but would that be dodging the possibility that
Ford is showing that in a world of revenge and the obsessive
exercise of power there are still moments when people can ask:
Is Heaven so bountiful (44)?

The scene closes on a note that is struck in other Renaissance tragedies, a calm acceptance of what is to come: *Now I can welcome death* (59).

1 sd **Enter Annabella above**   Should we think back to when she appeared *above* in I.ii.33?

1 **thriftless**   spiritually empty.

2 **spun**   This reminds us of the Fates, who spin the threads of people's lives before cutting the threads.
weary life   This is the ancient idea that sensual indulgence eventually leads to disenchantment. We might compare Annabella's heart-felt realization of the fleeting nature of earthly pleasure with the cynicism of Vasques' jaundiced moralizing in IV.iii.166–77 and 248–53.

3 **To**   from.

4–8 The controlling image is of *Time* as a messenger (*post*), to whom she says *stay thy restless course* (pause in your journey) to collect my story and *bear* it *to ages that are yet unborn* (carry it into the future).

7 **bear... unborn**   To a woman who is heavily pregnant, these words will be poignantly significant.

8 See Interpretations page 243.

9–10 The image of a court of law stands behind these lines. Her *conscience... stands up* as a witness *against my lust* with written testimonies as *depositions charactered in guilt* (decisive evidence).

13 **grace**   In Christian theology, *grace* – the unmerited gift of God – completes and transforms nature. Beauty, therefore, as the work of nature needs to be elevated and changed by *grace*.

14–16 In the Bible the song of the turtledove (*turtle*) is associated with spring – 'the voice of the turtle is heard in our land' (Song of Solomon 2:12). But there can be no love for the *mewed up* (caged) Annabella. Unlike the delightfully erotic Song of Solomon, she is without a sexual partner – *Unmated, I converse*. One of the meanings of *converse* was to engage in sexual intercourse. Like a caged bird she can *descant* on her *vile unhappiness* – that is, sing in the piping manner of a bird and comment on her outcast situation. *Vile* probably means of a low social order; Annabella is no longer treated as the wife of a noble.

17–18   It is a mark of Annabella's insight and moral generosity that she sees that both Giovanni and herself are victims of what they have done.

    17   **spoil**   Loss of virginity is like the invader who carries away precious things from a plundered town. But as the word is used of Giovanni, it might have another of its contemporary meanings – destruction.

19–20   Again Annabella sees that Giovanni is not to blame. See the headnote on page 171.

    21   **scourge**   small whip. Penitent persons would lash themselves with a *scourge* as a way of becoming aware of the stings of wrongdoing.

    23   **uncontrollèd flame**   The flame of passion has put her in danger of the flames of hell.

    25   **ceremonial knot**   the marriage bond. (We still talk of tying the knot.)

    28   **lethargies of lust**   *Lust* makes people spiritually unaware – as if asleep – of the consequences of their actions.

    29   **Hug their confusion**   This is an image of the bedroom. Just as the lustful embrace their partners, so those who are damned embrace their fate. See Interpretations page 194.

      making Heaven unjust   Either those who are lost in lust will wrongly think that *Heaven* (God) will overlook their sins, or they will blame *Heaven* for what they have done.

    32   **ends**   aims. But possibly there is a hint that she might reach her eternal end – heaven.

    34   The letter has two lines: the lines soaked in her *tears* and those written in her *blood*. In contemporary religious devotion and poetry, tears and blood were the sure signs of deeply felt repentance. See Interpretations page 229.

35–7   **I sadly vow... died in**   This is another extended comparison: Annabella *sadly* (solemnly) *vows* to repent and leave a life that has brought death.

    38   **providence**   the actions of God in the world to bring about goodness.

      ordained   established.

    39   **behoof**   benefit.

    42   Annabella has been speaking for herself, unprompted by another. Might the Friar be admitting that her confession in

III.vi might not have been *free*? A free confession is one in which her spiritual welfare – her *peace* – is in accord with who she is – *you*.

45 **favour**   In a play set in Roman Catholic Italy, this is an emphasis more in keeping with the Reformation. Luther taught that God's grace is irrespective of merit. Annabella has been given more than she *hoped*.

46 **Commend**   To *commend* is to entrust something to a person (in this case, her letter) and to commit oneself to the care of another.

49 **guardian**   Putana. Annabella, of course, does not know of Putana's fate.

50 **suspect**   concern, worry.

52 Although Soranzo was behaving considerately to her at their last meeting, Annabella – probably because of her imprisonment – tells Giovanni to mistrust him.

Act V Scene II

Both Vasques and Soranzo talk obsessively. Vasques emphasizes the disgrace of Soranzo's being a cuckold and tells him to *think upon incest and cuckoldry* (24). Soranzo talks of *my brother rival* (20) and imagines his revenge as a piece of theatre, with Annabella dressed as the virgin bride she never was. Vasques is aware of another aspect of the theatricality of revenge: the pressure of time (15–17). See Interpretations page 225.

In performance, a decision would have to be made as to what it is that most enrages Soranzo and what part, if any, Vasques has in controlling his master. If a production stresses Vasques' role, it might try to bring out the moral and psychological significance of a character who seems to strongly feel wrongs committed against another, who is eagerly energetic in devising plans, and who seems to relish the appalling cruelty he inflicts on Putana.

1 **believed**   Vasques is concerned with how he will be regarded, what his reputation will be.

2 **but** only.

3 **horns** It was a common joke that men who had been cuckolded (whose wives had been unfaithful) had horns on their heads.

   riot triumphantly exult.

5 **panders and bawds** These words are similar in meaning. A *pander* helped to arrange immoral sexual liaisons, while a *bawd* (the term could apply to either men or women) procured custom for a brothel.

9 **great** entirely filled up. The term was also used of pregnancy, as in 'being great with child' (Luke 2:5). See IV.iii.154 and Note.

11 **deck** cover, dress.

14 **ambush** Whom will the Banditti *ambush*?

18 **cunning** contrived, with the implication of being underhand.

19 **states** leading citizens.

21 **fail** i.e. fail to come.

25 **aspire** want, desire.

Act V Scene III

Giovanni's soliloquy is one of those moments in art from the past when the sentiments expressed surprise us with their apparent modernity. Giovanni values experience above principles and precepts. The *unexperienced* (3) might heed *opinion* (1), but he finds that his actual feelings do not accord with what is popularly believed. It is the kind of insight the post-war French existentialist philosophers insisted upon as proof that what matters are not ideas about human essence but the actual experience of living. Compare this speech with Annabella's soliloquy (V.i.1–23).

The exchange with the Friar about religion and love takes up the issues with which the play opened. Giovanni's quarrel with religion is complete by this scene (see Interpretations page 201). It is a good dramatic moment when the Friar resists the invitation to argue by giving Giovanni the letter from Annabella: *Look there,* '*tis writ to thee* (22). Giovanni thinks the letter is a forgery, but the audience know that Annabella wrote it. They also know her heart-felt remorse. Knowing this might prepare the audience for seeing that Giovanni's language works against him. He may say *pox on dreams* (35), but is it not he who is dreaming?

The Friar is still concerned for Giovanni's welfare. He must suspect that Soranzo has found out the truth, and might regard Vasques' rather wordy attempt to ignore the implications of *dare* (48) as a confirmation of his suspicions. Giovanni will not heed the Friar's warnings because he has determined to embrace the tragic denouement that awaits him. He is both foolishly reckless and staunchly heroic in wanting to go to the birthday feast, and there is a terrible purposefulness in his desire to *strike as deep in slaughter* (63) in the bloodbath that he senses Soranzo has planned.

The Friar acknowledges that this is the stage events have reached and bids Parma farewell, adding he wishes he had never known Giovanni. Do we feel he ought to have remained to see things through, even though the end is now horribly inevitable? Perhaps in Christian charity he ought to have stayed, but his departure may show that he is rejecting the tragic role that Giovanni has so dramatically adopted. From now on the tone of the play is unmistakably tragic (see Interpretations page 242).

1 This is a sneering dismissal of popular *opinion*: *Busy* means interfering and *idle* means ineffectual.
2 **school-rod** cane for beating pupils, which was displayed in a classroom as a threat.
3 **temper of the mind** mental disposition.
6–7 **no change... law of sports** Annabella's marriage, a *formal law*, has not altered his sexual desire (*sports*) for her.
8 **one** the same. It appears that incestuous relations have continued.
10 **reaped** harvested, obtained.
   privilege authority or licence. The word has a public and quasi-legal meaning.

11 **Entitled** This is another word with legal associations, suggesting having a claim to something. This language, like *privilege* (10), opens up the question of who has the right to Annabella.

12 **united hearts** This is the language of contemporary love poetry.

13 **book-men** scholars, very much a university term. Three lines later a *book-man* enters.

16 **Elysium** the home of the gods.

17 **jubilee** time of celebration.

18 **retired** private.

19 **prompted** put forward, suggested.

21 **slays** kills, with the implication of damnation.

25 **seething** boiling.

26 **congealed coral** Coral was thought to be a plant that hardened when out of the sea.

28 **factor** messenger, go-between.

30 **seared** made incapable of feeling, as in a wound that has been cauterized.

31 **stoop** submit.

33–4 It seems as if the thought passes through his mind that this is a warning from God (Giovanni's religious language is classical rather than Christian), but he scorns it.

38 **traitors** Giovanni cannot believe that they have betrayed each other. He does not consider that others – the Friar, Putana – might have revealed their secret.

39 **Confusion** Having discounted hell, Giovanni uses a word that elsewhere in the play means damnation (see II.iii.53). See Interpretations page 195.
   dotage senile writing. Giovanni implies that the letter has been *forged* by the Friar.

40 **peevish** silly, perverse.

45 **magnificoes** leading citizens.

46 **presence** attendance.

48 **dare** am willing to, but with the additional sense of accepting a challenge. Presumably Vasques pretends not to see the second meaning.

53 **miss** fail to attend.

57 **gage** stake.

58 **train**   lure, entice.

60–61 **plagues, blazing stars**   Both were signs of the end of the world. The *blazing stars* were comets. See Interpretations page 242.

62 **resolve**   show convinced determination. A tragic hero often shows resolution in the face of his final conflict. Vasques speaks of Soranzo's *resolution* in V.iv.22.

70 **aught**   anything. This refers to Giovanni; the Friar is saying he wishes he had never known anything of Giovanni.

71 **despair**   This was regarded as the worst of all spiritual states, because the one who despaired had lost any hope of salvation. Giovanni acknowledges in the next line that he is in a state of despair.

73 **set up my rest**   gambled everything. In the card game primero, the *rest* was the reserve each player agreed to at the start of the game. To stake one's *rest* was thus to risk all.

74 **baneful**   death-dealing. There is also an association with poison.

75–7 The *old prescription* is the set of laws by which people have always lived, including, of course, the precepts of Christian morality. He virtually prays that he will not lose his *gall/ Of courage* (courageous violence) and that his exploits will be written in the roll of honour of those who die *a glorious death*. Ford plays on another meaning of *gall* – a substance from the oak tree used in making ink, which will be used in writing out his name. The idea continues in the image of the *well-grown oak* (78).

79 **under-shrubs**   small bushes and plants of the undergrowth.

80 **splits**   splinters.

Act V Scene IV

The opening words show that the Friar was right to foresee violence and that Giovanni was equally right in bracing himself to meet his fate. The plotting of Soranzo and Vasques is very different from Giovanni's self-consciously tragic mode. Instead of the apocalyptic language, the sense of proud isolation, the bracing of the self in the face of the inevitable, Vasques is particular and practical; the talk is of killing, disguise, timing, *profit and preferment* (19). Perhaps this is the difference between tragedy and revenge; revenge is not necessarily tragic. See Interpretations page 241.

Once alone with Soranzo, Vasques heightens his language, bringing it close to the rhetoric of epic. The killing is *this great work*, and it requires *a great mind* (22–3). There may be the idea that Soranzo, who has played the part of the unrequited lover in II.ii, must now be instructed in the role of the revenger. Certainly, Ford gives Vasques the crucial word *courage* (25), which was central to Giovanni's soliloquy in the previous scene (V.iii.77). See Interpretations page 225.

Perhaps the somewhat excessive civilities of Soranzo in the presence of the Cardinal are Ford's way of establishing the high decorum of his birthday feast, and therefore providing a foil for the ghastly spectacle of Giovanni's entrance in V.vi.

2 **undertake for**   ensure.
5 **Liguria**   a dangerous and lawless mountain region north-west of Parma.
9 **want**   lack.
10 **noble**   This might be said to persuade the Banditti to commit murder, or it might be that Soranzo actually thinks it is *noble* to carry out revenge.
11 **free**   Banditti were outlaws; to be *free* was to be re-admitted to society, hence their cry of *Liberty* (12).
15 **watch-word**   cue for action.
17 **profession**   Does Vasques respect their *profession* because he is conscious of his own?
19 **ends**   aims.
21 **edge**   sharpen up.
28 **burn**   i.e. with desire for revenge. Perhaps his revenge is intensified because the one who burned for Annabella is the cause of his revenge.
30 **Italian**   Italians were popularly believed to be excessively revengeful.
32 **sharp set**   sexually intent.
    bit   colloquial term for a female sexual partner.

34 **hare** The term is used in Shakespeare to mean prostitute but here refers to Giovanni. Both hares and rabbits were regarded as lustful.

law freedom to do as he pleases.

35 **post to Hell** As incest is a sin, those killed in the act will *post* (go directly) to *Hell*. The pleasure of revenge, as in *Hamlet*, involves damning the victim.

40 **father** father-in-law.

states people of high rank.

43 **good housewife** typical wife; here, *good* means slow or lazy. There may be a play on 'hussy' – a sexually irresponsible woman.

45 **expect** greet.

48 **glut** literally stuff with food. The term is often used as a metaphor for sexual indulgence.

51 **grace** gracious acceptance of the invitation.

52 **vouchsafe** grant as a favour to.

54–6 As successor to *Saint Peter*, the Pope is the *vicar* of Christ. As his *nuncio* (representative) in Parma, the Cardinal is the Pope's *substitute*.

60 **walk near** pass straight in.

61 **with civil mirth** with due decorum.

63 **keep your way** proceed this way.

Act V Scene V

Giovanni and Annabella display quite different attitudes to what is to come. Giovanni has hardly changed; what he wants is sexual delight. Annabella is remorseful and fearful; she expresses her foreboding in the marvellous understatement that the preparations for Soranzo's birthday feast are *But to some end* (21). In 5–7 she expresses with eloquent sadness the appalling gulf between his insensitive joking about her anguish and his utter blankness as to the danger he is in. Is there a pathos that in this, their last scene together, the brother and sister seem so different?

He strikes the attitude of tragic defiance, while she is far quieter and perhaps more spiritually profound, as in her counsel: *be prepared to welcome it* (29).

His response is characteristically academic. He may have given up Christian belief, but he is still intrigued by its teaching, so turns thoughts about the future into a discourse about the theological image that the sea will burn at the end of the world (30–33). He is also concerned with another future: what people in the *after-times* (68) will make of their love. Perhaps only at this point do the two come close. She has plaintively talked about her future as A *wretched woeful woman's tragedy* (V.i.8), and Giovanni is concerned about *The story of my life* (53). What he wants of the future is that it will hear of their *fast-knit affections* (69) and exonerate them. At the moment of killing her, he claims he is doing it *To save thy fame* (reputation, 84).

One of the aspects of the scene that a production needs to bring out is Annabella's uncertainty as to what Giovanni intends. Although he talks about what people will make of them in *after-times*, she still responds to his *Farewell* with the question *Will you be gone?* (79). A good performance should also put the audience in doubt: is he really going to kill her?

As with many of Giovanni's speeches, a count of the number of times he uses singular personal pronouns (*I, me, my*) is revealing. It is characteristic of him that when he stabs her he says: *Thus die, and die by me, and by my hand* (85). It is important, however, to draw attention to two things in the scene. In his rhapsodic passage about their love (68–78) he frequently speaks in plurals: *yet when they but know/ Our loves* (71–2). He may be making fatal decisions about them, but might there be a recognition of their togetherness? The other point is surprising. Once Annabella is dead he thinks about the unborn child, yet very quickly it becomes an opportunity for Giovanni's linguistic invention. In a figure of speech that borders on being a conceit (see Interpretations page 194), he says the baby *Hath had from me a cradle and a grave* (96). The innocent child is buried in his language.

1 **changed** From what Giovanni says about *a trick in night-games* (novel sexual activities) it is clear that she is refusing to respond sexually to his persuasions.
sprightly lively. See IV.iii.31.

2 **trick** A sexual meaning – love-making – was current in Ford's day.

3 **simplicity** Giovanni means that they were new to (even innocent in) their love-making. The word also meant folly or silliness. Giovanni cannot be aware of the irony.

4 **fit** Giovanni uses this word as Putana did (II.i.45) to mean the impulses of sexual desire.
treacherous Giovanni regards Annabella's marriage as a betrayal. In line 8 he calls it *thy revolt* and in line 10 again her *treachery*.

5 **vows** Giovanni is thinking of their mutual promises (I.ii.258–64). He clearly disregards the marriage vows she has made to Soranzo.

6 **calamity** distress.

9–11 **Thou art... bent brows** He claims that she must be unfaithful, ill-willed or treacherous, for otherwise she would quake before his *bent brows* (frown). See Interpretations page 240.

14 **ebbing sea** This is an image of change. See Note to line 1 and the image of the tides in I.i.64–5.

15 **honest** respectable and sexually faithful to her husband.

18 **confusion** death and (possibly) damnation.

20 **gay attires** She senses that Soranzo had a sinister plan in making her wear her bridal dress (V.ii.11).

21 **solemn** splendid and bountiful.

22 **riot in expense** show that a lot of money has been spent.

23 **chambered** confined to a room.

26 **access** permission to receive guests.

27 **harbinger** messenger who goes ahead to announce an arrival.

28 **resolve yourself** settle it in your mind. This is a very different use of *resolve* from Giovanni's in V.iii.62.

30–33 **The schoolmen... waters burn** Scholars (*schoolmen*) believed that at the end of time the earth would be instantly consumed by fire. The sceptical Giovanni finds it *somewhat strange* that the sea should *burn*.

40 **kiss** Giovanni cannot imagine an after-life without sexual activity.

prate   chatter frivolously.

41 **do**   The sexual sense is probably intended.

42 **good**   dear, darling.

  mean   intend to do.

46 **Distraction**   mental disturbance.

47 **repining**   discontented, dissatisfied.

48 **weep**   Annabella has wept for her sins; Giovanni, we discover, is weeping for the imminent loss of his sister – at his hand.

54 **Be record**   bear witness.

  spirits of the air   bodiless presences, who made bodies out of air.

58 **mourners**   Giovanni is continuing the extended image of the *funeral* (49) by saying that all the tears he has shed over Annabella now gather as *mourners* do to weep. For tears, see Interpretations page 229.

59 **Never till now**   The phrase is used in Shakespeare's *Julius Caesar* (I.iii.9).

62 **Destinies**   the Fates. They are so *jealous* (possessive) that newly created beauty is *required again* (wanted back).

65 **Heaven**   Carried away by his own ardour, he speaks of that which he claims he has no belief in.

66 **drift**   direction of thought.

68 **after-times**   Like Annabella in V.i.8, Giovanni imagines what later times will make of their lives. She sees her life as a *tragedy*, while he sees that their incest will be overlooked because of the outstanding character of their love. Do we have to prefer one to the other?

70–71 **The laws of conscience... blame us**   He does now admit that *conscience* has a place in the justification of actions.

71 **but**   only.

72 **rigour**   extremity of action.

75 **constantly**   plainly, unambiguously.

76 **These palms do promise health**   She has all the signs of good health.

77 **cunning flattery**   Because she is shortly to die, her appearance of health is *cunning* (deceptive).

78 **forgive me**   Executioners begged forgiveness from prisoners they were about to kill.

79–83   What is to be made of these lines? Is it self-regarding bluster, or the attempt of a young man in love to give his actions significance?

81 **deed**   The actions of an epic hero were commonly referred to as deeds.

82 **Styx**   in Greek mythology, the chief river of the Underworld over which the souls of the dead were ferried. Giovanni only seems to be interested in the way poets have described its *sooty* colour.

86 **Revenge is mine**   The Bible speaks of revenge as belonging to God alone: for instance, 'To me belongeth vengeance' (Deuteronomy 32:35) and 'Vengeance is mine' (Romans 12:19). Giovanni cannot be unaware that he is taking upon himself what is reserved for God. And against whom is the vengeance: Soranzo, Annabella, public opinion that condemns incest, or God who created the great love of his life as his sister?

honour   Audiences today may feel a chill on hearing that *honour* commands that *love* kills Annabella.

88 **I'll give my reasons**   To whom, and for what?

dispute   This was the first word of the play.

90 **stagger**   falter, hesitate.

act   This is theatrical language. See also 106.

91 **glory**   See Interpretations page 241 and V.iii.77. In 103 Annabella is described as *over-glorious*.

93 **unkind**   There are two senses: cruel, and not according to nature.

94 **hapless fruit**   unborn child. *Hapless* means unfortunate.

98 **In all her best**   in her finery (her wedding dress) and also, very strangely, at her finest and most wonderful.

100 **prevented**   This has the sense of getting in beforehand to forestall an action.

reaching   scheming.

102–4 **Fair Annabella... infamy and hate**   See page 9.

105 **courageous**   Nothing he has done has made him question his use of this word. See V.iii.77.

Act V Scene VI

The entrance and the seating of the guests – *they take their places* – will take some time. This means that the re-appearance of Giovanni will not seem to come very soon after his exit in the previous scene.

Giovanni's entrance is the theatrical climax of the play. A murderer exultingly displaying his victim's heart impaled upon a dagger has all the shocking immediacy and horror of tragic revenge. As a piece of stagecraft, its impact is probably greater than anything that could be written about it. Yet one aspect of the scene might be considered through an awareness of its place in the play and its historical context.

The play works in part by the repeated use of certain words, some of which become visible in the action of the play (see Interpretations pages 194–5). One of these words is *blood*. In the closing scenes of the play, blood is seen: Annabella's blood on her wedding dress and her *reeking blood* (11) on Giovanni's dagger. The historical context concerns the seventeenth-century convention of the emblem book. Emblem books were an early example of what is now called 'word and image': a poem would be accompanied by a woodcut depicting the topic of the poem. The poems were often of a moral or religious nature, and the emblem had a representative or allegorical form. Henry Vaughan's *Silex Scintillans* of 1650 has a title page that bears the emblem of a flaming heart. Giovanni's parading of his sister's heart might be seen as the subversion of an emblem; it is a strong visual accompaniment – *Look well upon't* (29) – to Giovanni's 'message', but that message, unlike the elevated subjects of the emblem books, is one of revengeful pride.

An aspect of Giovanni's entrance that is difficult to present on stage is the reaction of those feasting. The players must present bewilderment and incomprehension. Vasques' question must stand for what all are wondering: *What strange riddle's this?* (30).

Giovanni clearly sees this moment as the triumph (see 57) of his life. He returns to the language he has used in the preceding scenes. He speaks proudly of *The glory of my deed* (22) and of himself as *a most glorious executioner* (34). He continues the atmospheric language of V.v.79–80 when he speaks of the *midday sun* being darkened (23). He uses the language of the theatre: *the rape of life and beauty/ Which I have acted* (20–21). Above all, the language is that of a tragic hero facing his ultimate trial. He says of himself that he has acted out of *courage* (67), speaks of his *brave revenge* (75) and, when faced with the Banditti, displays a Macbeth-like recklessness: *Welcome! Come more of you, whate'er you be;/ I dare your worst* (82–3). Perhaps there is also an element of display in his death, which is accompanied by a commentary upon his failing strength.

A feature of the scene is that the characters do not believe Giovanni. What is surprising is that he is surprised at this. He might be said to take it personally; as if his integrity is being questioned, he resorts to the elevated language of classical Greece and legal procedures: *'tis the oracle of truth;/ I vow it is so* (53–4). The audience, of course, know that as for the basic facts, Giovanni is telling the truth. What they might find more difficult is his disdainful bragging tone: *have you all no faith/ To credit yet my triumphs?* (56–7). There is no shame, no remorse; perhaps we feel that the incomprehension of his listeners (his audience) is understandable.

Once Giovanni has given expression to his turbulent feelings and assured self-estimations, the play becomes simpler and, strangely, in spite of the expressions of horror, quieter. It allows some final revelations of motive and character. Vasques' account of his life (119–25) opens with two important words: *Honesty, and pity*. Honesty is bound up with the rituals of loyalty, which have an important place in the play (see Interpretations page 230). *Pity* is more difficult to think about – but possibly more rewarding. We have only Vasques' word for this. Is he merely hoping for lenient treatment, or is it possible to play the character throughout as one who feels for his master's plight?

2 **resolute**   See Note to V.iii.62.

3 **fixed**   determined.

5 **coarse confections**   simple dishes.

5–7 **Though the use... your presence**   Although feasts such as this one are often given out of mere custom, I am honoured that you have graced us with your presence.

10 What can be the point of Soranzo's question?

10 sd *Enter Giovanni with a heart upon his dagger*   There has been speculation about how this was achieved on Ford's stage. It also presents an interesting problem for modern productions.

11 **trimmed**   decorated. The word was associated with fine clothing.
reeking   hot, steaming.

12 **proud**   Who speaks for whom? Giovanni is certainly *proud*, but is there any way in which Annabella can be said to be so?
spoil   that which is taken by the victors in a war. What meaning does it have here?

13 **Fate**   See Interpretations page 234.

14 **motions**   promptings, desires, inclinations.

15 **prevent**   forestall; as in Soranzo's: *Shall I be forestalled?* (16). See V.v.100 and Note.

17 **misgiving**   fearful, doubting.

18 **idle**   trivial.

20 **rape**   sudden and violent taking.

21 This is a crucial line in performance. The player must exhibit Giovanni's pride (the language is theatrical: *I have acted*) and the sudden change when his loss, and possibly the enormity of what he has done, comes upon him.

22 **glory**   See V.iii.77, and V.v.91 and Note.
deed   See V.v.81 and Note.

22–3 Compare with V.v.79–82.

26 **stone**   precious stone.

27 **balanced**   weighed as in scales.

28 **mine**   In the light of the image of mining – *a much richer mine* (26) – is this a pun?

32–3 **ploughed up/ Her fruitful womb**   Derek Roper (see Further Reading) points out that this is a perversion of a commonly used metaphor, which describes procreation in terms of ploughing. He adds that it is a grotesque equivalent of the delivery of a child.

37 See Interpretations page 236.

38–9 Perhaps Florio is right to call him *madman* (35) and *frantic madman* (43).

40 **moons** months. Annabella must have been heavily pregnant.

41 **throughly** thoroughly.

viewed i.e. realized her beauty, or saw her naked.

45 **sheets** This is a customary way of indicating sexual intercourse.

46 **monarch** This is a poetic image of male lordship in love.

48 **confounding** His *cheek* confirms the truth, and the truth destroys.

disgrace i.e. being a cuckold.

49 **bewrayed** showed, revealed.

50 **passage** course.

52 **Incestuous** As a churchman, it falls to the Cardinal to use the condemnatory word.

rage fury, perhaps even madness.

belies makes untrue. Florio cannot believe what is being said.

53 **oracle** In ancient Greece, the *oracle* was a prophetess who foretold the future. Again, Giovanni uses a word that is classical rather than Christian.

55 **strumpet** The husband condemns his wife, as before in IV.iii.1.

57 **triumphs** public festivities to celebrate a victory. This is another classical reference. In view of the earlier *triumphs* (12), Giovanni might be interpreted as enjoying what he regards as a victory.

58–9 Giovanni draws the distinction between what the onlookers *call sacred* and what he swears by, *the love/ I bore my Annabella*. The word *my* is another way of excluding Soranzo.

60 **ripped** This is the most disturbing case of a word becoming a reality. When the Friar used the word of Annabella (III.vi.2) it had a metaphoric edge: the soul is, as it were, ripped open to reveal its innermost secrets. Giovanni does not speak in metaphor here.

61 **'Tis most strangely true** This might apply to many things in the play.

63 **Monster** Compare Hippolita's curse: *may her womb bring forth/ Monsters* (IV.i.100–1).

66 **becomes**   is fitting for.

68 **gilt**   decorated (in the sense of gilded). The word sounds like 'guilt'.

69 **hapless**   unfortunate.

72 **twists**   sinews. He is holding Annabella's heart. In classical mythology, the thread of life was spun and cut by the Fates.

75 **brave**   This word often characterizes a tragic action: it suggests defiant and ostentatious display.

77 **insolent**   full of overbearing pride.

80 **fit you anon**   deal with you shortly.

81 **Vengeance**   This is evidently the *watch-word* of V.iv.15.

87 **Shift for yourselves**   look after yourselves. Are the Banditti denied the promises made to them in V.iv.11?

96 **my ever dearest lord and master**   See Interpretations page 231.

103 **impudent**   brazen, defiant – a word often associated with tragedy.

106 What sort of sense, if any, do you make of these words?

108–9 Even in death, Giovanni shapes his language. He has been a *guest* at a feast designed to kill him, and now in dying he welcomes *Death – I embrace/ Thee* – as a *guest*.

110–11 At his end Giovanni is close to Christianity; he asks the *grace* (a Christian word meaning the gift of God) to gaze upon *my Annabella's face*. Can it be known if he thinks this might be in heaven or a pagan paradise?

112 **justice**   For whom?

113 It is difficult not to find this remark absurdly comical.

115 **duty**   See Interpretations page 231.

119 **Honesty**   loyalty, honour, respectability. See also *honest* in 144.

120 **Spaniard**   Perhaps this is an indication of his fierce loyalties.

121 **forth**   from.

125 **ransomed**   saved. He regrets that he did not die for Soranzo.

127 **Of counsel**   in the know, complicit.

137 **this woman**   There is debate as to whether this refers to Putana, or to Annabella's dead body. Vasques has been talking about Putana, but the description *chief in these effects* fits Annabella.

140 **ashes**   Being denied burial is a sign of people's abhorrence.
just   Is it? See also IV.i.90.

146 **no Italian** Because he is not native to Italy, his punishment can quite properly be banishment.

148–9 **in this… thine offence** i.e. he will not exact the full penalty although he does not approve of what Vasques has done.

150–51 Who is the *Italian* and in what ways did Vasques outdo him *in revenge?*

154 **canons** laws.

155 **seize upon** take possession of.
proper own.

158 **pride and lust** Richardetto repeats what he said in IV.i.103–4.

161 **at large** fully.

163–4 See Interpretations pages 247–8.

163 **Nature's store** the plentiful gifts of nature.

164 **whore** See Interpretations pages 247–8.

Interpretations

Interpretation is usually a matter of saying what a work means and trying to make sense of the different reactions people have had to it. In the case of *'Tis Pity She's a Whore*, interpretation certainly involves recognizing its chief themes – love, marriage, revenge, and so on – and sorting out how we feel about the central characters. In the case of drama, one of the features of literary criticism over the past 50 years has been the attempt to do justice to the 'performability' of a play. Interpretation has taken on the issue of how something was performed, might be performed and whether, in performance, the play engages the audience.

Ford the dramatist

Changing reputations

The decades between the world wars saw the Hollywood film industry producing hundreds of 'westerns'. Many of them are now recognized as good, and a few – *Stagecoach* is an example – are considered masterpieces. The remarkable thing about these films is that they were not consciously aiming at being 'great works of art'. They were not serious or high-minded, but popular and entertaining. It might sound far-fetched, but Hollywood westerns have something in common with English Renaissance drama. Plays were written by the hundreds with the immediate purpose of packing in the crowds and giving them a comic or thrilling afternoon in the theatre. For well over two centuries, most of these plays were forgotten, but in the twentieth century theatres and scholars took a second look, and now some of them are seen as considerable works.

This has been the story of *'Tis Pity She's a Whore*. After it was performed in Norwich in 1663 it was not staged again until 1923.

Since then, there have been over 20 productions. It is not as popular as, for example, John Webster's *The Duchess of Malfi*, but it is now part of the English stage tradition and more popular than plays by Philip Massinger or James Shirley. So why has *'Tis Pity She's a Whore* returned to the English stage? There are a number of answers. Here are four.

Dramatic interplay

As with any good drama, its interest lies in the way we are engaged by the developing interplay between the characters. All plays unfold; that is, they have a moment-by-moment life in which characters exert pressure upon and respond to each other.

Sometimes the pressure and response are immediate. In the second scene (I.ii.205–208), Giovanni's high, though conventional, praise for his sister puzzles Annabella – *D'ee mock me, or flatter me?* After another speech in which her beauty is said to be above both art and nature, she teasingly says: *O you are a trim youth* (210–213). *Trim* is a term that probably comes from seamanship; Annabella's rejoinder is a playfully comic observation that Giovanni is in full sail. Then Giovanni produces a dagger. Annabella's brief *What to do?* (214) indicates a sudden puzzlement but not one that shows she is reduced to passivity. Although the mood of the scene has changed, Annabella is alert and, it might be said, still a forceful participant.

The life of one character can be shown to have been influenced by interplay with another character in an earlier scene. This shaping is particularly evident in monologues. When Giovanni enters in the second scene, we hear him in soliloquy:

> Lost, I am lost: my fates have doomed my death.
> The more I strive, I love; the more I love,
> The less I hope: I see my ruin, certain.

> (I.ii.150–152)

Many of the crucial words here are given weight because they were used in the opening exchange between Giovanni and the

Friar. Giovanni has talked a lot about *love*: *Must I not do what all men else may – love?* (I.i.19.) He ends the scene on a note that blends resolution with despair: *All this I'll do, to free me from the rod/ Of vengeance; else I'll swear, my fate's my god* (I.ii.83–84). By the second scene he believes that the *fates have doomed* his *death. Death* is one of the Friar's words – *lust and death* (I.i.58) – as, also, is *hope*: *the fruits of all my hopes* (I.i.55). Giovanni also owes *lost* and *ruin* to the Friar: *thou art lost* (I.i.35) and *thy ruin* (I.i.67). Ford follows the convention that in soliloquy, characters tell the truth. Giovanni's language, therefore, shows how seriously he has taken the Friar's words. Furthermore, the audience might feel for him when he says *What wit or art/ Could counsel, I have practised* (I.ii.160–161).

Activity

Discuss the interplay between Hippolita and Vasques in II.ii.155–165.

Discussion

The interplay between the two characters is shaped by Hippolita's request *Give me thy hand*. The scene therefore looks like one in which solemn promises are to be made, and given that the promise is to keep silent – *promise but thy silence* – the audience may sense that some sinister secret is to be disclosed. But before she gives details of a *plot I have*, there is what is virtually a promise of marriage – to *make thee lord of me*. It is now up to the actor playing Vasques to do two things: encourage Hippolita by his apparently welcoming response, and speak in such a way that he is not actually committing himself. He welcomes her by adopting the light tones of a man who cannot believe his luck – *Come, you are merry* – and, without making it obvious, is equivocal in his wording. By claiming he *can neither think or believe* in such *happiness* he withholds his assent, because, as is later disclosed, he neither thinks of an alliance with her nor believes that aiding her is right. He (and the one who plays him) is indeed a *special actor* who will *never disclose it till it be effected*.

The working of language

Ford's language lacks the imaginative richness of Shakespeare and, in spite of his depiction of horrors, he is not usually as surreal or chilling as Webster. Imagery is not a very important feature, though towards the end there are some striking passages, some of them close to being conceits – comparisons that can be developed at length and which initially strike the reader as odd rather than apt. In her soliloquy, Annabella speaks of how those who *sleep in lethargies of lust/ Hug their confusion* (V.i.28–29). The word *Hug* links the physical holding of a sexual partner with embracing a course of life that will lead to *confusion* (damnation). Although it cannot be a matter of context or history, there is something decidedly Italian about Annabella's expression of anguish; it is like an aria from an opera in which an abandoned heroine pours out her yearnings and griefs. See page 21.

With Ford, critics cannot play the old-fashioned game of searching for a family of images that embody the chief matter of the play. Ford's distinctive contribution to dramatic language – what W.W. Robson called 'the falling elegiac note' – will be discussed on pages 245–247. Three other things need to be commented on here.

- Ford builds up the thematic density of his play through the repetition of words. The following are prominent: *blood, brave, charity, confusion, death, deceit, delights, destruction, fate, fit, lost, lust, merry, privacy, resolve, rip, trust, vow.* Repeated words produce and reinforce thematic strands, and readers who recognize the recurrence of a word might appreciate the significance of the plot's movement. For instance, *blood* is used by Giovanni to justify his incestuous desires. He asks rhetorically whether he and his sister are not *each to other bound/ So much the more by nature; by the links/ Of blood, of reason?* (I.i.30–32). Because *nature* comes before *blood*, the primary meaning is the brother–sister bond. But because of his particular feelings for his sister, *blood* may already be taking on another of its familiar meanings – the heats of sexual desire.

- In a period when authors were revelling in the range of meanings a single word can have, Ford – though less adventurous than Shakespeare – could attune his language to indicate the significance of stage business. 'Confusion' meant ruin and destruction. Vasques uses it of the scheming Hippolita, who hoped to *laugh at* Soranzo's *confusion* (IV.i.82–83). But elsewhere it seems to means damnation, as in Grimaldi swearing he hates Soranzo *Worse than confusion* (II.iii.53). In Annabella's language it can mean both: aware of Soranzo's plotting, she warns her brother that *there's but a dining-time/ 'Twixt us and our confusion* (V.v.17–18). Annabella sees what Giovanni never does: their deaths may be their damnations.

- Ford follows both Shakespeare and Webster in linking words to future actions. The climax is linguistically anticipated in the use of the words *rip, unripped* and *ripped*. Giovanni says *Rip up my bosom* to Annabella (I.ii.215); the Friar, hearing Annabella's confession, says she has *unripped a soul* (III.vi.2); and Giovanni fits the word to the deed: *These hands have from her bosom ripped this heart* (V.vi.60).

Activity

Explore the use that Soranzo and Giovanni make of the word *heart*.

Discussion

An audience would expect that in a scene in which love is declared, the word *heart* would be prominent. Soranzo, a disappointingly unoriginal lover, protests to the unmoved Annabella: *Did you but see my heart, then would you swear* (III.ii.21). He is cut off by Annabella's belittling literalism: *That you were dead*. But the undaunted Soranzo returns to conventional love language: *I'm sick, and sick to th'heart* (33), only to be rebutted in a similar fashion by the deliberately obtuse comedy of Annabella's *Help! Aqua-vitae!*

But her brother-lover's use of the word *heart* is uncomfortably close to its plain, anatomical meaning. He affirms that he is speaking in *earnest* when in his wooing scene he says that were she to *Rip* his *bosom* she would *behold/ A heart, in which is writ the truth I speak* (I.ii.215–216). His usage prepares the audience for his horribly literal enactment of such an idea at her death. The heart on his dagger when he enters at V.vi.10 is real. What increases the horror of her death, however, is that Giovanni continues to use *heart* as a conventional lover or tragic hero would. He speaks of *the tribute which my heart/ Hath paid to Annabella's sacred love* (V.v.56–57), and once she is dead he calls upon his heart to show a proper tragic resolution: *Shrink not, courageous hand; stand up, my heart* (V.v.105).

Parallels

It is better to talk about the plots (in the plural) of *'Tis Pity* rather than a single plot. It is a play in which there are a number of distinct pieces of dramatic action. As some of these actions share common features, there are parallels between them.

One of the most important is that between Giovanni and Soranzo. Both woo Annabella and, in wooing, suffer the pangs of the unrequited lover. Both succeed – Giovanni is the lover who takes his sister's virginity, and Soranzo the suitor who marries her. Both come to see the other as a rival and both pursue revenge. What is the effect of this?

Paralleling makes irony possible. Soranzo soliloquizes in the manner of the (rather conventional) yearning lover. Like many Renaissance lovers, he finds that poets mislead (II.ii.5–17), not least in their failure to imagine the overwhelming beauty of the beloved. (Giovanni has already spoken like this in I.ii.197–200.) The poet whose work Soranzo is reading (*Sannazar*) would have given up writing the poetry that earned him considerable wealth *for one only look from Annabell* (II.ii.16). Irony in drama is always recognized by the audience and it is always against a character or characters. What do we understand that Soranzo does not? The answer is that Giovanni has had much more from Annabella than *one only look*.

In the case of irony we have to reckon with the shifts that take place with the passage of time. What one age reads unambiguously, a later one can see ironically. The scene in which

Annabella repents and accepts the hand of Soranzo (III.vi) works by unexpected ironies. The threat of hell that the Friar delivers in such horribly graphic detail (8–23) looks as if it is a frightening disclosure of a mind steeped in the gruesome specifics of an essentially medieval imagination. This is a judgement that comes easily to modern audiences. But when its place in the unfolding of the plot is considered, ironies emerge. The list of punishments ends with the murderer and the wanton:

> There is the murderer forever stabbed,
> Yet can he never die; there lies the wanton
> On racks of burning steel, whiles in his soul
> He feels the torment of his raging lust.

> (III.vi.20–23)

The ironies become evident in the last two scenes of the play. Before he murders his sister, the pair talk of heaven and hell (V.v.33–41), and before Giovanni stabs Annabella, his imagery is close to that of hell:

> Be dark, bright sun,
> And make this midday night, that thy gilt rays
> May not behold a deed will turn their splendour
> More sooty than the poets feign their Styx!

> (V.v.79–82)

The *sooty* air may remind audiences and readers of the Friar's *A lightless sulphur, choked with smoky fogs* (III.vi.12). In the last scene, Giovanni dies the deaths of both a murderer and an incestuous lover. Soranzo asks him *hast thou a thought/ T'outlive thy murders?* (V.vi.70–71), and his dying words are: *let not that lecher live* (V.vi.94).

Activity

How do you think Donado's words in I.iii might be received by an audience that is responsive to what has happened in the preceding scenes?

Discussion

The audience will not find it difficult to view the negotiations between Donado and Florio in terms of what is happening offstage – the love-making of Annabella and Giovanni. The audience, therefore, sees a grotesque parallel between the frankly commercial propositions of Donado and the aim of all wooing – the pleasures of sexual intercourse. That Annabella is no longer what everyone assumes her to be – a virgin – becomes a plentiful source of irony. If in the third scene the audience imagines what is happening elsewhere, Donado's easy, conversational remark *If the young folks can like* (15) has a quite different meaning, as also do his words about enclosing a *jewel* (86) in a letter. The audience might reflect that in a parallel, though unseen, piece of action, Annabella is at that moment losing her *jewel* – a common term for virginity.

Stage business

Those who study the text of a play must always ask how printed words can be performed. How, for instance, might the various exchanges be played? There are also passages such as the fight between Grimaldi and Vasques, the death of Bergetto, and the scene outside the Cardinal's palace, all of which provide enticing theatrical opportunities.

There are two scenes in which the action is viewed from the balcony: the 'parade' of suitors (I.ii) and Soranzo's proposal (III.ii). It is difficult to decide how the uncomfortable moment of Giovanni's appearance *above* (III.ii.16) should be played. Does his intrusion on the privacy of a proposal make us feel more for Annabella, or for Soranzo? Perhaps for Annabella, because it shows Giovanni has no trust in her, and for Soranzo because it shows how horribly different the situation is from what he imagines. The power of the scene in part depends upon the essentially theatrical business of who is watching whom. Giovanni watches Annabella and Soranzo, and is watched in turn by the audience. This 'framing', as some critics call it, might de-stabilize the position of Giovanni. Rather than being the one at an advantage (he thinks he sees without being seen), he is being viewed, perhaps more critically, by an audience, who might regard his glee as possessive and selfish.

Activity

What performance opportunities are offered by the marriage feast in IV.i?

Discussion

The marriage feast offers several opportunities for solemn splendour: the grandest entrance in the play, formal speeches of celebration, and Hippolita's masque. A masque was a theatrical spectacle of words, music and dancing, often performed against an elaborate set. They were written for special occasions such as marriages. (Shakespeare's *The Tempest* includes a wedding masque.) Ford here is following an established theatrical practice in making his characters use entertainments to effect their plans. (Hamlet stages a play in order to test his uncle.)

Ford uses the masque to stage a dramatic unmasking. Hippolita evidently regards the moment of recognition as pivotal. She intends her *'Tis she* (39) to lead to the tragic/triumphant winding up of the plot. She certainly plays the part of the wronged woman who, because of her past, can speak with authority: *What I have right to do, his soul knows best* (49). Her horrible death and the scornful words of Vasques, whom she thought was her faithful accomplice, turn the scene into a subversion of what a marriage should celebrate. A spectacle that marks fidelity and concord becomes a confused riot, which foregrounds heartless seduction, betrayal and revenge.

The ideas of the play

Disputing

The play opens in an academic manner. Its first word is *Dispute*. To *dispute* was to partake in a formal debate between two speakers (the disputants), who analytically examined each other's arguments in favour of or against a proposition. This exercise in logic was called a disputation. Although the word did not enter the English language until 1600, the disputation had been a feature of university education throughout Europe during the Middle Ages. The methods of argument were derived from Aristotle and had been refined by generations of 'school men' – the philosophers of medieval universities. We must assume that the Friar, who refers to the classical philosophers as the *philosophers/ Of elder times* (II.v.31–32), had taught Giovanni how to dispute. The academic opening gives the play an intellectual edge; whenever Giovanni and the Friar meet, there is the stuff, if not the exact pattern, of a disputation. They argue about two things: atheism and incest (see page 204).

The courtyard of Bologna University; Giovanni's education is
at Bologna

The Atheist's Tragedy is a play of 1611 by Cyril Tourneur. It plots the schemes of D'Amville (the name is no doubt a pun) who, believing in nothing but the impulses of nature, lives for power and sensual indulgence. The play is a tragedy in the sense that his scheming fails and in his downfall he comes to see that there is more to life than the satisfaction of natural desires. Giovanni's tragedy will be discussed on pages 238–239. But what of his beliefs?

The first thing that needs to be said is that because disputation was essentially an exercise in reasoning, neither participant was required to believe in the truth of the argument he was defending. The impatient tone of the Friar's opening speech indicates that he thinks Giovanni is treating grave moral matters merely as a topic for dispassionate debate. The Friar's remarks about those who on the *foolish grounds of art* strove to prove that God did not exist and thereby filled the world *with devilish atheism* (I.i.6, 8) show that he thinks Giovanni's speculations might lead him astray.

Giovanni does not start the play as an unbeliever. In this he differs from Tourneur's D'Amville, who sets out his atheism in the opening scene. Ford shows that Giovanni listens to the Friar and tries to pray. His unbelief is something that he comes to later. By V.iii he scornfully dismisses the claims and, in particular, the sanctions of religion. *'Tis Pity* is about a man who changes his mind. But do we see that change as it happens?

The answer is: not really. Audiences might find it disappointing that Ford does not give us scenes in which Giovanni examines his beliefs. There is an early soliloquy, but this is chiefly taken up with his sexual desires (I.ii.150–168). Nowhere does Ford show him arguing the case for unbelief. Moreover, there is an element of personal antagonism against the Friar. Do we feel that he is too keen to shock his old tutor rather than seek the truth and work out the implications of what he has discovered?

There are, however, early indications in Giovanni's language that he is beginning to abandon Christian belief. Two things are significant. First, he talks of the classical gods rather than the Holy Trinity, and at one point says *as I do kneel to them* (I.i.23). This may be hyperbole – extravagant language typical of the young in love – but the absence of what is explicitly Christian may indicate the direction of his thinking. The second point is that he introduces what might be called political and social relativity. The prohibition on incest he calls a *customary form* (I.i.25). Morality, in other words, is just a matter of custom, and customs differ from one society to another. It might follow from this that the force of religion is used to impose what is nothing other than a local custom. This is the view he later comes to (V.iii.18–20).

It is not very clear what Giovanni does believe. He does not take a set of reasoned steps to a consistent and rational atheism. If there is an important factor in his thinking it is nature. Once nature became the object of scientific investigation (as it did in the work of the philosopher and scientist Francis Bacon, 1561–1626) it was possible to view it as unrelated to the God whom Christians believe is the creator of all things. But once nature is cut off from God, the question becomes: what is it like? Is it, as Edmund in Shakespeare's *King Lear* says, a goddess who favours amoral ambition?

Giovanni's language is much more elevated than that. His view is that nature is good and purposeful. At one point he tells Annabella that *Wise Nature in your creation meant/ To make you mine* (I.ii.241–242). Here Giovanni gets uncomfortably close to the Christian tradition that nature is fundamentally good. Natural law, for instance, taught that there is a purpose in the way God has made the world, and if we follow that purpose we are doing his will. For Giovanni, however, this will (of God or nature) is to commit incest. Earlier he has said to the Friar that nature formed him and his sister for mutual delight: *One soul, one flesh, one love, one heart, one all* (I.i.34). He sets out his argument for incest in II.v.13–26. See pages 208–210.

What then can be said about Giovanni's unbelief?

- An aspect of Giovanni's drift from belief in God is his use of religious language for non-religious purposes. It was customary for poets to speak of their beloveds in religious terms (*Romeo and Juliet* is an example), so to speak of Annabella as a kind of goddess is not unusual. But is Giovanni being no more than conventionally poetic? In his fullest dispute with the Friar, he says to the Friar that were he not old, *You'd make her love your heaven, and her divine* (II.v.36). Notice the word *make*. Were he being poetic, he might have used language more appropriate to speech: 'talk of', 'claim', 'say'.

- It is not easy discussing the 'big questions' of life without resorting to religious words. This, of course, was particularly so in a society where more or less everyone was a Christian. In moments of crisis, Christian language was virtually inescapable. Giovanni does talk of *heaven*, though the classical name of *Elysium* occurs in I.ii.269 and V.iii.16. When he is dying (very often a revelatory moment in Renaissance tragedy) his language is significantly ambiguous: *Where'er I go, let me enjoy this grace,/ Freely to view my Annabella's face* (V.vi.110–111). *Grace* is an important religious word meaning a free gift of God, and the gift here is to see in heaven. In Christian theology this usually means the beatific vision – the sight of God in his love and beauty. But for Giovanni, *Freely* sounds like 'free from interference', and the object of sight is not the face of God but that of Annabella.

- Giovanni's path to whatever it is he comes to believe is circuitous. He starts as a doubter and then adopts the role of his sister's ardent lover. When she marries, he becomes the jealous lover and finally plays the part of the revenger. This is not unrealistic; people's feelings and ambitions vary in strength from moment to moment. It is certainly possible to entertain doubts about God and to be passionately in love. Yet at the end of the play, we have to ask what was the relationship between atheism and incest, and whether one of these was of chief importance to Giovanni. In discussing the matter of unbelief in *'Tis Pity*, we have to see it in relation to his incestuous desires.

Activity

Consider how Giovanni's expression of unbelief is presented in V.iii.1–21.

Discussion

Giovanni speaks scornfully of *Busy opinion*, by which he means not religious belief, but commonplace ideas about the fading of sexual desire. It is only when he has relished his still-continuing love that he compares earthly pleasure with religion: *Let poring book-men dream of other worlds* (13). Scholars (*book-men*) looking down upon dusty books (*poring*) might be implicitly compared with Giovanni gazing down upon the one to whom he is making love.

When the Friar enters, Giovanni's attack on religion is delivered in an authoritative tone: *Now I can tell you* (18). *Hell* is dismissed as *slavish and fond superstitious fear* (20). We never hear the arguments that *could prove it* (21), but perhaps the aggression of the earlier part of the speech is enough to show that Giovanni's chief mode of argument is the insult. Religion is often presented as the opposite to superstition; Giovanni identifies the two things together.

Atheism and incest

It might be said that two of the chief themes of *'Tis Pity* are atheism and incest. Both of these are enacted in the life of Giovanni. The important question, as indicated above, is the relationship between the two. Three points need to be made.

- The first is one about theatrical (and probably cultural) conventions. Atheism was believed to result in immoral behaviour. D'Amville – the atheist in *The Atheist's Tragedy* – is a sexual predator. Is this convention used in Ford's presentation of Giovanni? This is a difficult topic. Perhaps the main moral problem of the play is how the audience view the brother and sister (see page 206). What is inescapable is

Giovanni's desire and the way that, once it is satisfied, he treats his sister. Is his conversation in the opening of II.i too proud and teasing? Does he appreciate Annabella's feelings? And is his statement that he will *lose* her (21) chiefly concerned with himself?

- The intertwining of desire and unbelief is present at the beginning and the end of the play. The first scene raises two questions: which matters most to Giovanni, and how are atheism and incest related? These questions might trouble an audience throughout the play. The first seems to be answered when he asks whether a religious prohibition should form *a bar/ 'Twixt my perpetual happiness and me* (I.i.26–27). He starts with incestuous desire, and then encounters the religious question. The second question might receive an answer through the working of irony. As by definition *perpetual happiness* can only be attained in heaven, the audience might see that Giovanni's unbelief is chiefly related to the fact that he sees religion as thwarting his desires (the placing of the word *me* looks significant). At the end of the play we may be prompted to ask whether we favour the young and are critical of those who disapprove of them. In V.iii Giovanni brings incest and belief together when he says *all of happiness, is here* (14) and *I'd not change it for the best to come:/ A life of pleasure is Elysium* (15–16). When the Friar enters, his response is *Thy blindness slays thee* (21). It is possible for an audience to decide that the Friar is right – that talking about sexual love as *Elysium* obscures what matters, morally and religiously.

- Is one of the links between incest and atheism the fact that Giovanni is educated? In their last scene together Giovanni, a clever young man experiencing sexual desires, introduces an intellectual debate about the end of time, possibly because Annabella has refused to have sex with him. If, he says, he can believe that water might burn, then *There might be Hell or Heaven*. To Annabella's earnest *That's most certain*, he dismissively replies *A dream, a dream* (V.v.35–36). Is Giovanni using his education to taunt Annabella? If he cannot subject her to his sexual power, does he use his mind, sharpened by the techniques of university learning, to exert control? Might it also be said that because Annabella is thinking they both face death, it is nothing short of cruel that he should treat *Hell or Heaven* as merely a debating point? (Interestingly, an unbelieving man tormenting a believing woman has become a topic for literature. In Thomas Hardy's *Tess of the D'Urbervilles*, Angel Clare admits to Tess that he does not believe in an afterlife.)

Incest was known in the ancient world. In the Old Testament there is the case of Lot and his daughters (Genesis 19), a story that was used as a subject in seventeenth-century art. Incest is the terrible secret revealed at the end of Sophocles' *Oedipus Rex*. Nor was it new to the Renaissance theatre when Ford wrote *'Tis Pity*. In Thomas Middleton's *Women Beware Women* (dating from the 1620s) there is incest between an uncle and niece. More importantly, Ford introduced incest into his poised, melancholic tragedy *The Broken Heart*. This play (probably written in the same period as *'Tis Pity*) has a scene in which incest is presented as the ugly suspicions of a disturbed and jealous husband. But *'Tis Pity She's a Whore*, as Derek Roper says, 'is the first English play to take incestuous lovers as its main protagonists, and treat them with some sympathy' (the Revels edition of the play, see Further Reading page 257).

Incest was a crime. Roper draws attention to a notorious episode in which a man, accused of killing a baby he had incestuously fathered upon his sister, escaped prosecution by transferring his estate to the Lord Chief Justice, Ford's great-uncle, John Popham. Most cases of incest were less lurid. They were dealt with, on the whole leniently, by Church courts. There seems to have been a general understanding that incest was an understandable consequence of crowded living conditions. Obviously, *'Tis Pity* is not to be understood as similar to these cases; Florio is rich, so can provide spacious accommodation for his family.

Portrait of an Italian merchant and his family by Lorenzo Lotto, 1547

It is also unlikely that much illumination can be gained from anthropologists who have studied cases of incest. Derek Roper discusses some of the theoretical approaches both to incest and to its presentation in the play. Whatever is to be made of them, the 'theorizing' that chiefly matters is that which occurs in the play itself. Incest is, like atheism, potentially a matter of debate.

Activity

It is often pointed out that the Friar does not clearly state why incest is wrong. Why is this?

Discussion

There is probably nothing strange about this. The assumption of the audience would be that there is no point in giving a reason when nobody believes incest to be right. Giovanni, however, is ready with justifications. In the first scene he says that as they were children of the same womb, they are essentially one body and one soul, and that therefore to separate them would be sinful. Those who remembered the marriage service might have seen this as a grotesque variation on 'Those whom God hath joined together let no man put asunder'.

The argument about incest

What emerges from the Friar's angry confusion is a terse summary of his judgement when he says that Giovanni has *left the schools/ Of knowledge, to converse with lust and death* (I.i.57–58). Two points need to be made.

- First, the word *converse* links the university with his life of incestuous desire. In both there is talk – the standard meaning of *converse* – but as the word 'conversation' was also used for sexual intimacy, the audience can see that the association Giovanni seeks in Parma is not of the intellectual kind.
- The second point is that in the phrase *lust and death*, Ford has raised two of the play's major themes. But the relationship between them is not easy. Giovanni may talk like an ardent lover but once he has conquered Annabella, his tone is very rarely loving. Indeed, his exultant pride and aggressive possessiveness lead to *death*.

Giovanni argues for incest in a philosophical manner:

> What I have done, I'll prove both fit and good.
> It is a principle (which you have taught
> When I was yet your scholar) that the frame
> And composition of the mind doth follow
> The frame and composition of the body.
> So where the body's furniture is beauty,
> The mind's must needs be virtue, which allowed,
> Virtue itself is reason but refined,
> And love the quintessence of that. This proves
> My sister's beauty, being rarely fair,
> Is rarely virtuous; chiefly in her love,
> And chiefly in that love, her love to me.
> If hers to me, then so is mine to her;
> Since in like causes are effects alike.

(II.v.13–26)

The shape of this argument looks to be as follows.
1 The mind and the body are alike in their make-up.
2 Virtue is to the mind what beauty is to the body.
3 Virtue is reason purified and has love as its essential nature.
4 Therefore, as his sister is exceptionally fair, she must be exceptionally virtuous.
5 This virtue is seen above all in her love for me.
6 Because similar causes have similar effects, her love to me is the same as my love to her.

What can be said about this argument?

- It is expressed in the formal language of reasoning. Giovanni sets out to *prove* that his love is both *fit* (appropriate) and morally *good*. He marks the stages in his reasoning with the standard 'scaffolding' words of logic: *So*, *must needs*, *If* and *Since*.

- The argument has some of the characteristics of a syllogism – a form of reasoning in which a conclusion is deduced from two statements or premises. It departs from a syllogism in the middle, when a new idea is introduced (stages 3 to 5).

- The argument depends upon the neo-platonic idea that the mind and body are similarly composed, and that virtue is reason and finds its best expression in love. The trouble with this is that it is vague: is virtue exactly the same as reason, and reason exactly the same as love? Arguments are not won by sliding from one term to another on the assumption that the words involved are equivalents.

- A further problem is that even if the argument is successful, it does not prove what Giovanni wants it to. All it would prove is that it is right for the brother and sister to love each other. But why should such a love be sexual? The trouble is that Giovanni assumes that love means sexual love. Arguments cannot be won by assuming what you want to prove.

- In performance, the speech might work well if it were delivered confidently and quickly. The audience could then see Giovanni's passionate desire to win his case, and the speed would obscure the fact that, as an argument, it has failings.

• It is worth asking whether Giovanni is being knowingly dishonest. Is he trying to baffle the Friar with the kind of logic the Friar has taught him? And how does this passage relate to Giovanni elsewhere? He lied to Annabella about love. Are there other ways in which he has misled her?

But what of Annabella? How might she be described? Twice, in IV.iii.125 and 136, Soranzo uses the word *tempted*. He, of course, thinks Annabella is just the victim of a seducer; but we, who know what has happened, might wonder whether there is some truth in the word *tempted*. There is no reason for disbelieving Annabella when she tells Giovanni that what he has *urged*, her *captive heart had long ago resolved* (I.ii.250–251). If sexual relations with her brother were something she had long desired, then temptation is what she is facing – doing what is desired but known to be wrong.

Activity

How might we respond to the Friar's speech about the damnation of those who have committed incest, III.vi.7–30?

Discussion

An immediate response, particularly today, might be that as Annabella is clearly penitent, the speech with all its graphic horror is cruel. It might also be felt that it was not necessary to imagine Annabella and Giovanni suffering the punishments of the incestuous (24–30).

But perhaps the play needs a statement of the sin Giovanni and Annabella have committed. And the Friar is not unsympathetic; he knows how difficult it is to stop sinning (39–40). Furthermore, what he says is psychologically right: those suffering for their sins blame not themselves but those with whom they have sinned (29–30). It might also be observed that the picture of damnation – sinners tortured with a version of their own wrongdoings – prepares us for the close of the play, in which Giovanni acts out the ghastly punishment of Annabella and then dies as both a *murderer* (20) and a *wanton* (21).

Actions and themes

People leaving the theatre or readers closing the book must sometimes wonder what *'Tis Pity She's a Whore* is about. More precisely, people might ask what themes emerge through the movement of the plot. The answer to this question is probably on the following lines: it is a play of a number of plot strands (each with their own distinctive pieces of dramatic action), and these strands embody a number of thematic concerns. The question as to which of the plot strands is the most important is something that, perhaps, should be left to individual productions and readings.

Shakespeare's influence

Unlike many English Renaissance plays, *'Tis Pity* can itself be seen as an interpretation: an interpretation of a well-known Shakespeare play. Shakespeare dominated his own era and the ones that followed. In *The School of Shakespeare* (see Further Reading) David L. Frost shows that Shakespeare was a force in English drama until the closing of the theatres in 1642. Shakespeare was performed, published, discussed, quoted in sermons and – a sure sign of his prestige – credited with writing plays that were obviously not his. One of the experiences of watching post-Shakespearean drama is hearing his voice echoed in phrasing, and seeing his dramatic actions repeated. To take a single example, the brooding, indeed obsessive, opening of *The Revenger's Tragedy* (Middleton, published 1607) parallels the gravedigger's scene in *Hamlet* with Vindice, the revenger of the title, holding a skull.

Ford's debt to Shakespeare is fuller and perhaps more puzzling than any other seventeenth-century playwright. *'Tis Pity She's a Whore* might be seen as an interpretation of *Romeo and Juliet* from the perspective of incestuous love.

Shakespeare's play about the 'star-cross'd lovers' was popular from its initial appearance (it was probably written in 1594–1595) until the theatres closed. There were four editions of the play before 1642, and two of Middleton's works – *Family of Love* and (with Thomas Dekker) *Blurt, Master Constable* – use parts of its plot.

There are strong links between Ford's play and Shakespeare. Characters are paralleled. Both plays are about young lovers, who are guided by a Nurse and a Friar. Both the young women have firm but considerate fathers. In both plays the two main characters confess their love, consummate their desires, suffer separation, and die. Their deaths are in part due to the unforeseen consequences of the Friar's actions. There is fighting in the streets at or near the beginning of both plays, and this fighting is stopped by an authority figure – the Prince in Shakespeare, and Florio in Ford. As befits the young who are new to love, the language is richly and conventionally poetic. (In *Romeo and Juliet* I.v, the two lovers share a sonnet.) The love language is drawn from what is usually called the Petrarchan tradition: images that elevate the beauty of the beloved to an almost divine level. Giovanni uses such language in I.ii.201–212. In addition to the desires of young love, both plays deal with the courtship of the central female character by other ardent suitors, the eluding of traditional authority, revenge, and the relationship between love and death.

Yet who would say that the two plays *feel* alike? The differences are to do with the ways in which *'Tis Pity* plays variations upon *Romeo and Juliet*. And some of the variations are significant. Some variations will be mentioned later; for the moment, here are two.

- The roles of the 'guardian' figures – the Nurse and the Friar – are importantly different. Shakespeare's Nurse indulges in sexual wordplay, but Ford's Putana is openly (and outrageously?) coarse: *if a young wench feel the fit upon her, let her take anybody, father or brother, all is one* (II.i.45–46). Such crazy notions are what a guardian should protect her charge against. The worst that can be said of Shakespeare's Friar is that things go wrong with his scheming. Ford's Friar is not so compromised as Putana, yet he has limitations. Might he be too ready to persuade Annabella to enter a marriage that has little to be said for it but the hope of respectability?

- One of the achievements of Shakespeare's Romeo is that the presence of his friends helps to place him as a fashionable, affluent, enterprising and witty young man. Romeo belongs to the class of swaggerers that could be found in Italian cities or the streets of London. Giovanni has no such company. Throughout the play he is defined by his entrance in I.ii as a lonely, brooding man who *with such sad aspect/ Walks careless of himself* (139–140). He argues with the Friar, but with whom else does he talk for any length of time?

Activity

What do these parallels and differences with *Romeo and Juliet* tell us about Ford's play?

Discussion

Here are three interpretations of what Ford is doing with the *Romeo and Juliet* plot.

- David L. Frost takes the line that the parallels with *Romeo and Juliet* work emotionally to bring home the horror of what the audience is viewing. Writing about the bedroom scene (II.i) in which Giovanni harps on Annabella's loss of virginity, Frost says 'the horror is heightened by the similarities and terrible differences when compared with the arising of Shakespeare's lovers'. Two things are in favour of this view: first, it does justice to the way audiences regard Shakespeare as a benchmark, and second, it accords with what is almost universally felt about incest.

- The second possible view is that Ford is doing to Shakespeare's plot what Shakespeare himself seems to do to the conventions he uses in what we call his 'problem plays': *All's Well That Ends Well*, *Measure for Measure* and *Troilus and Cressida*. To take one example, comedies often have a character who controls the plotting. What happens in *Measure for Measure* is that things go wrong – very wrong – with what the plotter hopes for. Perhaps Ford is conducting another such experiment: what would *Romeo and Juliet* be like if the lovers were brother and sister? This might help to explain the divided sympathies of audiences and readers.

In spite of what they do, are Annabella and Giovanni close to us, and do we feel for them in the tempests of their passions?

- The third option is an extreme version of the second. Perhaps Ford is here subverting the themes and conventions of the dramatic tradition, which he inherited. Is he showing that the language of Petrarchan love, with its dwelling on the aloof, almost unattainable beloved and the ardent, sorrowing lover, is just a charade played out to win sexual favours? And is he showing that sexual desire can be so strong that it overwhelms all the courtesies of civilized behaviour? Certainly, Annabella's other suitors are, in various degrees, unattractive, and perhaps this prompts us to think that the whole of Parma society is without integrity.

The test of these ideas is the standard one: can performances of the play that follow these interpretations convince audiences? This is a question that we should bear in mind when looking at individual scenes and thinking about what the play as a whole adds up to.

Love

A play that owes a lot to *Romeo and Juliet* must show us something about love. What, then, is the picture of love that emerges from the action of *'Tis Pity She's a Whore*?

Perhaps the biggest difference between Shakespeare's and Ford's worlds is a moral one. *Romeo and Juliet* has characters driven by the passions – anger, jealousy, sexual desire – yet no one would want to say that any of them act out of *evil* motives. It is impossible to be so sure about this in *'Tis Pity*. Even if we leave aside the problem of Annabella and Giovanni, we still have to come to terms with Soranzo and Hippolita. In II.ii she accuses him of corrupting her, and he makes the counter-accusation that her behaviour was the cause of her husband's death. Neither denies their adulterous liaison. Ford's world is one in which love can breed corruption.

What is absent from the play is the moment when Giovanni awakes to the beauty and desirability of Annabella. We have no insight into the origin or nature of his passion. His love for Annabella is an inexplicable 'given'. When Romeo first appears, he too is preoccupied with thoughts of love, but he is woken from these by the sight of Juliet. The actor needs to show that Romeo is really discovering what it is to love. In the case of Giovanni, he is already in love. This makes him argumentative in the first scene and forlorn in the second, someone *Wrapped up in grief* and reduced to *some shadow of a man* (I.ii.143). Because we are denied that moment of glad realization, we see the strains and painful longings of love more than its wonder. The same is true of Annabella; she merely announces that she has long loved him (I.ii.249–251). The audience, therefore, can only judge as people have always judged incest, as 'a perversion of nature which... is defended by no one' (T.S. Eliot), and await the development of the action.

Audiences should not forget that although Giovanni's desire for Annabella is incestuous, his wooing of her is not. He attempts to court her as any ardent young man would. In this he is hardly different from Soranzo in III.ii. His praise of Annabella's beauty (I.ii.197–212) is detailed and utterly conventional. He resorts to all the standard comparisons made by love poets: her *forehead* (a conventional mark of beauty) exceeds Juno's; her *eyes* would give life to inanimate objects; her colouring is the ideal of white and red; her *lips* and *hands* would tempt saints, and she is more beautiful than anything *art* or *nature* could fashion. This might be judged embarrassing, though an actor should try to show that although the imagery is reach-me-down stuff, his feelings are real.

As so often in the play, Annabella's response to the experience of love is interestingly distinctive. Derek Roper (see Further Reading) makes the point that Annabella finds her voice when she confesses her love for Giovanni: 'she flowers into expressive speech for the first time'. And this is something that she is aware of. The tears she has shed have been *not so much for that I have loved, as that/ I durst not say I loved* (I.ii.255–256). Her eloquence is beyond dispute, and it raises an interesting problem. Should we resist the view that whatever moral objections there are, her incestuous love leads to lyrical self-fulfilment?

One of Ford's most interesting dramatic moments comes at the close of the 'wooing' scene when the brother and sister kneel and make vows. This should be viewed against the background of the ceremony of betrothal. When two people agreed to marry, they would promise themselves to each other before witnesses. Then the father of the woman would join their hands as the sign of the binding nature of their promises. The ceremony was not a marriage, but it prevented either of the pair from contracting a marriage with another person.

Giovanni regards what they have done as binding. Both promise not to *betray* the other, and he later regards Annabella's marriage as such a betrayal (V.v.8–9). But should we endorse his judgement? Their mutual promises do not make it a betrothal. There are no witnesses. Is Ford perhaps suggesting that there is something perverse about a private ritual, a ritual in which the only people who understand what is happening are the participants? But what of our feelings: are we moved by the innocence of the lovers? Is there a kind of charm in their devising of this ritual? Yet can we exclude the thought that this is all folly?

A betrothal ceremony as depicted in 1470; note the importance of witnesses

There is not very much joy in *'Tis Pity*. Although we know that Romeo and Juliet are 'star-cross'd lovers', the play only works if the delights of mutual love are acted out. Ford allows his lovers one scene of post-coital pleasure, but the exchange is brief and troubled, perhaps even tainted, by Giovanni's careless (or even callous) talk about loss of virginity and his fears for the future (II.i.1–34). There is also a disquieting contrast between his witty talk about her change in status from *sister* to *a name more gracious* and her confession to Putana: *what a paradise of joy/ Have I passed over!* (II.i.39–40). The scene is very different from the awakening of Romeo and Juliet (III.v).

Instead of the eloquence of new love or some probing of why characters love as they do, there is plenty of talk about sexual desire, particularly from Putana. She says a woman might *Commend a man for his qualities, but take a husband as he is a plain-sufficient, naked man* (I.ii.102–104). *Qualities* included natural gifts, achievements, social and economic status, and what might be called style. By contrast, it is clear what the plain-speaking Putana means by *a plain-sufficient, naked man*. It is worth asking whether Annabella is any better: are there *qualities* that lead Annabella to take Giovanni? See IV.iii.36–49.

Furthermore, Ford shows how the language of love, particularly the convention of making excessive claims, can lead people into confusion. When Hippolita angrily denounces the treachery of Soranzo, we can pick up in her words what the ardent Soranzo must have said to her in the linguistic intoxication of his desire:

> Didst thou not swear, whilst yet my husband lived,
> That thou wouldst wish no happiness on earth
> More than to call me wife?

> (II.ii.70–72)

He does not deny that this is what he said. It is the kind of thing a young man might say when he is searching for a way of expressing the intensity of his devotion. The rapture of desire leads characters to excessive claims they cannot live up to.

The imagery of love poetry can also turn sour. Giovanni uses the image of lordship when he says he does not *envy... the mightiest man alive*, because *in being king of thee* he counts himself *More great, than were I king of all the world* (II.i.18–20). This is youthfully exuberant and not unlike John Donne's triumphant assertion in his poem *The Sun Rising*: 'She is all states, and all princes, I'. Although Donne's image is one of mastery, we may catch in his rhythms and tone the sheer delight of possessing a beloved. But this is not always so in Giovanni. A later claim to mastery comes in Soranzo's wooing scene, when Giovanni appears on the upper balcony to witness his sister being courted by Soranzo. When Annabella says that *the fates* will dispose whom she loves, Giovanni, with the knowing power that comes from the sexual possession of his sister, says (exultingly?) *Of those I'm regent now* (III.ii.18). His position above Annabella and Soranzo clearly acts out the superior position he regards himself as occupying. He may gloat, but does he show any delight?

If we use the contemporary critical idea of multiple discourses – different attitudes and beliefs expressed in ways of talking – then it might be that Annabella knows the discourse of female frailty: women are weak creatures who cannot help sinning. Soranzo, when playing the part of the reasonable and understanding husband, says *'tis as common/ To err in frailty as to be a woman* (IV.iii.146–147). But it is clear from her subsequent behaviour that she does not submit to that discourse. Perhaps her apparent submission later in the scene is her way of coping with his rage.

Activity

Consider how male and female power work in IV.iii.1–76.

Discussion

It is a commonplace to say that the only power a woman had in the past was that of refusal. Once she was married, a woman (so the argument goes) was the possession of her lord and master – her husband. Judging by his actions and threats, Soranzo is acting as a dominant male, but Annabella refuses the role of the submissive wife. She is discovered to be pregnant (and was presumably discovered not to be a virgin on her wedding night) but does not accept the language of male authority.

She does not bother to counter Soranzo's accusations (if that is really what they are) that she has had sex with many men, but instead taunts him with hints of the masculine splendours of the man whose child she is bearing. This may remind us of the way that she reacted to his poetic ardour in III.ii with remarks that seem like jeering and parody (13–36). Here again, Annabella controls the dialogue. To his frenzied demand that she tell him who the father is, she replies with the teasing assurance of one who knows she is in control: *We are not come to that* (IV.iii.43). She even says of her marriage: *I scarce dream yet of that* (49). Perhaps what is most impressive is her refusal to be intimidated. The exasperated Soranzo asks: *Dost thou not tremble yet?* (68).

Suitors, courtship and marriage

A good deal of the dramatic action of the play is taken up with courtship, or wooing. Of the 15 main characters, seven either court or are courted, and others encourage or control them. Soranzo, who makes high claims for the intensity of his love, accepts the formal conventions of wooing: a man makes his courtship public by approaching the father, negotiating a financial settlement, and only then seeking an interview with the beloved. It is part of the convention that the beloved is praised in elevated terms. Courtship, therefore, can be studied in stages.

The second scene opens with fighting. This may remind us of *Romeo and Juliet*. The difference, however, is important: in Shakespeare the dispute is between dynastic families, while in Ford it is a feud about love which, though essentially domestic, is fierce and violent. Florio, the father, puts a stop to the brawling and endeavours to make peace with Soranzo. This brings out an important feature of the courtship plot: he makes it clear that he wants Annabella to marry Soranzo. He expresses surprise at

Soranzo's impetuous behaviour, particularly when Soranzo must know that he is the favoured suitor: *this is strange to me,/ Why you should storm, having my word engaged* (I.ii.57–58). *Engaged* is a strong word: it means to pledge one's word or make a binding promise.

The next piece of stage business is a discussion of the various merits of the three suitors: Grimaldi, Bergetto and Soranzo. After the fight, Annabella and Putana *Enter above* (on the balcony) and see, but probably do not hear, Florio restoring order. When those on the main stage exit, the women see Bergetto's posturings. The stage direction *Walks affectedly* turns the scene into something of a parade, which concludes with the entrance of Giovanni. *'Tis Pity She's a Whore*, we should remember, is a play that foregrounds public display (see page 9).

The 'parade of suitors' may owe something to another Shakespeare play: *Troilus and Cressida*. This is set in Troy during the Trojan War. Like *'Tis Pity*, it opens with a young man, Troilus, opening his heart to Pandarus, an older man. The second scene shows Pandarus visiting Cressida, his niece, and gossiping about the ladies and heroes of Troy. The retreat is sounded to indicate that hostilities have ceased, and Pandarus and Cressida watch the soldiers returning from 'an excellent place', probably the balcony. Pandarus comments on them all and praises several, including the legendary figures of Aeneas and Hector. His highest praise, however, is reserved for Troilus. Cressida is wittily non-commital.

The parallels with *'Tis Pity* are evident: fighting, public viewing, discussing the merits of notable men, and an older character persuading a young girl to choose a suitor. The important difference is the responses of the two young women. Whereas the canny Cressida declares her love in soliloquy and decides to resist Troilus on the admirably worldly ground that 'Men prized the thing ungained more than it is' (I.ii.275), Ford's Annabella moves quickly. She descends to Giovanni, he courts her, she yields and they exit to consummate their desires.

Cressida, by contrast, does not comply until III.ii. The rapidity of Ford's plot development raises awkward questions. Is Ford unable to present characters making up their minds? The decision Annabella takes is far more serious than Cressida's, and yet where is her struggle? It is strange that Ford avoids the suspense of expectation that often gives life to drama.

The business of marrying off Annabella makes Florio an important character. In his first speech (I.ii.25–30) he presents himself as a private man who, the audience may infer, has been unreasonably bothered by suitors – in particular, Grimaldi. His concern for public order and his daughter's future happiness combine in a clear statement that he does not want the courtship of his daughter to *cause the spilling of one drop of blood* (I.ii.66). In the very next scene he makes a liberal declaration to Donado:

> As for worldly fortune,
> I am, I thank my stars, blessed with enough.
> My care is how to match her to her liking;
> I would not have her marry wealth, but love.

> (I.iii.8–11)

This strikes all the right notes. After remarks about his wealth, he does not say, as might have been expected, that because he is wealthy he has hopes of marrying her into the aristocracy. His *care* (in the sense of care for) is that she may be matched *to her liking* and that she should not marry *wealth, but love*. All those things that make for a standard plot – whether one should marry for love or money, the freedom of a daughter to marry for love, the tensions in a family over marriage partners – are excluded.

Is there reason to doubt his hope that Annabella will marry for love? Derek Roper (see Further Reading) trenchantly makes the point that 'Florio's genial statement' about wanting Annabella to marry for love 'gives a pleasant idea of what a father might be, and (as we already know) Florio is not'. So what is to be made of his conversation with Donado? From what he has said to Soranzo (I.ii.57–60), he surely cannot mean it when he says *if she like your nephew, let him have her* (I.iii.12). And perhaps his duplicity shows. As he has no doubt received several proposals of marriage for his rich and beautiful daughter, the actor might introduce a note of irritation in his opening line: *you have said enough* (I.iii.1).

So playing Florio is not easy. He adjusts what he says from suitor to suitor. Perhaps he can be played as the wily merchant who wants the best deal. Hippolita draws attention to his profession when she disdainfully refers to Annabella as *Madam Merchant* (II.ii.49). But to think of him as a man trying to strike a good deal does not end the matter. Good deal for whom? Might he be sincere when he says that if Annabella likes Bergetto, she is free to marry him? And although he makes it clear that he favours Soranzo, he never actually orders her to marry him. His speech at the opening of III.ii can be played as an expression of his hope rather than a strong direction that she should accept Soranzo.

Any production has to decide whether to play the final suitor, Bergetto, as the other characters, in particular his uncle, see him. Is he to be presented merely as a figure of fun? He certainly is the occasion for laughter, but should we be quite sure that it is directed against him? For instance, his role as the wooer of Annabella might be played as exposing the artificiality of the conventions of courtship. More positively, he does seem to enjoy being a young man seeing city life, and when he meets Philotis he is delighted with her and relishes the sexual feelings she arouses. Her character is only lightly sketched, but from what we see she is sensible and practical. Would she have accepted Bergetto if he were an idiot rather than an innocent? And she delights in love. Upon kissing her, Bergetto gasps with pleasure – *Aha, Poggio!* – and she responds with a promise of further intimacies: *You shall have enough, sweetheart* (III.v.43). In a play where so much love feels sour, it is good to know that the young find pleasure in kissing.

Activity

What does Soranzo's wooing scene (III.ii) reveal about the treatment of courtship?

Discussion

The consummation of Giovanni's incestuous desires might cast an uncomfortable irony on Soranzo's courtship of Annabella. In III.ii the appearance of Giovanni on the balcony makes the irony visible. When Soranzo says he is drawn to her not by *hope of what you have, but what you are* (III.ii.30), Giovanni's presence forcefully reminds us that one important thing he does expect her to have – her virginity – is no longer a part of what she is. It is interesting to ask what the effect of this is. Might Giovanni's superior sneers make us feel sorry for Soranzo? This is something we do not usually feel in the play, and may therefore be an indication that Ford's presentation of character and theme is sensitive and subtle.

Revenge

When wooing fails, several characters become revengers. Giovanni, Grimaldi, Hippolita, Richardetto and Soranzo all seek revenge because of thwarted love. Only Bergetto and Philotis have nothing to revenge. Vasques has no personal wrongs to prompt him, but he becomes a kind of revenger because he acts on behalf of his master, and pretends to do so for Hippolita.

Revenge is one of the impulses that drives the plot. Most of the revengeful contriving is against Soranzo. Grimaldi plots against him, and the cuckolded Richardetto assists. Hippolita, whom Soranzo has abandoned, recruits Vasques in order to revenge herself on his master. Giovanni seeks revenge because he has lost Annabella to him, and part of that revenge is the killing of his sister. As he stabs her, he says: *Revenge is mine* (V.v.86).

Soranzo, the object of several characters' revenge, becomes a revenger himself. When he learns that Giovanni is the father of Annabella's child, he seeks revenge against both brother and sister. He says to Vasques: *all my blood/ Is fired in swift revenge* (IV.iii.151–152), and the *watch-word* (V.iv.15) Vasques gives the Banditti turns out to be *Vengeance* (V.vi.81). In his death, Soranzo is consoled with the knowledge that (as he sees it) he is revenged: *well pleased that I have lived/ To see my wrongs revenged* (V.vi.91–92). To put it bluntly, there would be little action in the play were it not for the impulse to exact revenge.

Activity

Does Ford do any more with revenge than use it to drive the plot?

Discussion

There are several answers.

Revenge was popular in Renaissance drama. Typically, it involved important state matters, and the revenger was someone who, though highly placed, could not right wrongs by recourse to law. Hamlet, for instance, is the son of the late king, but because his only evidence is what his father's ghost has disclosed to him, there is no way of bringing the murderer (if that is what the present king is) to justice. Ford, however, is not writing that kind of play. *'Tis Pity* is not concerned with high politics. What prompts revenge is love, not injustice. In that it is more like *Othello*. Othello seeks revenge because he believes his wife has betrayed him. This is the case with both Soranzo and Richardetto. Hippolita has been betrayed by Soranzo, though he is not her husband. But it does not apply to Grimaldi (see below).

What might make Ford distinctive is his presentation of Giovanni. Ford shows that in Giovanni's mind, his right to Annabella is greater than Soranzo's. His revenge is a consequence of his incest. He has made Annabella his, so to kill her is a proper response to Soranzo. Ford raises the question of whether Giovanni has a right to say, no doubt with the triumph of a great achievement, *Revenge is mine* (V.v.86).

Ford also shows a disturbing aspect of characters stirred by the passions of love: the triviality of the provocation, and the readiness to seek revenge. Grimaldi says:

> I, to be revenged,
> (For that I could not win him else to fight)
> Have thought by way of ambush to have killed him.

(III.ix.45–47)

Soranzo has only *wronged* him by refusing to engage in a duel over Annabella and by employing Vasques as a protector, yet Grimaldi offers this, in the presence of the Cardinal, as his reason for seeking revenge. Something of the same unreasonable excess is found in Hippolita, who has no real claim upon Soranzo, yet not only seeks to kill him but does so by virtually offering herself to Vasques. Morally speaking, all revenge is excessive. Ford also brings out that it is bizarre.

It is part of the depth of Ford's understanding that he shows that the impulse to revenge must be strenuously maintained. Vasques has to keep Soranzo fixed on the wrongs he has suffered in case his master (we remember that he is a young man) should fail in his resolution. Vasques, not Soranzo, harps upon cuckolding and insists that Soranzo does not trouble himself with *other business than your own resolution* (V.ii.15–16). There is an implied cost in this; Soranzo will have to close his mind to any tender feelings or moral scruples. Vasques tells him not to allow *pity* to *betray* him but to *think upon incest and cuckoldry* (V.ii.23–24). Sounding not unlike a child who is trying hard to show that he will behave as required, Soranzo closes the scene with a frighteningly glib couplet: *Revenge is all the ambition I aspire;/ To that I'll climb or fall: my blood's on fire* (25–26).

Vasques continues to brace Soranzo for his terrible act by implying that revenge is a sort of right. He reminds Soranzo of what he has suffered: *Call to your remembrance your disgraces, your loss of honour*, and then says Soranzo should *right those wrongs in vengeance which you may truly call your own* (V.iv.23–27). In marrying Annabella, he has made her his own, but now she has, as he sees it, betrayed him, what he can now call his own are his feelings of being wronged.

Almost inevitably, Ford sees the irony in revenge. (Does incest necessarily make plots ironic?) The marriage feast begins with Soranzo saying that he knows he has been the object of revengeful contriving, but that *The hand of goodness/ Hath been a shield for me against my death* (IV.i.7–8). The irony is immediate: if he knew the truth about Annabella, he would not talk about the generosity of the *hand of goodness*. Further ironies are present if we recall an earlier scene in which *hand* occurred. Grimaldi, waiting in the dark to stab Soranzo with a poisoned blade, said *now guide my hand, some angry Justice* (III.vii.6). The irony is enforced by Hippolita: *lend's your hand... take this hand from me* (IV.i.46, 52). Hippolita is parodying marriage and also intends that Soranzo will die by her hand. Soranzo is again the victim of irony when, having discovered Annabella's pregnancy, he exits saying: *Delay in vengeance gives a heavier blow* (IV.iii.165). The blow is a heavy one, for he himself is to become a victim of *vengeance*.

There is a logic to revenge. The revenger acts in the painful knowledge that wrong has been done, and as there is no judicial way in which the perpetrator can be punished, the revenger must take responsibility. But as to exact revenge is also to break the moral law, the revenger must die. Sometimes revengers die in the act and sometimes, as at the end of *The Revenger's Tragedy*, they effectively ask to be executed. In *'Tis Pity*, revengers suffer various fates. Hippolita dies in the course of her revenge, but only because Vasques, who has something of the revenger about him, deceives her. Of the other revengers, two die. Soranzo's death has something in common with Hippolita's in that both were bent on revenge but encounter their ends in ways they did not expect. Giovanni is lured to the feast and there, as planned, he is cut down by the Banditti, but only after he has already killed Annabella and Soranzo. Killing his sister might look more like jealous cruelty than revenge, but once he has seen Soranzo die Giovanni is content, even ecstatic, in his own death because he has achieved his goal.

Two revengers do not fit the conventional pattern: Grimaldi and Richardetto. Grimaldi is urged to revenge himself on Soranzo by Richardetto, but when their plot misfires, he seeks sanctuary in the Cardinal's palace and is later sent to Rome. Richardetto is very interesting, in part because he is a revenger who repents. He is the instrument of the death of the man who was due to marry his niece; but after the ghastly spectacle of his wife's death, he leaves matters to take their own course. He survives with his secret: his part in Bergetto's death.

Audiences very often find revenge difficult to cope with. In particular, they are inclined to recoil from scenes in which revenge is discussed and plotted. There is something horrible about planning the death of another person in clinical detail. Ford seems to know this, so when he wants to temper the effect of plotting revenge he can make a revenger more sensitive than the audience expects. The result is an unexpected moral complexity. This is how he treats Richardetto. Because the intelligent Philotis (who has noticed that Annabella does not favour Soranzo or any suitor) has already seen that her uncle is planning revenge, he asks her to leave before his plan is described. This means that she would not be guilty if the matter came to court. Her *ignorance* will *plead for* her (II.iii.16).

One feature of revenge plots is the intensification of mood and atmosphere as the play moves towards its close. This intensification is achieved by the strengthening of emotions, the clarifying of intellectual issues, and by the impression that the pace is increasing. This sense of things moving ever more quickly to a bloody conclusion is evident in many plays of the English Renaissance. It is there in the works of Middleton, Tourneur and Webster. Above all, it is found in Shakespeare's *Hamlet*.

Ford's ending features the revenge plots of Giovanni and Soranzo. Vasques, Soranzo's agent and director of revenge, reminds his master that *time lost cannot be recalled* (V.ii.17). Interestingly, the character who voices most clearly the play's increasing pace towards its ghastly winding-up is one who is no longer a player in the action – Annabella. She is confined to her room and only overheard by the Friar. The visit of Giovanni is not of her designing. Yet in her poetry she expresses the unnerving sense that events are gathering to their terrible denouement. Alone on her balcony, she laments:

> Thou precious Time, that swiftly rid'st in post
> Over the world, to finish up the race
> Of my last fate; here stay thy restless course,
> And bear to ages that are yet unborn
> A wretched woeful woman's tragedy.

(V.i.4–8)

Like Faustus in the final scene of Marlowe's *Dr Faustus*, Annabella senses the swift passage of events and wants to halt them – *here stay thy restless course*. But unlike Faustus she recognizes that there can be no *stay*, so instead she pleads that the gallop of time will act for her. Time the messenger (*post*) will carry into the future the tale of her tragedy. It is a consciously theatrical moment. A character in a play talks to the audience about her own *woeful woman's tragedy*, and those viewing the action might realize that they, as the theatre of the future, are seeing now those things that she is hoping time will *bear to ages that are yet unborn*.

Activity

Does Ford's presentation of revenge add up to a consistent view of its nature?

Discussion

The case for thinking that Ford has a consistent view of revenge is that he sees it as a consequence of thwarted love. The characters are passionate and purposeful. What chiefly drives them is love (or sexual longing) for another, and this is of such force that when the object of love is unattainable it takes the form of a resentful violence against whoever stands in the way. This is the case of Grimaldi. With other characters, however, it is not failure to attain but the jealousy of a man who fears losing his beloved. In those cases, the revenge is against the one who has cuckolded him.

Against this is the view that Ford treats revenge as a device to create a number of exciting pieces of stage action. Is Grimaldi's revenge a convenient way of clearing up the Bergetto plot?

Can these two views be reconciled?

Tears and oaths

Not every character seeks revenge. At least one seeks repentance and its expression, tears. In this the Friar is a crucial figure. He has been Giovanni's confessor and becomes Annabella's. He witnesses one of the most important differences between the two: Giovanni never acknowledges his failings, whereas Annabella repents. In the scene of her confession, the Friar makes much of her tears: *But weep, weep on,/ These tears may do you good; weep faster yet* (III.vi.4–5).

Tears were an important part of the religion of the seventeenth century, particularly in its baroque aspect (see page 9). There were books of devotion that included meditations on the tears of characters in the Bible. Poets such as John Donne, George Herbert, Robert Southwell and Richard Crashaw wrote of tears as signs of remorse and repentance. Crashaw's *The Weeper*, a poem of 186 lines about St Mary Magdalen, is possibly close in time to Ford's play, being dated 1634 (see page 9).

There are tears in the first scene of the play. Giovanni says to the Friar: *in your eyes I see the change/ Of pity and compassion* (I.i.38–39).

The actor playing the Friar could wipe his eyes to indicate that he is indeed weeping. Here Ford handles his characters with considerable resourcefulness. Giovanni immediately interprets tears as an indication that the Friar is weakening and, in pity, will sanction incest. What Giovanni does not realize is that the Friar's tears may well be tears of pity, but that the pity is for Giovanni's lost soul. Do we see that it is Giovanni who ought to be weeping tears of repentance?

The Friar speaks of tears in what might be called the standard devotional sense. Tears are evidence of sorrow for sins and the desire to repent by turning away from folly and sin: *wash every word thou utter'st/ In tears (and if't be possible) of blood* (I.i.72–73). The reference to blood is part of the elaborate code of tears in seventeenth-century literature. Tears of deep remorse were called 'tears of blood'.

It is against that understanding of tears that Annabella's tears should be viewed. Audiences today should be careful not to underrate the importance of tears and the significance in the plot of Annabella's repentance. And even if it is hard to look at Annabella in terms of a code of seventeenth-century spirituality, it might still be found moving as a courageous expression of her self-knowledge.

If Annabella is right to repent, it does not follow that she is the character who embodies the standards by which all the other characters are to be judged. The play does not work like that. All the characters have significant moral failings. The point is that when the chief moral matter is incest, it is not necessary to have a character who embodies virtue. As most people do not engage in incest, the moral standard is not in the play but in the audience. And what goes for incest also goes for the other moral matters – truthfulness, fidelity, resisting revenge, the proper exercise of power. As no character fully embodies these, it is we who have to do the judging.

One of the judgements an audience might make is that characters exhibit loyalty. The late medieval period valued the bonds between subjects and their lords. A man would swear loyalty to the local lord, a vow that brought certain duties – legal, social and military. The public swearing of an oath of loyalty was the expression and the guarantee that society worked through a complex web of obligations. The importance of loyalty and the oaths that cemented it is central to *'Tis Pity*. Characters take oaths seriously, otherwise Hippolita could not accuse Soranzo of breaking a promise to marry her (II.ii.69–73).

Vasques is relevant here. He plays a number of roles: the reasonable man, the low schemer, and the sympathetic friend. He adopts these roles to exert control. The audience sees him manipulate Hippolita and his youthful master. One of his most deft manipulations is his persuasion of Putana to disclose who is the father of Annabella's child (IV.iii.178–236). He has planned it carefully; the Banditti are waiting for a summons.

In addition to his role-playing and scheming, he is something of a moralistic malcontent. The malcontent was a familiar figure in English Renaissance drama. (John Marston wrote a play called *The Malcontent*, published in 1604.) The malcontent is something of an outsider who broods on the evils of the times. In his soliloquy at IV.iii.166–177, Vasques disapprovingly observes the sexual dishonesty in the people around him.

But there is more to Vasques than a set of roles. There is a motive for what he does; he is the loyal servant of a master whom he thinks has been wronged. At the close of the play, Vasques says this in justification of what he has done: *I have paid the duty to the son which I have vowed to the father* (V.vi.115–116). We might wonder whether this is just another role. Alternatively, is there a good reason (or any reason) for not believing his words to the dead Soranzo: *my ever dearest lord and master* (V.vi.96)? His conspicuous devotion to Soranzo is recognized by the Cardinal, who acknowledges that *what thou didst was done/ Not for thyself* (V.vi.145–146). Yet loyalty is a questionable virtue. We should ask: loyalty to whom? And there might be consequences. Sparing Vasques the death sentence might sow seeds of corrosive revenge, which would blight future generations.

Activity

How should the loyalty of the servants and 'guardian' figures be judged?

Discussion

Putana hardly merits a mention. She is concerned to make money out of suitors to Annabella and encourages incest. The two characters who might be interestingly compared are Vasques and the Friar. Both serve, advise and plot. A major difference is that Vasques serves his master to the end, whereas the Friar abandons Giovanni before the terrible denouement. But Vasques appears to be willing to do absolutely anything for Soranzo. Furthermore, it is hardly a mark of moral worth to be spared by the Cardinal. The Friar does make moral compromises, but his sincerity is unquestionable and his pastoral concern extends far beyond Giovanni.

The 'guardian' character it is difficult to fault is Poggio: he enjoys the company of Bergetto, protects and advises him, and his grief is real.

Motivations and fate

It is the immediacy of drama that sometimes raises the question of why characters act as they do, although the kind of answers we try to give varies from play to play and era to era. Ford, like other Renaissance dramatists, presents characters who speak of being controlled by a superintending power. This power is sometimes called Fate, and at other times Destiny. Some characters see the stars as controlling human actions. The most famous statement of this view comes from the Chorus in *Romeo and Juliet*, who speaks of 'star-cross'd lovers' (Prologue 6). One character in Webster's *The Duchess of Malfi* imagines the stars controlling people with the apparently random indifference of tennis balls struck off the walls of an enclosed court: 'We are merely the stars' tennis-balls, struck and bandied/ Which way please them' (V.iv.53–54).

As plays are not works of philosophy, there is little point in trying to distinguish between fate, destiny or the stars. What matters is not which superintending agency is at work but what characters mean when they speak of a control exercised by an agent beyond them. In this way, Renaissance playwrights explored the puzzling matter of human freedom: to what extent are we the authors of our own actions, or is what we do the work of other and greater powers?

There is much talk of fate in *'Tis Pity She's a Whore*. One of the characters who uses the word on significant occasions is Giovanni. This should not surprise us. One of the dramatic functions of Giovanni is to voice the themes of the play. He provides the argument, and not just the impetus, of the incest plot, and later we will see that the claim that *'Tis Pity* is a tragedy depends very largely upon Giovanni's interpretation of his own behaviour (see page 238). How, then, does Giovanni speak of fate?

At the end of the first scene, Giovanni sets out stark alternatives: *All this I'll do, to free me from the rod/ Of vengeance; else I'll swear, my fate's my god* (I.i.83–84).

The point of this looks to be that he will embrace the life of repentance urged on him by the Friar in order to escape the avenging *rod* of God's wrath. The *else* implies that if this fails, he will have to accept that he has no control over his desires and that it is his *fate* to follow them rather than the laws of God.

In his soliloquy in the second scene, Giovanni reveals that in spite of *What wit or art/ Could counsel* he is *still the same* (I.ii.160–163). He puts his case to himself: *'tis not I know,/ My lust, but 'tis my fate that leads me on* (164–165). As characters in soliloquies rarely tell lies, we must assume that, at least in his own mind, Giovanni thinks that some power – *fate* – is controlling him.

When he encounters Annabella, his language is 'fatalistic':

> I have spent
> Many a silent night in sighs and groans,
> Ran over all my thoughts, despised my fate,
> Reasoned against the reasons of my love,
> Done all that smoothed-cheek Virtue could advise,
> But found all bootless; 'tis my destiny
> That you must either love, or I must die.

(I.ii.228–234)

What he says is consistent with the two speeches quoted above. This is not the heightened language of seduction; Giovanni means it. He might have tried to defy (*despised*) his *fate* and *Reasoned* (this presumably refers to moral reasoning), but he has come to see that his *destiny* is either the love of his sister or his death. What is undeniable is that what he calls his *destiny* drives the plot. Once he has committed incest, the pattern of events unfolds.

It might be accepted that Giovanni believes what he says. But is he right? Should we accept Giovanni's account of himself, that he is subject to a force beyond his control? Audiences are not obliged to judge matters in the same terms as characters. It is also dangerous to confuse what a character thinks with what the playwright believes. Occasionally, characters appear to be speaking on behalf of the playwright, but in nearly all cases the point of drama is that characters speak for themselves. It was not Shakespeare who said 'To be or not to be', but a character called Hamlet.

Activity

Is Giovanni consistent in his apparent insistence that he is driven to his *destiny* by *fate*?

Discussion

Giovanni does not think like this throughout the play.

At the end of the play he talks of wilful action. When Giovanni kills his sister, his language indicates a deliberate decision: *Thus die, and die by me, and by my hand* (V.v.85). Giovanni's preoccupation with himself – with his thoughts and feelings – is one of the ugliest things of the play, but he could not be condemned for egocentricity if he were not a free agent choosing his abominable actions. His emphasis on *me* and *my* is morally offensive – but only if these words are true. Killing his sister is his action. He believes this in the last scene of the play:

> Fate, or all the powers
> That guide the motions of immortal souls,
> Could not prevent me.

(V.vi.13–15)

This moment should be viewed in the intellectual terms that have shaped Giovanni's speech. He has struggled to make sense of his own feelings and at times has felt he could resist the forces of nature. Here, however, he presents himself in heroic and even glamorous terms as a lone individual who has striven to be the sole author of his own actions. *Fate* is something over which he has triumphed.

Giovanni is not the only character who talks of *fate*. Hippolita, for instance, indicates that what drives her is passion. When she talks about her husband, she says that *The devil in my blood… Caused me to counsel him to undertake/ A voyage to Leghorn*

234

(II.ii.74–76). Hippolita, in thinking back on her actions, sees that she was not in control but driven by evil and irrational forces: *The devil in my blood. Blood* can mean a number of things – including murder, and family bonds – but here it looks like a blend of lust and spite. The crucial point is its location – *in* her *blood*. Hippolita sees that what drives her is not in the stars, but in herself.

Fate sometimes means what will happen. There is a moment when Annabella seems to call a curse down on herself. When Soranzo angrily questions her about the father of the child she is carrying, she defiantly replies that he will never know. She follows this up with: *Never; if you do, let me be cursed* (IV.iii.52). We need not take this to mean that she believes some superintending power will blight her if she discloses the name of the father. Her words may simply be a rhetorical flourish or a recognition that if the truth were to be learned, the consequences for her would be catastrophic.

Seeing the inevitable consequences of actions can give an ironical edge to language about the future. A character may presume there will be one outcome, but events might turn out otherwise and expose the presumption of the speaker. Thus, in the light of the plot movement, Hippolita's words that Soranzo *contemns his fate* (II.ii.103) apply not only to him but to herself.

Characters can talk about an unavoidable future but not necessarily commit themselves to a belief in fate. In the scene in which the Friar tries to cope with Giovanni's actual rather than intended incest, he warns the young man: *Thou art a man remarked to taste a mischief./ Look for't; though it come late, it will come sure* (II.v.10–11). The repeated *it* (the coming but unspecified *mischief*) makes his words menacing, and the falling cadence at the close enacts the sense of some inescapable nemesis. But is that exactly what the Friar means? Certainly, the language is of some external agent working for Giovanni's downfall but, given his religious calling, this agent might well be interpreted as the moral law or the divine lawgiver.

Perhaps the Friar is typical of the play. He uses the language of inevitability, but without being committed to the idea of a fate. The language of fate might be a metaphor for the way things work out.

And so we are back with Giovanni. Is the language of fate a convenient image for his compulsions and desires? They seem so strong that he feels as if they are ordained. Moreover, talk of fate is in keeping with his references to classical gods. His comments at the end of the play (see the Activity above) can be understood as Giovanni deciding to use the term metaphorically. When his father asks whether he is himself, Giovanni's reply affirms that killing his sister is what he has lived for: *Yes, father, and that times to come may know/ How as my fate I honoured my revenge* (V.vi.36–37). Here, *fate* is close to a chosen path, an end or goal that it is his life's fulfilment to achieve.

It should be added that although Giovanni voices many of the play's themes, it is Annabella who talks with the greatest clarity. When she laments the mutual harm she and Giovanni have done, she says: *Would thou hadst been less subject to those stars/ That luckless reigned at my nativity!* (V.i.19–20).

The qualification *less subject* shows how difficult it is to be certain about human actions. Even if we feel that there is some superintending agent that controls them, can we be sure that the control is absolute, and that there is no scope for human choice? Perhaps, as on other occasions, we feel that Annabella comes nearer to the truth of things.

But we still have to ask whether she speaks for Ford. This is not impossible, because most of the characters show that they struggle against mighty forces (whatever those forces are), but not that they are entirely controlled. Or perhaps Ford is simply showing that the matter of human freedom in a world in which so much constrains people is not something that can easily be understood. It may be that the furthest he goes is to show that this is a vital matter that puzzles and will continue to puzzle people.

Activity

What does the Friar's speech in V.iii.64–71 reveal about the place of fate in the play?

Discussion

The language is fatalistic. He speaks of seeing *thy fate* drawing to *an end* and uses the traditional language of fate bringing about the tragedy of Giovanni's *fall*. But *The wildness of thy fate draws to an end* (65) indicates that this is something that pertains to Giovanni alone. The *wildness* could be a comment on Giovanni's life. It may be significant that the Friar talks of *a bad, fearful end* (66). Does the indefinite article – *a* – indicate that Giovanni has brought his *end* on himself rather than it being what some superintending fate has preordained?

This portrait of the friar and mathematician Luca Pacioli with an unknown young man was painted in 1495–1500, and is attributed to Jacopo de' Barbari

The significance of the action

What matters in *'Tis Pity She's a Whore*? This section offers some tentative answers to this question.

Tragedy

Ford wrote tragedy when the genre was losing its appeal. Twenty to thirty years before, Middleton, Shakespeare, Tourneur and Webster had created a distinctly English kind of tragedy. Ford turned to it when the fashion was for comedy or tragic-comedy. And, like Shakespeare, his tragedy is varied. *Hamlet* is different from *Othello*, and *'Tis Pity She's a Whore* has a different tone from *The Broken Heart*. In one sense, *'Tis Pity* has more in common with earlier works than the stately and almost serene *The Broken Heart*, and in Giovanni, Ford has created a figure that has many of the characteristics of the tragic hero. Yet Giovanni is not a tired conventional figure drawn from the stock of tragic conventions. What Ford manages to do is bring out just how difficult for audiences the tragic figure can be.

Activity

In the early parts of the play, does Giovanni appear to be a tragic figure?

Discussion

Giovanni has many of the qualities associated with a tragic hero. In the first scene he is described by the Friar in fulsome terms: *A wonder of thine age*, distinguished for his *government, behaviour, learning, speech,/ Sweetness*. He has *all that could make up a man!* (I.i.49–52). The significance of this is that from the very start he is marked out as the kind of character who, either through some personal whim or the unfortunate circumstances of life, comes to grief.

Tragic characters are often morally ambiguous. Many audiences cannot forget the way Hamlet treats Ophelia, and yet most are drawn to him. A feature of critical writing about *'Tis Pity* is the claim that audiences respond more sympathetically to Giovanni than the other characters – Florio, the Friar, Soranzo and many others. Nor is this a feature of recent and more consciously 'liberated' writing about the play. Back in 1933, G.B. Harrison even claimed that what we see in the play are the feelings of the playwright: 'Ford's sympathies are clearly with the defiant, not the repentant, sinner' (*Webster and Ford: Selected Plays*, Everyman's Library, 1933).

But those who want to admire Giovanni have to reckon with his lies. In the first scene the Friar tells him that he may love, but does not say he may commit incest. In the second scene, Giovanni's ardent wooing of Annabella includes what he claims is the permission of the Church: *I have asked counsel of the holy Church,/ Who tells me I may love you* (I.ii.246–247). As her own profession of love immediately follows, Giovanni's words can be played as the final persuader. Is he deceiving her or, perhaps even more corruptly, has his desire so distorted his own language that he imagines the Friar has sanctioned incest? Only ten lines later, Giovanni shows he is aware of the difference between reality and dreaming. When Annabella confesses her love for him, he says: *Let not this music be a dream* (I.ii.257). In the joys of requited love, such language is understandable, but we might ask whether his belief that the Church permits incest is also a *dream*, a piece of self-deluding fantasy.

Giovanni arouses sympathy because his youthful passion is felt to be preferable to the cynical calculations and compromises of the older generation. But this sympathy is in part a response to Giovanni's own self-approving judgements. A tragic hero often does what the Greeks and Romans said was against natural justice: he becomes his own judge. This is present in the first scene when the Friar holds out the hope that Giovanni will listen to his *counsel* (68), and Giovanni replies *As a voice of life*. What he seems to be saying is that if the Friar sanctions Giovanni's incestuous desires, then this will lead to *life*. Perhaps those who want to defend Giovanni are taken in by his strident affirmation that his desires are life-enhancing, and, of course, the dramatic irony of the play works to undermine Giovanni's pride. Incest does lead to life – the life of the unborn child Giovanni kills when, in jealous pride, he murders his sister.

Being one's own judge arouses tragic fear and even terror when the act is monstrous. Othello does not just believe his wife is unfaithful, he thinks it is right to kill her. Giovanni kills Annabella. His reason is that she is *a faithless sister* (V.v.9). The only meaning this can have is that she has broken the vows they made when they first declared their love (I.ii.258–264). He thinks that in promising themselves to each other they are as morally bound as any married couple. He does not see what Soranzo sees about his vows to Hippolita:

> The vows I made, if you remember well,
> Were wicked and unlawful; 'twere more sin
> To keep them than to break them.

(II.ii.86–88)

Although Soranzo's motives are dubious (he just wants to be rid of Hippolita), the argument is worth taking seriously. No one should promise to do what is wrong, and once such a promise has been made, fulfilling it would not make the deed a good one.

Giovanni has no idea that an immoral promise should not be kept. He therefore stands very firmly in the traditions of tragedy in that he does what is forbidden. Peter Coveney expresses this idea with brevity and force: 'the tragic hero is always wrong' (*The Image of Childhood*, Rockliff, 1957). Tragic figures need to be outstanding and many are awesome, but what makes them tragic is their firm commitment to doing what is wrong. Ford shows that deliberately doing wrong is to go against nature. Contrary to Giovanni's argument, nature does not sanction sexual relationships between siblings. Furthermore, nature is independent of the human will. It is in the nature of sex that children are conceived. Giovanni's killing of his child is a terrible act because it expresses his relentless ego's desire to control the very processes that sustain all life.

In Giovanni we see more than wrongdoing. Like many tragic figures, Giovanni embraces his task with gusto and acts it out with pride. He may, in the manner of an executioner, have begged forgiveness from his sister, but he kills her with exultant triumph – *Revenge is mine; honour doth love command* (V.v.86). The stress surely falls on *mine*. At her death, his pride has a weird kind of joy in *this act/ Which most I glory in* (V.v.90–91). Glory is one of our weightiest words; it denotes splendour, lustre and wonder. He has no hesitation in using it of killing his sister.

Tragedy, like revenge (see page 226), has its own logic. The plot is one that leads inevitably to catastrophe. And catastrophe has two senses: the popular meaning of 'disaster', and the more technical one of the ending in which the tragic hero dies. Sometimes the shape of the tragic plot is signalled to the audience through terms that anticipate the ending. And quite often, anticipation creates irony. In the scene in which Florio performs the betrothal ceremony for Annabella and Soranzo, the word *resolved* is used twice within five lines. Florio asks Annabella *are you resolved?* (III.vi.49), and the Friar says their union is *Timely resolved* (III.vi.53). The word means both to answer a question and sort out a problem. Is it too ingenious to see its use as anticipating the resolution – the sorting out – of the plot? The end, though a resolution, is one that neither Florio nor the Friar expect or want. The reason for this is that they have left Giovanni out of consideration. He wants a resolution that is bloody and revengeful.

The tragic hero is often offensively self-centred. King Lear, for instance, is chiefly concerned with his status. Giovanni's preoccupation with himself and his power is distastefully evident when he views Soranzo wooing his sister. Rather than praising her fortitude and courage, he is only concerned with his own position in her affections: *I'm confirmed* (III.ii.39). Perhaps this is so throughout the play; he is egocentrically preoccupied with his feelings and what he believes are his rights. One form that egocentricity takes in tragedy is bravado – the deliberate and pleasurable playing out of one's role in order to impress onlookers with awe and win their approval. The tragic figure struts and frets, particularly in the theatrical spectacle of the plot's close. The word 'bravado' does not feature in the play, but the adjective derived from it does. The revengeful Hippolita, speaking of her plans to kill the faithless Soranzo, says: *I'll do it bravely* (III.viii.7). In Hippolita's mind, the brave act will be public.

It is consistent with the element of public spectacle that the tragic figure usually presents himself against a huge background. He is taking on fate, death and facing up to the possibility of damnation. The language is often apocalyptic. Thus Giovanni, resolving to go to Soranzo's birthday feast, casts himself in the role of the one who is defying not just death but the terrors that will wind up history:

> Not go! Stood Death
> Threat'ning his armies of confounding plagues,
> With hosts of dangers hot as blazing stars,
> I would be there.

> (V.iii.59–62)

Giovanni is a lone individual facing many – *armies* and *hosts* – and yet he exults that he is unflinching. Neither *plagues* (of which there were frequent occurrences in Ford's London) nor *armies* (Europe was enduring what is now called the Thirty Years' War) can daunt him – and that is what he wants everyone to know. Perhaps deliberately echoing the Friar's words in the first scene, he sees himself fulfilling the calling of a man: *Be all a man* (V.iii.75). And that might be what, in spite of many things, makes him attractive to audiences. Tragedy is double-edged.

Ford is clearly interested in one of the tensions that Shakespeare recognized. The point may be put like this: do we respond more to tragic heroics than to practical plotting? On this matter, Shakespeare implicitly invites the audience to compare the actions of his leading characters. At the heart of Shakespeare's *Julius Caesar* is the difference between Brutus's painful scruples over killing his friend and the efficiency with which Antony, Octavius and Lepidus calmly draw up a list of those they wish to kill. Brutus is undoubtedly a man of conscience, but the other three are more open and entirely honest about what they are doing. Ford handles this tension by the immediate juxtaposition of scenes. In V.iii Giovanni displays several highly tragic qualities: defiance, awareness of mortality and a sense of the horrors he is planning. Yet does the efficiency of Soranzo and Vasques in the following scene show him up as too concerned to play a role, too preoccupied with the theatricality of his enterprise?

And what of Annabella? She describes her life as a tragedy. In her touching soliloquy, spoken after she has been imprisoned in her room, she asks *Time* to *bear to ages that are yet unborn/ A wretched woeful woman's tragedy* (V.i.4–8). Although she only uses the indefinite article – *a* – we might be enticed into regarding her fate as typical of all women. Is she 'the' *wretched woeful woman*, who is the victim of male jealousy? Interestingly, the overhearing Friar does not think that way. To him she is essentially a penitent sinner. But to us the reference to the future might be the important thing. Does Annabella know that in the world of Parma she will not be seen as tragic (think of the final line of the play) but that the future – we who now see the play – will see that there is such a thing as female tragedy, and that its special quality rests in woman as the object of male desire and dominance?

Activity

In what ways does Giovanni's entrance in the last scene (V.vi.10–15) establish him as a tragic hero?

Discussion

Giovanni's entrance might be seen as consciously theatrical. Each of the characters presented either has a vital plot link to him or, as in the case of the Cardinal, a representative function in Parma society. All is ready for his performance. Giovanni's first words – *Here, here* – constitute a public gesture; with what might be called baroque gothic language (*trimmed in reeking blood*) and actions, he displays Annabella's heart and in doing so creates a visual parable that encapsulates his claim that he and not Soranzo owns Annabella's heart. His words refer to her heart, but can equally apply to him: he is *proud in the spoil/ Of love and vengeance.*

Do we also experience the terrible ambivalence of the tragic hero? He stands alone and defiant, but his defiance is egotistical and without any obvious sympathy for his dead sister. His behaviour is open to the judgement that this is not really tragedy at all, but the wilful showing off of a petulant young man.

Ford's verse

There are deaths aplenty in *'Tis Pity She's a Whore*: Bergetto is murdered in the dark; Hippolita, intent on murder herself, is poisoned; Annabella is not only murdered but, in the grisly manner of a public execution, virtually disembowelled; Florio dies of shock and, presumably, a broken heart; Soranzo is killed in a swordfight; Giovanni is overcome by the Banditti; and Putana, who has already had her eyes gouged out, will perhaps (see Notes, page 189) be taken out of the city and burnt to ashes. On its body count, the play still seems to live in the world of horrors created by Thomas Kyd in *The Spanish Tragedy* and Thomas Middleton in *The Revenger's Tragedy*. Not all of these events (thankfully) are presented on stage. Unless a production wishes to go further than the text, we do not see Giovanni ripping out Annabella's heart. What we do see is her bleeding heart upon Giovanni's dagger. It might stand as an emblem of the kind of world Ford has created.

And there is the incest. No doubt many audiences (or readers) new to the play know beforehand that it deals with incest. Nevertheless, they may be surprised that this topic is the first one to be aired, and that by the end of the second scene the brother and sister exit to consummate their incestuous desires. Any production will have to cope with the fact that the subject matter is distressing.

Yet it must be asked whether *'Tis Pity* feels quite as disturbing as a summary of its deaths and distinctive love interest might lead audiences and readers to expect. The play now has a place in the

British theatrical tradition. It has, for instance, been performed by the Glasgow Citizens Theatre, the National Theatre, the Royal Shakespeare Company, and the Young Vic. There was a BBC production in 1980. At English A level it is, along with plays by Jonson, Marlowe and others, an alternative to Shakespeare. Parents do not insist on withdrawing their children from classes.

Might it be concluded that either the world has supped too full of horrors, or that there is something about the play that orders and tempers what would otherwise be simply horrible? It is hard to take the first alternative seriously. The seventeenth century had its own horrors. Can whatever we see of blood and guts in a film or video game compare with what was witnessed at public executions? What, then, about what the play does? Plays about violence need not be violent plays. So what does Ford do to temper the horrors he is dealing with?

One answer is a feature that critics have singled out as distinctive of Ford's art. This is the movement, textures and tones of his verse. The movement of Ford's verse is measured and evenly paced. Even when a character is agitated – ardent or revengeful – the steady tread of the verse can be felt. Listen to Giovanni in the opening scene arguing against the prohibition on incest:

> Shall a peevish sound,
> A customary form, from man to man,
> Of brother and of sister, be a bar
> 'Twixt my perpetual happiness and me?

(I.i.24–27)

Giovanni has thought through what matters to him, so his words – the enactment of his thought – have a weighed, deliberate quality. Because he thinks of his sister and himself, his thought forms a series of pairs or doubles: *man to man, Of brother and of sister, my perpetual happiness and me*. These doubles are given emphasis, though not loudly or stridently, by the unobtrusive alliterations, whether close as in *man to man* or distant as in *peevish* and *perpetual*. And as for pace, it is difficult to deliver the polysyllabic words *perpetual happiness* quickly.

The 'sound values' of those lines are typical of the textures of Ford's verse. His smooth lines usually flow with lyrical ease. It hardly seems to matter (and this may be a limitation in Ford) what the scene is about. Annabella's confession to the Friar might have been written in tense, emotionally fraught verse, but the opening words of the Friar (even in spite of their subject matter) are controlled and gentle:

> I am glad to see this penance; for believe me,
> You have unripped a soul so foul and guilty,
> As I must tell you true, I marvel how
> The earth hath borne you up. But weep, weep on,
> These tears may do you good.

> (III.vi.1–5)

The textures of the second line are significant, for in spite of the potentially disturbing *unripped*, there is the mellifluous *a soul so foul* in which the alliteration and assonance sound like a pleasurable set of variations on the 's' and 'l' sounds. Another feature of Ford's characteristic timbre is the run of monosyllables. After *marvel* the next 17 words are of one syllable. The effect of this is that the speaker must consciously articulate each word, as if they are small pebbles dropping into a still pool.

Of course, terms such as 'movement', 'texture' and 'tone' are just that – words we use to talk about aspects of verse. And those aspects can be seen in many lines of the play. For instance, the tone of the above passages is evident in the notes of yearning and melancholy. Such notes are characteristic of Ford. Listen to Annabella in her last scene with Giovanni:

> Brother, dear brother, know what I have been,
> And know that now there's but a dining-time
> 'Twixt us and our confusion. Let's not waste
> These precious hours in vain and useless speech.

> (V.v.16–19)

Although the object is different, Annabella yearns as did Giovanni in the first scene. And what she shares with the passage from the Friar (III.vi.1–5, above) is a sadness, a melancholy, a ground-note of regret. We hear this in the falling cadences – the movement in pitch a voice makes at the end of a phrase or sentence. Noticing cadence is a matter of listening. Do we hear remorse in the falling cadence of *what I have been*, and a bleak sense that time is short in *vain and useless speech*? Interestingly, in line 17 an early text of the play prints *dying* instead of *dining*. It may be that we can hear *dying* in *dining*. Certainly the cadence dies away.

Activity

Consider the way that Ford handles language in the first 11 lines of Annabella's 'valedictory' speech: V.i.1–11.

Discussion

How does Ford create the poised, stately and moving quality of the soliloquy? Think, for instance, about its grammar. In the opening words – *Pleasures farewell* – and the line *To these my fortunes now I take my leave*, the normal word order is reversed, so that the object comes before the subject and the verb. The effect of this might be to foreground what it is she is losing. The solemnity of the speech is created by the formal address to *Time*. The audience might get the impression that she is rising above the turmoil of human emotions and speaking to the stable and eternal aspects of human experience.

A similar effect is created by *My conscience now stands up against my lust*. Conscience becomes like an allegorical figure in a poem debating the moral life, or a figure in a court masque. The traditional image of *Time* as a swift rider is given fluency, though not a hectic pace, by a series of restrained alliterations.

Title

A difficulty with the title of the play is that in the ordinary sense of the word, Annabella is not a *whore*. She is not, for instance, like Bellafront in Thomas Dekker's *The Honest Whore* – a confident and quite brazen prostitute. As the Notes point out (see Note to IV.iii.1), words usually used of prostitutes, such as *harlot, strumpet, whore*, could also mean an immoral woman. Annabella is clearly no prostitute, rather she is a young woman who yields to desire. That much is not in dispute.

What Ford seems to be interested in with regard to his title is what today we might call 'the politics of discourse': the way subjects (and people) are treated in speech or writing, and who controls this. Plays can be read as competing ways of talking about whatever is crucial in the plot. Hamlet talks of Claudius as 'that adulterate beast' (I.v.42), though as the king he is, according to Rosencrantz, 'That spirit upon whose weal depends and rests/ The lives of many' (III.iii.14–15). The question in *'Tis Pity She's a Whore* is: who controls the discourse, and what does the audience make of that control?

As far as control of the discourse goes, Soranzo and the Cardinal are the centres of power. Soranzo is full, if not inventive, in his denunciations: to him, Annabella is *strumpet, famous whore* (IV.iii.1) and *Whore of whores* (IV.iii.20). The Cardinal literally has the last word in the play, and though what he says meets Ford's need of a rhyming couplet to close the drama, the word *whore* is the last one the audience hears. But audiences can think for themselves, and may insist that the controlling discourse is not the one they wish to endorse. Audiences may wish to see her as a woman who is a victim and may, in the way she responds to her situation, rise above her confining circumstances. Although Vasques is being diplomatic, perhaps he is right in saying *she shows the nobleness of a gallant spirit* (IV.iii.97–8).

She is clearly a victim of both Soranzo's rage and the Cardinal's imperious exercise of power, and she might also be said to be a victim of her father's desire to make a satisfactory marriage deal. The biggest question is whether she is a victim of Giovanni. Is he the man who releases in her a desire for love and independence, or the one who unfeelingly bullies her to gain his own satisfactions?

Any production must decide where to place the moral emphasis. It is easy (particularly today) to see Annabella overcoming her inferior position by her defiance of Soranzo. Before he begins his proposal, she opens with a plain demand: *Sir, what's your will with me?* (III.ii.13), and she shows that she knows the rules of the game she is being invited, or obliged, to play. Her wordplay is quick though blunt: she cuts off the textbook ardour of Soranzo's *Did you but see my heart, then would you swear* with a plain bit of (very English?) common sense that treats tired metaphors literally: *That you were dead* (III.ii.21–22). Her resistance in the wooing scene and her defiant and colloquial *O yes, why not?* (IV.iii.21), or her fearless interjection *do not beg for me* (IV.iii.94) appeal to current notions of female empowerment. Certainly the play can be performed to bring out those features.

The other way in which she might be said to overcome her circumscribed lot is by recognizing her faults and warning her reckless brother. It may be an unpopular view, but possibly she is at her most magnificent when she weeps before the Friar (III.vi) and, on her balcony (the position might suggest that she looks upon the moral confusions of the plot with a clear authority) laments her state and then implores the Friar to give her letter to Giovanni so that he may *read it and repent* (V.i.47). It may not be an easy reading today, but it might be what the play should make us think.

John Ford and literary criticism

It was only in the twentieth century that a critical tradition about John Ford was established. It effectively starts with T.S. Eliot's essay of 1932, and M.C. Bradbrook's response to some of his judgements in her important historical and critical enquiry *Themes and Conventions of Elizabethan Tragedy* (see Further Reading). Two of the most fruitful contributions to critical debate have been editions of the play and, because stagings are inevitably interpretations, productions in the theatre. The following points have emerged as attracting critical interest.

- A great deal of work has been done by theatre historians such as Andrew Gurr on the physical properties of the early seventeenth-century stage. This work has established the differences between the indoor hall theatres and the much larger outdoor amphitheatres. Understanding the circumstances of the initial performances has raised matters such as the domestic character of some plays, the presentation of privacy and, possibly, the freedom of the small and expensive hall theatres to tackle delicate topics such as incest. Interestingly, earlier twentieth-century productions were in private theatres. See page 21.

- There has been work on the context of the play. Ford wrote for Caroline London (the London of King Charles I). Charles's queen, Henrietta Maria, was the patron of the company that performed Ford's plays. In Simon Barker's words (in his Routledge edition of the play, see Further Reading), Caroline London witnessed debates about 'the modern family, marriage convention and gender stereotyping'. He adds that Ford shows how unstable the pattern of family life could be. Another relevant context is the trade that marked the life of London (and Parma). In terms of other literature, it used to be suggested that the presentation of Giovanni's behaviour owed something to Robert Burton's observations in his *The Anatomy of Melancholy* (1621, with further editions in 1624, 1628 and 1632). Another aspect of contextual study is the treatment of the Roman Catholic Church. The Cardinal's behaviour can easily be taken as an example of English hostility to the Catholic Church, though it is not necessary to be anti-Catholic to disapprove of the abuse of power, and such abuses are not confined to Italy. An interest in the contemporary fashion for baroque can be found in the presentation of Annabella in V.ii.10–11; dressing her in her bridal robes turns her into a powerful work of art.

- Critics and theatre producers seem consistent in their sympathetic presentation of the lovers and their corresponding criticism of Parma society. See Derek Roper's remarks quoted on page 206. Roper says that the 'presentation of their society is more like a satire upon the established order than a defence of it'. Roper makes the point that this hostility is evident in productions that bring out 'the greed and hypocrisy of bourgeois society'.

- Hostility to society is particularly evident in feminist readings. Marion Lomax (see Further Reading) says that the play deals with the plight of 'intelligent, passionate women' who, in trying to manipulate men, 'bring the full force of the patriarchal system against them'. Lomax makes much of Annabella as a victim of Giovanni's self-absorption, pointing out, as have other critics, that when the lovers make their mutual promises, Annabella swears by *our mother's dust*, while Giovanni excludes her by invoking *my mother's dust* (I.ii.259, 262).

- Feminism is now treated as one of several literary theories. Because a theory is a starting point, any conclusions reached will be in accordance with the particular outlook of the theory. Derek Roper gives a helpful account of some theoretical approaches. Interpretations that follow Freud emphasize the enclosed nature of incest. An extension of this is the insight that Giovanni wants to dissociate nature from society and its political discourses. That this cannot be done becomes obvious when Annabella's pregnancy is discovered. Another aspect of the enclosed character of incest is that it makes for class exclusiveness.

- T.S. Eliot saw Ford's greatest achievement as a mastery of 'cadence and tone in blank verse'. Following Eliot, Brian Morris (in his New Mermaids edition of the play, see Further Reading) writes of Ford's 'plain, still voice, at once simple and grave, cadenced and wonderfully austere'. Oddly enough, it is harder to hear his voice in the theatre than in the study.

What appears to be absent in writing about Ford is the identification of major critical problems. Criticism continues to offer a number of perspectives, and productions are sympathetic to some characters and hostile to others (the Friar has often been presented unsympathetically). But unlike Marlowe (and clearly unlike Shakespeare) there are no big things to argue about. Yet all that tells us is that Ford is not like Marlowe or Shakespeare. He is a good theatrical craftsman (probably a better one than Marlowe) and he wrote simple yet eloquent verse that lingers in the memory. It is the combination of those two things that have established him as a significant figure in the English theatrical tradition.

Essay Questions

1 Discuss the view that in a manifestly corrupt world, the love of Annabella and Giovanni is the most attractive feature of the play.

2 Does the play present a consistent view of the morality of incest?

3 What is the dramatic purpose of the love story of Philotis and Bergetto?

4 How does Ford use irony in the play, and what effects does he achieve?

5 In what ways does Giovanni embody the main themes of the play?

6 What do you think is the main theme of the play, and how does Ford explore it?

7 Explore Ford's presentation of Vasques. How far does the character arouse interest or sympathy in the audience?

8 What dramatic options does the character of Florio present?

9 What do the intellectual debates add to the presentation of character, the interplay between characters, and the tone of the play?

10 How does Ford present the various revengers?

11 Discuss the view that Annabella is the most remarkable and original character in the play.

12 Is it true that the play concentrates on violent emotions rather than softer and more gentle feelings?

13 What does the variety of Ford's dramatic language contribute to the plot, themes and overall effects of the play?

14 Explore the significance of the way various characters speak about fate and destiny.

15 What view of the society of Parma emerges from the play, and how is it presented?

Chronology

1607 *The Revenger's Tragedy* by Thomas Middleton published.

1611 First performance of Shakespeare's *The Tempest*; Cyril Tourneur writes *The Atheist's Tragedy*.

1613 Ford's *The Golden Mean* (prose) published; Ford's *An Ill Beginning Has a Good End* performed.

1614 Probable date of Webster's *The Duchess of Malfi*.

1616 Death of Shakespeare; the Cockpit Theatre built, probably to designs by Inigo Jones.

1617 Ford is possibly censured for joining in a protest about the wearing of lawyer's caps.

1621 Ford collaborates with Thomas Dekker and William Rowley in the writing of *The Witch of Edmonton*; publication of *The Anatomy of Melancholy* by Robert Burton.

1625 James I dies; Charles I becomes king.

1629–30 Inigo Jones builds the Cockpit-in-Court theatre in the royal palace of Whitehall.

1633 *'Tis Pity She's a Whore*, *The Broken Heart* and *Love's Sacrifice* first published; publication of John Donne's *Poems*.

1634 Publication of *Perkin Warbeck*, Ford's history play.

1639 Ford leaves London. No more is known of him.

1642 Civil war; London theatres are closed.

Further Reading

Editions of the play

Simon Barker (ed.), *'Tis Pity She's a Whore* (Routledge English Texts, 1997)

Marion Lomax (ed.), *John Ford: 'Tis Pity She's a Whore and Other Plays* (Oxford World's Classics, 1995)

Brian Morris (ed.), *'Tis Pity She's a Whore* (New Mermaids, 1968)

Derek Roper (ed.), *'Tis Pity She's a Whore* (Revels Student Editions, 1997)

Martin Wiggins (ed.), *'Tis Pity She's a Whore* (New Mermaids, 2003)

Critical books

M.C. Bradbrook, *Themes and Conventions of Elizabethan Tragedy* (Cambridge University Press, 1935)

A.R. Braunmuller and Michael Hattaway (eds), *The Cambridge Companion to English Renaissance Drama* (Cambridge University Press, 2003) See Chapter 10 Caroline Drama, by James Bulman

T.S. Eliot, 'John Ford' (1932), in *Selected Essays 1917–1932* (Faber, 1932)

David L. Frost, *The School of Shakespeare* (Cambridge University Press, 1968)

Andrew Gurr, *The Shakespearean Stage, 1574–1642* (Cambridge University Press, 1992)

Lisa Hopkins, *John Ford's Political Theatre* (Manchester University Press, 1994)

Robert Ornstein, *The Moral Vision of Jacobean Tragedy* (The University of Wisconsin Press, 1965)

Eric Partridge, *Shakespeare's Bawdy* (Routledge & Kegan Paul, revised edition 1968)

Emma Smith and Garrett A. Sullivan, Jr (eds),*The Cambridge Companion to English Renaissance Tragedy* (Cambridge University Press, 2010) See Chapter 19 *'Tis Pity She's a Whore*: The Play of Intertextuality, by Emily C. Bartels

Rowland Wymer, *Webster and Ford* (Palgrave Macmillan, 1995)